TO
MARK DESAUTEL
AND THE REST OF
THE folks AT
ART ATTACK!

NOW you're all
BRAIN Robbers....

MURRAY
Aphel
10 10 94

The GREAT BRAIN ROBBERY

How to Steal Ideas . . . and Make Money!

The Great Brain Robbery

Ray Considine and Murray Raphel

The Great Brain Robbery
1360 East Rubio Street
Altadena, California 91001

Library of Congress Catalog Card number: 80-506-55
ISBN: 0-86558-000-6
Designed by Bernard Schleifer

6 7 8 9 10

I want to thank (make that THANK) Murray Raphel,
creative/loving/tender/caring/pushy friend
(make that FRIEND) for pushing me to put down
on pages some of the best Ideas I have Heard,
Said, or Thought.
Without his Push . . . these pages never would've
been put down.
Thank you Mur . . . for putting me down. Finally.

And to Betty Considine for putting up with. . . .

RAY CONSIDINE

To Ray, the Number One Brain Robber, who shared
the ideas, prepared the philosophy, and taught
the techniques making the Brain Robbery possible.

And to my wife Ruth, who makes everything possible.

MURRAY RAPHEL

Contents

Preface

ONCE UPON A TIME we saw a movie that fit the missing piece into a puzzle and made us think, "Aha!"

It was *Butch Cassidy and the Sundance Kid.*

Here were two of the West's worst outlaws. In a railway robbery scene, they put too much dynamite in the safe and blew the dollars and box car all over the territory.

They were constantly running from a posse, trying to outwit the competition.

One afternoon, after riding over rock and through riverbeds to elude the lawmen following them, they wound up high atop a mountain range, convinced they "won the day."

And then, Paul Newman, looking down the mountain to the distance, saw the faint outlines of the plodding, on-their-trail small group of stalkers. Still following. Still coming. Closer all the time.

Unbelieving and frustrated, Newman (Butch Cassidy) turned to Robert Redford (Sundance) and, in a puzzled, unbelieving voice asked, "Who are those guys? How do they do that?"

And Redford, looking at the same sight in disbelief, shook his head slowly and said, "I don't know. I just don't know . . ."

For years we shared the frustration of Redford and Newman.

Here we were, two rather good idea guys (ask us, we'd tell you) who did not know why what-we-did worked. Or how to make it work . . . better.

As successful as we were in our selling, in our speechmaking, in our promotions, there were others who were even better. We found ourselves constantly talking about the rare idea people we all read about, know, admire . . . and envy.

The more we talked about these stellar performers to groups all over the country, the more clearly a pattern began to emerge.

We discovered certain characteristics that made these individuals different. Certain things they did that others did not. And though most of them did not know one another, their styles and conquests and reputations had common themes. An admiring world examined their achievements and wondered, "How do those guys do that?" And asked one another, "Do you know how those guys do that?"

So, like scientists spending years in the laboratory to find the secret components of a successful formula, we finally extracted the basic ingredients. When we tried them . . . they worked for us! And when we described the formulas, to others, they worked for them too!

The first chapter tells you about some of these outstanding individuals and why they became sought after as idea men, problem solvers, corporate fire fighters—and money makers.

In the rest of the book we explain their techniques, tell how they did it, how it worked for us, for others, and how it will work for you too.

After you finish reading, the moment will come in the future when you pull off a mind-boggling deal. Or come up with a solution "they" thought impossible. Or changed your life when others said it was too late. And when you leave the room, you will hear a familiar half-whispered sentence from an admiring group, "How did he do that? Do you know how he did that?"

Read on. The answer's in the book . . .

RAY CONSIDINE
MURRAY RAPHEL

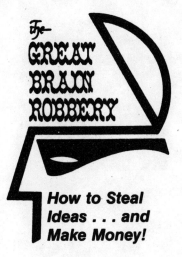

*How to Steal
Ideas . . . and
Make Money!*

Introduction

It ALL STARTED with a box.

The box was a puzzling brain teaser we found both tormenting and enlightening. Intrigued, we placed it in that un-named what-will-we-do-with-it Idea file.

There it stayed for a couple of years until we came up with the concept of The Great Brain Robbery seminars. We needed an opening to describe what the Brain Robbery was all about.

"Non-traditional ways to solve problems," one of us said.

"Stealing other people's ideas and making them work for us," the other said.

"Coming up with unusual ways to solve usual problems," we said.

What single illustration would show all this? The box! Great. It worked. We can show people how they work themselves into a box . . . and can't get out . . . and then they can.

Here's the puzzle. (In fact, here's two of them. One to practice on.)

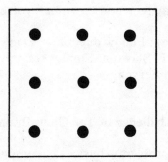

Connect all 9 dots in the box with 4 consecutive straight lines, not repeating a line or lifting your pencil.

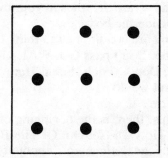

Connect all 9 dots in the box with 4 consecutive straight lines, not repeating a line or lifting your pencil.

Now, read the instructions and come up with the answer.

We will pause for a few moments while you decide how to do it.

Take your time . . .

(The answer's on the next page.)

Here's the answer:

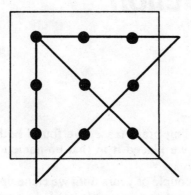

"But," you say defensively, "you went *outside* the box."

Right. We did. For where was it written to stay *inside* the box?

It wasn't. Read the instructions again. They said, "Connect all nine dots *in* the box"—that's where the nine dots *are*. It doesn't say "Connect all nine dots and *stay* in the box," does it? Ummm. No.

But you *assumed* you had to.

The borders around the box were a barrier to you in thinking of a solution.

And so are the rules in your everyday life. You "assume" you cannot go outside the box.

You are conditioned to think this way: Follow directions. Don't cross the line. Don't pass GO. WALK. WAIT. Stay out. Employees only. Wet Paint, Don't Touch. Stand Here To Be Served.

And we do it.

Wow.

This, then, is the beginning of the challenge of The Great Brain Robbery: How To Get Out Of The Box.

The next time you encounter a problem—business, personal, or intellectual—remember the image of the box. We are all constantly *trying* to break through years of conditioning, layer after layer of earlier influences all of which unconsciously affect our present mental attitudes and our ability to accept new ideas or the ideas of others. It is a natural feeling. And it IS difficult to change, to do things differently. Here's an example:

Fold your arms in front of your chest as you normally would.

Got it?

Fine.

Now, look at how your arms are folded. Is the right arm over the left? (or the left arm over the right?) Now, unfold your arms slowly—*and put the opposite arm on top.*

Uncomfortable? Sure. The arrangement doesn't work comfortably. But is it wrong? No. In fact in any group of people, half will put their right arm on top, the other half will put their left on top. Who's wrong? Nobody. It *IS* different. And it is NOT wrong.

Just different.

Don't be afraid to *get out of the box.*

You must admit to yourself there are others who have faced the same problems you have . . . and solved them! When problems occur you may feel you are the only one ever placed in that position. Suddenly several people who had the same problem come to you and tell you not-to-worry, they attacked the same problem and won! You are no longer alone. There really are others who have the same worries, frustrations, and unhappiness as you do.

Some overcome the problems.

Some stay in the box and complain.

In one of our Brain Robbery opening workshops, we handed out the illustration of the nine-dot puzzle. We explain this non-traditional thinking. That anyone could solve this problem any way they wanted to. A few moments later one smiling member of the group shot his hand in the air and said, "I solved the problem."

He held up his paper with the dots in the box erased, "There is no problem now," he announced smugly, "I eliminated it."

Hmmmmmmmmmmm. Very non-traditional.

Who says THAT solution is not acceptable?

In another session, one bright banker lady carefully folded the puzzle paper which put all three rows of the dots on one line, drew her pencil back and forth and quietly announced, "I have it." Aha.

Although it IS true you do not eliminate problems by pretending they do not exist, it is also true, if you can eliminate the problem, it no longer exists!

The next few hundred pages will give you examples of the best reactions to problem-solving, money-making, life-changing Ideas we have heard, collected, and added to during the seven and a half years of exchanging ideas with audiences from all over the country. You will find the word Idea capitalized throughout the book because we feel it is the greatest single change agent in our lives. An Idea whose time has come. For you. For me. For us.

There is no last word on the subject. We are constantly "topped" by people in our seminars. One time, after we went through the story of the nine dot puzzle and the box, one scholarly fellow asked, "Why do you have to do it with *four* lines. Why not three?"

"Three?" we asked, "Can that be done?"

And in the best student-showing-the-professor-how-to-do-it style, he held his solution aloft for all to see. Here it is:

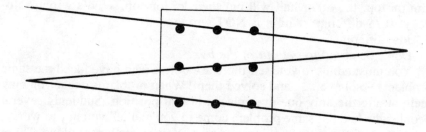

He had just nipped the outer corners of the dots—enough to "shave" out a new solution. Non-traditional.

Queen Isabella challenged members of her court to stand an egg on end. All the courtiers failed. One young sailor walked in, surveyed the problem, lifted the egg, jabbed its end against the surface of the table, and while the gooey insides drained over the wood Christopher Columbus simply said, "It stands." Non-traditional.

Did the members of the court get mad? Probably. But Chris wound up with money and ships to sail away, as one contemporary put it, "over the edge of the world into oblivion." (Yes, the reasons-why-it-won't-work fraternity were at it even then.)

Alexander the Great was confronted by the Gordian Knot, an inextricably complex weaving that defied unloosing. Dozens of would-be experts and leaders had picked, pawed, and pulled at the knotted rope mess. He looked at the problem, reached over, grabbed the hilt of his large sword and with one fell swoop, Swat!—the knot was not.

How different is that from our friends in the seminar who erased the dots or who folded the paper? In terms of problem solving, same thing.

The point: practice solutions—at least mentally—whenever you hear your cohorts grumble that "it-won't-work-because . . ."

Case in point: Who is your competition in life? In your business?

Banks say banks are their competition. Retail stores say other retail stores are their competition. Food outlets point to other food outlets as their competitors. Are they right?

Partly. But each is thinking in the box of his own business.

Their real competition is *every other place where consumers spend their money.*

Each business advertises and hopes consumers will spend money with "me" rather than . . . with ANYONE else. For the competition REALLY IS . . . EVERYONE who is not . . . you.

If you have been thinking your competition is merely everyone in the same business as you, you have fallen in the habit of how everyone ELSE thinks.

Get out of THAT box.

Take a quick walk outside your door. Look down the main street of your town, no matter how big or small it is. See all those signs outside all those stores? Aren't they all *really* your . . . competition?

Now, how do you convince customers to spend more of their dollars with you? Or your boss to spend more of his dollars ON you?

In the following pages you will find concepts, gimmicks, angles, techniques—Ideas you can use to your own advantage. None are really new. Bright, fresh, "original" applications of old Ideas . . . or new combinations of existing Ideas. The best Idea people will tell you they see, capture, remember, mark down, file, and keep—whatever "flashes" in their minds, what impresses them as . . . a Good Idea. Then when the occasion arises, they dig down into that file of Ideas and come up with and use—the Right Idea at the Right moment. Its called Being Creative.

We call it the Eleventh Commandment.

Most people remember the Ten Commandments. This is the Eleventh. It goes like this:

> *Thou Shalt Steal Every Idea Thou Can Find . . . and Make It Thine Own*

(We'll never tell.)

The following pages present a wide selection of Ideas. Peruse them as you would the menu in your favorite Chinese restaurant. Take some from Column A and some from Column B. Mix, match, share. Whatever pleases your creative taste.

And it all begins with some of the Great Idea People We Have Known, Admired, Read About, and Envy.

The question is: How do those guys do that?

1 Great Idea People We Have Known, Admired, Read About . . . and Envy

Reese Palley

"Everybody wants to think and act rich.
So we should charge VERY high prices
to make them VERY happy."
— REESE PALLEY, Merchant to the Rich

THE TROUBLE with writing about Reese Palley is the feeling his newest, most outrageous idea will explode the day before this chapter is published. And people will then ask "Why didn't they mention THAT one in the book?"

Ahhhh, but where to start to write about Atlantic City's self-proclaimed "Merchant to the Rich" (who has that snobby phrase emblazoned on all the shopping bags from his posh Atlantic City Boardwalk art and gift shop.)

Shall we begin with the multimillion dollar sale of Boehm Birds? Or his fascinating scheme to fill the empty hotels on the Boardwalk with private Palley Parties, B.C. (Before Casinos)?

Or the birth of his art galleries in New York, San Francisco, Paris? What about his ingenious purchase of Atlantic City's Marlborough-Blenheim Hotel from its proper Quaker owners who sought a buyer because they couldn't envision their hotel becoming a gambling casino— only to have Guess Who do his abrupt turn-around sale to Bally to transform that same hotel into . . . a casino?

How about the Palley promotion where the giant game of Monopoly, played out in the open on a board thirty-two feet square with bikini-clad girls as "pawns"? Or should we talk of his recent chairmanship of the New Jersey Lottery where he watched over how other people gamble. Who is watching the watcher? Almost everyone.

His list of non-traditional activities grows almost daily with one more mind-boggling than the other, in the classic Brain Robbery pattern.

All have made Reese Palley a very rich man. And one who is already ready to greet the news media with an appropriate headline quote, glib and newsworthy enough to make the six o'clock TV news *tonight*. Like, after the casinos arrived, Reese was asked by the press to comment on the major change in Atlantic City since gambling. He said, "The prostitutes are looking much better!" That made the news.

For this very short chapter on Reese Palley (it rhymes with "peace rally"), one of our great promotion men, we touch briefly on his background, on how he has constructed some of his infamous schemes and how they have worked out. Most of the time.

You can see Reese coming. Physically, he is a sharply contrasted "black and white production." His appearance is his identification. At the top, a wild shock of crazy messed-up white hair that looks like it is combed with an egg beater. Black horn-rimmed glasses on a grinning elfish face complete with small scruffy goatee white beard. Black turtle-neck shirt, black pants, black socks, black shoes—with one splash of color: a western red bandana in his back pocket to wipe off his clients' kisses.

He began in Atlantic City by being born there and is there still (actually never "still," always active, into everything that touches his world). Early on, his father and grandfather had a jewelry store and Reese worked part-time in the store while growing up. "Hustled" is Reese's phrase. At one point he decided to be an optometrist. (Does Reese see the world through his tinted horn-rimmed rose-colored glasses? Answer: Yes! Does Reese possess vision for projects unseen by others? Answer: Probably.) Watch what he does with his optical training now . . .

During World War II his high IQ gave him a shot at Officer Candidate School. He missed graduation, flunked inspection, and was shipped up to Alaska, the Aleutian Islands, where he says, the Army sent all its communists, homosexuals, and trouble-makers. A perfect place for Reese, who was one of the latter.

He set up shop, examined eyes, and asked the innocent enlisted men, "Do you want Army-issue glasses or real glasses?" Every one of his "customers" opted for the "real" ones which—uh—cost just a few more dollars and these dollars went to . . . Reese, "merchant to the myopic."

After wartime, he studied economics in New York and London. Toured Europe and returned to selling in Dad's jewelry store. Within four years his business had the highest annual dollar volume per capita of any jewelry store in the United States. (Who's to dispute?) But that store was dear old Dad's. Reese wanted to get his own game going. How to do this?

He borrowed $700 on an insurance policy in 1956 and opened a classy *objet d'art* shop in the Marlborough-Blenheim Hotel (which he would someday sell to the casino folk).

One day Helen Boehm walked in from her nearby Trenton, New Jersey, studio to tout her husband's handsome porcelain birds. Palley bought a few. Sold them. Bought a few more. Early on through his far-sighted lenses he perceived the collecting craze. He built his Boehm Bird customer list and began to trade each of them up, up, up. He urged them into the collective craziness with this sales message: "Buy now! Buy! Buy! . . . If you bought this gorgeous bird from me ten years ago, it would have tripled in value by now. Don't wait this time. Buy now!" Hustle, hustle, Reese is busy with the bird game.

In 1971, Reese convened the collectors at a national convention in his Atlantic City hometown and sold out the next year's entire production of Boehm birds!—in advance. A two million dollar sale.

How did he do that?

Well . . . if it worked with a collectors' convention, how about trying it in December? In the 1960s the Reese Palley Hoo-Ha parties began. December was the slowest month of the year in Atlantic City in those days—people stayed home with their families for the holidays, out of the wind, off the Boardwalk. Could Reese bring his "guests" to his party in December in Atlantic City?

First he contracted with the big empty hotels, for their empty rooms. Reese reminded the owners repeatedly their rooms were empty—without him. He told the owners he would fill their place with hundreds of customers who drink at the hotel bars and eat the hotel food. Now, how much would those expensive empty rooms cost Reese? How about $25.00 a couple??? Done! Reese sent out 20,000 direct mail pieces inviting his entire list to a weekend party. Here in typical Palleyesque prose was part of the invitation:

> Be my guest any of these three December weekends in Atlantic City. I'll provide the bed for two nights and three days. You supply the bedmate. Bring (check one) your wife, a concubine, somebody else's wife, a casual acquaintance. We take no responsibility for pregnancies begun on this weekend. . . The party is formal. If you do not have formal clothes you should not be my customer. If you expect me to pay for your food you are wildly overestimating my generosity.

Reese Palley does not feed the pigeons.

The invitations were richly illustrated with rather suggestive, ribald sketches. Reese attended as Henry the Eighth, the King of the thousand couples who attended! "No one was required to buy anything," says Reese, "they just weren't invited back if they didn't buy. Or if they were a pain in the ass in the store."

How much did each couple spend with Reese at these extravaganzas? No one is saying, but the promotion of the off-season Hoo-Ha parties did go on until recently when Reese struck casino oil on his Atlantic City homeground.

All Palley promos are not boffo. In fact, one smelled. In March of 1970 he opened a gallery in New York City's SoHo, the lower Manhattan art district. It was short-lived. Managing directors came and went like so many revolving doors. But what sent most people through the doors (in the wrong direction) was his outstanding exhibit. This classic was an anti-war show by artist John Freeman. It consisted of Plexiglass boxes filled with ox blood. Within a few days, the ox odor was so rancid most of the people walked in, breathed once, had sudden waves of nausea and ran, not walked, to the nearest bathroom.

If you were not close enough to the entrance to catch the essence of the ox blood, maybe you'd like the essence of Reese's *New Yorker* ad when the gallery opened. There Reese was on a full page of the *New Yorker* magazine standing beside the life-size blow-up of himself with this headline: "The only thing better than one Reese Palley is . . . Two Reese Palleys."

Which was probably true until he came up with the idea of 700 Reese Palleys! Which in turn brings us to the most-remembered self-promotion of all: The Palley-Dali Paris Birthday Party.

"How can I celebrate my fiftieth birthday in style?" said the Merchant to himself. With that one question, he proceeded to put together THE most flamboyant of his nonsensical, Never-Neverland schemes. Even in his wildest dreams (some of which out-Fellini Fellini), could he conceive that this self-centered celebration would make headlines from the Fiji Islands to Fairbanks, Alaska, the New York *Times,* the Washington *Post,* Paris *Match,* three major TV networks, and the Voice of America? This one did.

There are always those who say he didn't know what he was doing. Other practiced Palley-watchers laughed and said, "Of course he knew . . ."

Well, what he does know—and is the only one who DOES know—is how many dollars eventually were entered on M'sieur Palley's banque balance. Some say he made a million dollars on the deal. Others say the "take" was potentially over a million. Who knows? The Shadow does . . .

What says Reese Palley? He wears his best Mona Lisa smile, looks heavenward as if he were expecting celestial instructions, chuckles slightly, and, depending on his mood and the moment purrs, "Enough." Or, shrugs his black-turtle-necked shoulders and says, "Who knows?" Or confidently, "Millions."

How did this crazy idea of giving himself a birthday party in Paris begin? Where did the idea come from? He stole it.

The concept is simple enough. Cosmetic firms have been doing it successfully for years. They call it purchase-with-purchase. You buy something, you get something free. Or at a ridiculously low price.

The basic ingredients were on hand: Reese wanted to celebrate his fiftieth birthday. Reese was opening an art gallery in Paris featuring artists well known in the United States. (The theme: "Bring something American home from Paris.")

How could he bring people to the opening of his Paris art gallery? He needed a hook. A dazzling hook.

An agent of Salvador Dali happened to approach Reese with an art offer. It seems crafty Dali had done paintings of the face cards in a playing deck: the four jacks, queens, kings, aces and one joker. Dali would offer them as a limited edition of lithographs. *One hundred seventy prints of each card.* Total: 2,890 renditions. *Voila!* The bait for the hook.

Reese later said, "Dali made them for me." (Hmmmmmmmm. If so, how come they were gathering dust in Dali's studio since 1967—four years earlier? And how come they were seen on playing cards for twenty-five dollars a deck?)

But who cared? Or knew? Apparently not the customers Reese had on file.

So! Reese said he would buy *all* 2,890. Uh, yes, of course with an option to cancel if he found he could not sell them.

How much did he pay for each lithograph?

Again, no one *really* knows except you-know-who.

Some dealers say in this huge quantity he could have bought them for fifty dollars each. Reese is horrified at the thought. "My God," he says, "Dali lithographs sell *wholesale* for $180!"

He put together an inexpensive, rather crudely done mailing piece—a booklet. ("Cost me about a nickel apiece," he admitted.) The front page headline said, "This one you won't believe."

Inside, the copy explained it was his birthday and he wanted to spend the day in Paris opening his new gallery and wanted his friends to travel there with him. He described the Dali lithographs, and as a kicker, offered the "joker" (there's always one in Reese's deck) to his customers for $650.00 which entitled them to a round trip passage to Paris for two for a four-day weekend including jet fare and hotel room.

And, he guaranteed to buy the lithograph back for the $650.00 at any future date.

He mailed the invitations and figured on sending out a follow-up. After all, he had chartered a 747 with about 400 seats!

In four days, he was sold out.

In ten days he had sold out TWO 747s!

For the first time in commercial airline history, one person had chartered TWO 747s. Oh well . . .

That's 700 people. That's 350 lithographs @ $650 = $227,500 and we are just beginning.

Naturally on the flight over he assembled a major art collection and there was . . . a special offer. The price of each painting was *less* going over, but would be slightly *more* going back. Ahh, Reese was in full action.

Before the plane arrived he had a couple of treats ready. To make sure everyone in the world knew he was giving a free trip, he preprinted postcards with Paris scenes, already postmarked, with the message ready to be sent to friends of his birthday-celebrating friends (after all he would be sixty someday). The cards each said: "Free at last. Free at last. Reese Palley has given me something free at last . . ."

Now the plane arrived. Plural: Planes. Armed with their postcards and luggage, everyone was ready to head for customs. But wait! Here, let's have some real fun! Everyone put on these face-sized photographic masks with the rubber-bands to hold the faces on. Whose face? Who else? The Benevolent One. Can you begin to picture the consternation and shock of the custom officials who looked up the corridor and saw coming at them, bag and baggage, *700 Reese Palleys!*

Small wonder this made the news wires and world-wide press.

When he arrived in Paris and checked in at the Intercontinental Hotel (just down the street from the new gallery location), Palley held his press conference in the hotel's magnificent red and gilt Baroque Room. No Hoo-Ha Henry VIII costume here. This time . . . Napoleon! There he was, holding court, lolling in an Atlantic City Boardwalk wicker-back rolling chair (brought over on the plane, naturally).

Reese set up a temporary shop in the hotel lobby and took orders on Boehm plates. Why not? Four hundred sets at $300 each. And a few more Dalis. His customers who bought the jokers wanted jacks, queens, kings—complete sets. Money, money, money, money . . .

To liven up the return plane trip, he announced his new organization called the National Association of Friends of Rare Porcelain. Dues were $5.00 a year and everyone joined on the trip home.

How much did Reese realize from this Dali-Palley-gallery gaiety?

Figure it out. Cost of all the Dalis—the 350 prepurchased to qualify for the round trip for two, plus another 350 the travelers snatched up on board (at the "going" rate). About 700 Dalis.

Probable cost: Around $50,000.

Plus a hotel bill of $32,000.

Plus the two 747s. Another $110,000.

Total in the area of $192,000. Let's throw in another $28,000 for expenses here and there, which gives us $220,000. Cost. Maybe.

How much did he take in?

Well, for starters, there's the 350 people times the $650 which equals $227,500.

Gee, only $7,000 profit?

Well, not quite.

Remember the extra 350 lithographs. That's ANOTHER $227,500. Plus a profit of about $60,000 from the Boehm plates. And the art he sold on the plane coming and going. If Reese didn't make a million from just the trip and the promises-to-buy-more after the trip, well, he at least made (as he says and you look for the tear in his eye) "a lot of friends . . ." who went to Paris to wish him Happy Birthday and who, of course, are all members of the National Association of Friends of Rare Porcelain. Gotcha!

The following year he planned a similar trip to Tahiti. And then there was the 747 he chartered to bring a wedding party to Rome and invited all his friends. And then there was the time . . .

His career is like a real-life Saturday cinema cliff-hanging serial—always another chapter.

What happens to Reese Palley next?

What will he conjure up? What will he promote? What outrageous, reckless idea will he concoct to raise the temperature of the traditionalists who keep saying "It can't be done . . ."—and all the while, he's doing it.

Only the headlines will tell. Few of us would plot the unchartered course of this reckless sailor. For sailing, says Reese, is his true pure passion. Maybe that's why he sails his thirty-two-foot sloop *Unlikely* repeatedly into the Bermuda Triangle.

Taking chances is simply the Reese Palley way of doing business.

THE SAYINGS OF CHAIRMAN REESE

ON MERCHANDISING: "If a product doesn't sell, raise the price."

ON RE-MERCHANDISING: "If it sells fast, it's too cheap."

ON THE MEDIA: "You can get all the publicity you want if you follow the two basic rules. Be honest. Give them a quotable quote."

ON HIS EMPLOYEES: "They're scared to death I'm going to open my fly in public."

ON HIS EX-EMPLOYEES: When former Palley New York Museum director Dave Hickey left, his departing remark was, "I felt like a ship leaving a sinking rat." To which Palley answered, "When I saw his comment in the paper I almost hired him back. That's a creative line! Shows very good thinking."

ON SELLING ATLANTIC CITY IN PRE-CASINO DAYS: "Change the beaches to nude bathing. That'll bring the crowds."

ON SELLING ATLANTIC CITY IN POST-CASINO DAYS: "I'm working on a book called *Atlantic City on $1,000 a Day.*"

ON SELLING CONTEMPORARY ART: "It reminds me how little I understand."

ON PRICING: He bought some Japanese lead-glass ash trays. Cheap. Put out a dozen at $5.95. Sold the dozen in one day. "Ooops," he said, "wrong price, too low." Put out another dozen for $10.95. Sold those in one day. Moved the price immediately to $25. Sold six in one day. "Getting closer to the right price," he reasoned. Eventually sold them all at prices ranging up to $100 each. Then there was one left. Put a price tag on it for $295.00 with a note, "Last of its kind"—which it was, right? "The person who bought that tells me to this day how everyone that comes into his home admires that marvelous rare Japanese ash tray. *THAT* was the right price!"

ON THREATS TO HIS LIFE: "I received a phone call the other day saying they were going to cut my throat with a razor blade. I thought about that and figured if I was going to die, I wanted to die like a kosher chicken."

Update

Reese made his fortune in Atlantic City. And left. He bought the Marlborough-Blenheim hotel where he was a tenant because he knew the Quaker owners would not want to be involved in gambling. And then, within a few months, he sold the hotel at a few million dollars profit. How many million? As with the lithographs, he's not telling. . . .

He has reversed Horace Greeley's advice and went west. To China. To build boats.

He likes the wages he has to pay ("15¢ an hour") and the fact that everyone from the janitor to the boss receives the same wage.

"If you walk the streets of Shanghai you can find anything you want. Or ask someone and the next day they have either (1) found what you want or (2) opened a factory to make it."

Does working with a communist country bother him? His answer:

"When I was young and poor I was a communist. Now that I'm old and rich, I'm a capitalist."

Bill Veeck

"There's nothing wrong with stealing other people's ideas. And anyone who doesn't is presumptuous. Because there simply aren't that many new ideas. You simply take something used somewhere else and adopt it for your own use."

—BILL VEECK

IF NON-THINKING is the theme of The Great Brain Robbery (and it is), then its resident high priest must be Bill Veeck (and he was).

His many and varied promotional ideas bring out the best from the crowds and the prose from the press (some of it rather purple). He is a maverick, marked and much admired not just for *doing* the non-traditional—but for doing it in the most traditional game: Baseball.

Rules are NOT meant to be broken in baseball, they kept telling Bill Veeck, from the early days of his ownership of the Milwaukee Brewers through his ownership of the Cleveland Indians, St. Louis Browns, Chicago White Sox, and, the White Sox again.

Like most prophets who propose and practice unusual and non-traditional ideas, he was "turned out" by the traditionalists. Society-Establishment doesn't sanction the sensational. And, like most prophets, many of Bill's "unthinkable" ideas and philosophy—once violently opposed by team and league presidents, are now, as a matter-of-stride, the way the game of baseball is officially played.

And the Great American Pastime boasts of higher attendance than ever—a fact hopefully to be acknowledged by some future sports historians—because of the foresight and uncommon sense of Bill Veeck, who was, clearly, a man before his time.

He was the man who, in the best non-traditional sense:

● Signed Larry Doby, the first Negro player in the American league. Veeck received 20,000 letters—most were violent and obscene. He answered each one, including a paragraph congratulating each correspondent on being wise and fortunate enough to have chosen parents of correct color and beyond prejudice!

● Was the first to use the exploding scoreboard, which he admits he stole from the final scene of William Saroyan's play, The Time of Your Life.

● The first to have players' names printed boldly on the back of the uniforms ("Oh! That's who 37 is!")

• The first to have the grandstand managers call the plays. Veeck provided huge hand-held billboards saying "Yes" or "No" which fans held aloft to direct the player to hit, steal, bunt, whatever . . . (By the way, the team won that night.)

• The first thing he did as new manager of a club: Took off the doors of his offices and listed his phone number so anyone who wanted to call him for anything could get him directly without any nonsense about switchboards.*

He persuaded the city of Cleveland to cancel midget auto racing at his stadium because the cars chewed up the playing turf. When the customers complained, he agreed to provide his own midget racing. He did: Six midgets in six kiddie cars pedaling madly across the infield toward home plate! The winner received a large lollipop. One of the drivers was Eddie Gaedel (whom you'll hear more about in a minute).

The closing feat when he was boss of Suffolk Downs Race Track in Boston: He stages a real, honest-to-goodness chariot race. (Asked Charlton Heston to come. Heston declined. Said he only participated in chariot races that were fixed for him to win.) He found half a dozen Roman chariots with the help of MGM and Billy Weinberger, then head of Caesar's Palace in Las Vegas, now head of Bally's Park Place Casino in Atlantic City—which he bought from Reese Palley. See, there really are only 400 people in the world (see our chapter on this).

Back to baseball. When fans complained vendors and candy butchers always seemed to block the view of the playing field, he promised this would positively NOT happen on the opening day in 1961. (It didn't. He had midget vendors selling *midget* refreshments—including fast-pedaling Eddie Gaedel, the Little Man.)

But with all his novel, different, daring and crowd-pleasing events, one stands out above the rest by sheer magnitude (or perhaps, lack of magnitude) of its impact on the baseball industry, the sportswriters of America and the American public. Fans in neighborhood bars or in front of TV sets with beers in hand will even now occasionally pause during commercials to turn the volume down and once more talk about the day that wily William Veeck sent The Midget Up To Bat . . .

Bill Veeck came into baseball naturally. His father, William Veeck, Sr., was a sportswriter for the *Hearst-American* in Chicago. One day, he wrote a piece criticizing the Cubs. Owner William Wrigley took the classic stance of "If you know so much, why don't *you* run the club?" Veeck,

*Calling Bill Veeck direct still works. We very much wanted Bill to write us a quote for ; book. How to do that? Murray snapped his fingers and said, "Veeck always lists his ie phone, remember?" We dialed Chicago information, asked for the number and heard l ar ˌˇ with a brisk "Veeck." "We had worked with you three years ago." He remem- ˌsted we make it fast. He had a night game and was leaving in five minutes. ote for the book?" we asked. He laughed and said, "Can I read it first?" ., as in "wreck." As in Great.

Sr., accepted. One of his first moves was to hire Joe McCarthy, later legendary leader of the Yankees. And the Cubs won their first pennant in twenty-one years.

A quiet, reticent man, he was unlike the flamboyant son he sired. Veeck, Sr., was also a man of high moral character. Knowing the infamous Black Sox gambling "fix" was a scandal endangering the future of baseball, he was instrumental in hiring Judge Kenesaw Mountain Landis—a close personal friend who brought integrity back to baseball.

Veeck, Sr., himself brought the fans back. His Chicago Cubs were the first team to draw more than one million customers in one season.

Bill worked in baseball at an early age. (Note: part of the difference in father and son was their first names. The father was always William, the son always Bill.) Bill worked the baseball concession stands and quickly discovered the faster he worked between innings, the more he sold. The short break, comparable to TV's commercial in sporting events, meant the closer he could place his merchandise within arm's reach, the more food and drink he would sell. If he could grab a dog and a drink without moving . . . terrific. His sales formula: "One extra step costs ten percent of your gross."

At the young age of twenty-six, Bill bought the Milwaukee Brewers Triple-A team with $25,000 of borrowed money. In just four years, he took the team from the brink of bankruptcy to the pinnacle of minor league attendance records—plus winning three pennants.

When asked the secret of his success, he said, "I decided very early in my life that while I couldn't outsmart anybody, I could work harder and longer than anyone else was apparently willing to work." (Winners work harder.)*

And so Bill would stand at the gate to greet customers as they arrived and as they left. EVERY game. He never sat in the owner's box. He sat with different groups of fans in every inning. And would ask, "What do you like? What don't you like?"

With the Brewers—and with each subsequent club or organization he bought—he would get to the park/club/turf early in the morning and check everything from the concessions to the seats to the rest rooms. He's everywhere. He always takes the extra step. People soon know . . . he cares.

In 1943 he joined the U.S. Marines. A recoiling artillery piece injured his right leg in Bougainville. Operation after operation failed to save the leg and in November, 1946, it was amputated.

---

*Calvin Coolidge said something similar years before: "Nothing in the world ca⬛⬛⬛⬛ the place of persistence. Talent will not—nothing is more common than unsuc⬛⬛⬛⬛⬛⬛th talent. Genius will not—unrewarded genius is almost a proverb. Educ⬛⬛ world is full of educated derelicts. Persistence and determination⬛ (Probably the longest sentence Cal ever wrote . . .)

In 1947, a syndicate headed by Veeck bought the Cleveland Indians. The next year, they doubled their attendance. The following year (1948), Cleveland won its first pennant in twenty-eight years! Attendance hit a record high of 2,620,677—never topped as of this writing.

And helping set that record was Veeck's inability to say "no" as a speechmaker anywhere in Ohio. He averaged better than a speech a night and there were times when he made as many as fifteen separate appearances in one day!

After the 1949 season, Veeck sold the Indians. He bought the St. Louis Browns in 1951 and sold them two years later.*

In 1959, he bought the White Sox and the club won its first pennant since 1919 and set a home attendance record. In 1960, he topped that record with 1,644,460 attendance—due in some part to Veeck's introduction of the sensational "exploding scoreboard."**

He sold the White Sox in 1961 and, a few years later, took over Suffolk Downs Race Track.

Then there was the moment when he nearly bought the Ringling Brothers Barnum and Bailey Circus, and there are those who have wild hallucinations on what would . . . could . . . have happened if THAT deal had gone through! Elephants on trapezes?

In 1975, he stopped the White Sox from leaving Chicago to move to Seattle. He took the oldest ball park in the big leagues, cleaned it up, added murals, paintings, and created an attractive, exciting, fun environment that set a home park attendance record—again—breaking the one he himself set originally nearly twenty years ago.***

All of these accomplishments and achievements seem to pale against the time Bill Veeck sent the midget up to bat.

Says Veeck, "He was, by golly, the best darn midget who ever played big league ball. He was also the only one . . ."

Baseball is the most traditional and sacrosanct of professional sports

---

*In his speeches, he tells classics like this: "Business was so bad in St. Louis, as general manager I had to answer the phone. One day a lady called and asked what time the game started. I said, "Lady—what time would be convenient for you?" She wanted to know if she could be sure to get a seat. I said, "Lady—how about second base, we haven't used it for a week!"

**Once at Lake Geneva in an appearance with us, he told the World Hockey League they were too traditional. "With all the action on the ice," he said, "if the guy in front of me stands up, I can't tell if they scored a goal. Why don't you have the net blow up, shoot up to the roof, have sirens go off? Create excitement!" If hockey had Veeck, that would happen.

***Ever aware of what people love and hate, Veeck cleverly staged an Anti-Disco Rally between games at a double-header. The fans were invited to stream onto the playing fiel̶̶̶tomp and destroy a huge pile of disco records. So ferocious was the destruction, ̶̶̶̶d was rendered unplayable and the second game had to be canceled! Did ̶̶̶the national publicity that riot got?

in this country. That simple fact became an almost daily challenge to Veeck, the non-traditionalist. He rewrote the rule book throughout his baseball career.

But the most shattering breaking-of-rules took place on a fateful day in 1951 when more than 18,000 fans witnessed a scene which was immediately teletyped, announced, and broadcast to the rest of the world and made sports history. Break-the-rules Bill sent a *midget* up to bat!

And baseball would never be the same.

It began simply because Veeck was looking for an angle to bring in crowds. Looking for a reason-how, he used the American League's fiftieth anniversary theme that year and tied in his brewery sponsor, Falstaff beer, for their birthday celebration as well. Not that it WAS their birthday. But since none could prove it was NOT their birthday . . .

To convince Falstaff management he had a terrific idea, Veeck did what any good promoter would do: He told them he had a terrific idea. When pressed for details, he would look around suspiciously and whisper he could not give exact details because he was afraid the information would leak out. In truth, he did not know, at that moment, exactly what he was going to do. In fact, he had NO idea of what he was going to do. The conspiracy worked.

The beer people figured good-old-Bill wouldn't let them down. Their distributors and dealers hustled tickets all over the state. Result: more than 18,000 packed the stadium for a Sunday doubleheader against the last place Detroit Tigers.

How do ideas come about? What happens when inspiration strikes? Does it really happen like in the comic books? Does an electric light suddenly go "on" over your head?

Most often it is simply a case of bits and chips of information piled atop information inside the thinking apparatus atop our heads. When the right moment comes, like a giant volcano undisturbed for centuries, there is a tremendous explosion. Some say it is "spontaneous." Those of us who know better say, "It had been a long time brewing." (A more appropriate phrase could not be found as far as Falstaff beer was concerned.)

There are those who say Veeck stole this fabulous idea from James Thurber's "You Could Look It Up" which had a similar premise. And though Veeck believes in the Eleventh Commandment as all good promoters do (see "Introduction"), he remembers the inspiration from his childhood idol, John J. McGraw, good friend of his father and former manager of the New York Giants. McGraw had a little hunchback named Eddie Morrow. He kept him around the club and often threatened he would "send Eddie up to bat" one day before he left the game of baseball.

The fact the idea originated with McGraw did not bother Veeck. In true Brain Robbery fashion, Bill's philosophy is: "If you're a promoter, you've got to take credit for other people's ideas." Why not? But update 'em.

And here he was with the Browns looking for an idea to make Falstaff happy. Why not send a small man up to bat—a little Brownie. In fact . . . a midget.

Veeck called a booking agent who found tiny Eddie Gaedel in Chicago. He was three feet, seven inches tall and weighed sixty-five pounds, suited up. The idea was happening—and Veeck kept the secret to a handful of inner sanctum friends.

Veeck told Eddie what he had in mind. Gaedel would be a big-league ball player. Well, at least for a day. And he would be appearing before thousands of people. Could he handle it?

Gaedel was an actor and snapped at the one-day, one-time, once-in-a-lifetime job. Veeck showed him how to crouch at the plate (crouch? yes) like a ballplayer. Only more so. Which narrowed the normal strike zone down to a miniscule one and a half inches!

Gaedel mastered the crouch. And then, suddenly, began to swing his imaginary bat at the imaginary ball.

Veeck was thunderstruck. What was his new friend doing? He was not supposed to swing. He was supposed to wait. Four balls, one at a time. And then walk dramatically to first base. But no, Veeck warned—no, never . . . *swing!*

Veeck put it succinctly and simply to Gaedel. "Eddie, I'm going to be up on the roof with a high-powered rifle watching every move you make. If you so much as look as if you're going to swing, I'm going to shoot you dead." Eddie stopped swinging and nodded his head.

Amazing how an actor can understand directions when a director breaks it down into specific threats.

The day of the game. Veeck was ready and, he hoped, so was Gaedel.

The stadium was full. Falstaff's men had done their job. Eddie's uniform was borrowed from a small seven-year old. The number "1/8" was custom-sewn on the back. Eddie's name was printed on the program, an official contract was prepared, signed, and mailed to league headquarters. Nothing was missed. Everything was ready for the magic moment . . .

The sell-out crowd was happily drinking their free Falstaff beer, eating their free birthday cake and ice cream.

Everyone knew Veeck, the great promoter, the show-off genius, the fun-lover. He would have something unbelievable for the between-game show. The Falstaff people waited for the something special whispered by Bill.

The show began with a parade of antique cars, a bicycle they built for four. Musicians marched high through the stands! A hand balancing act was happening at first base. A trampoline act at second and jugglers at third. A clown who performed all over the field and the Browns' own band with Satchel Paige on the drums . . .

Not bad for a between-games show.

But the Falstaff people waited . . . There must be something else. Veeck's philosophy had always been to put together half a dozen ideas and then, at the last minute add something unexpected, unadvertised, uncharged-for . . . the basis for Added Value.

A special giant Falstaff birthday cake was brought to the center of the field, and, on cue, out popped a little brownie, complete with elf shoes—our friend Eddie Gaedel.

A smattering of applause and small laughter from the crowd. And the Falstaff people sat, nervously smiling, waiting for the punchline . . .

Nothing.

"That's it, Bill?" they asked, not quite believing.

"He's a real live Brownie," answered Veeck, calmly emphasizing *Brownie*.

The sponsors complained the idea was not new, Veeck had done the cake gimmick before and where was the spectacular idea Veeck had promised. Was . . . that . . . it?

"Well, uh, yes," said Veeck.

Strained silence.

The second game started and as the Browns came up for their half of the first inning, suddenly little Eddie Gaedel emerged from the dugout waving three tiny warm-up bats. And the announcer's voice echoed over the stadium, "For the Browns, number one-eighth, Eddie Gaedel!"

There is that very special moment of stillness in any dramatic event. When the actor has brought the audience to heights . . . and is on the stage. When the tornado is about to hit and you are in the exact middle or "eye" of the storm . . . and everything is stark silence. When a stunning announcement is made to an audience, they are first amazed, then unbelieving, and then suddenly the rising, murmuring sound waves become overwhelming, as if on cue, the giant crowd realizes what has happened.

Such was this moment.

The Falstaff sponsors sat bolt upright.

The home plate umpire, Hurley, took one look at Gaedel and stalked over to Browns' manager, Zack Taylor, demanding an explanation. Out came Taylor coolly, handing over the copy of the contract, copy of the telegram to league headquarters and the listing of little Eddie on the official roster.

Photographers swarmed around home plate. The audience was in a constant roar. The Detroit pitcher and catcher laughed, chatted for a few minutes, knowing this was only one of those crazy Veeck gags and the midget would soon disappear—they hoped.

Not so. Bill had promised Eddie his moment in history.

Hurley, faced with the authentic papers and a ball game, did what any self-respecting league umpire would do: He shooed away the photographers and bawled the classic call: "Play Ball!"

The Detroit pitcher was not sure what to do. The catcher came to talk it over seriously now and made the logical decision. Back to plate the catcher went and got down on both knees to offer some kind of target.

In the press box, the typewriters were chattering away, the announcers pace had shifted to high, the Falstaff people were laughing and cheering and Veeck, oblivious to all the pandemonium around him was watching little Eddie Gaedel and wondering, Would the enthusiasm of the audience flow down to the small figure at home plate? Would Eddie, in the excitement, forget Veeck's instructions? Would Eddie, above all, do the unforgiveable—and swing at the ball?

But no, Eddie the actor did as directed. Curled in the tight crouch, trying to look threatening to the pitcher, who by now was laughing so hard he could barely throw the ball. Ball three, then four, then Eddie trotted down to first base. He waited for the pinch runner, patted him on the rump, posed for pictures and, like a pro, trotted across the field to the dugout in slow motion—stopping every few steps to tip his hat to the enthusiastic crowd, turning, bouncing, and then disappeared into the dugout, a happy man . . .

Baseball tried to turn its vengeful wrath on Veeck by threatening to censor the moment out of written baseball history, but Veeck, who had promised Gaedel his moment in history, struck back and said if Gaedel's name was to be cut out of official records, so must the game—and would baseball, traditional, sanctimonious baseball, try to say that, in fact, a game with 18,000 witnesses had never been played? Reluctantly, oh so reluctantly, the league backed down and Eddie's name remains a one-day, one-time official playing appearance in baseball records.

When Gaedel died, he received a front page obituary in the New York *Times,* realizing even beyond the dreams of his mentor, Veeck, a firm place in history.

And that is Veeck, the super-promoter, the entertainer, the original idea-entrepreneur, the man who made pennant winners out of last place ball clubs, the man who shattered more tradition, and who at the Suffolk Downs battled the state and officials—and won. The man who surrounds himself with talent that produces dozens of new and novel ideas, and yet he knows he will always be remembered for this one memorable fact: The Man Who Sent The Midget Up To Bat.

THE QUOTABLE VEECK

"The exploding scoreboard I stole from Saroyan's *The Time of Your Life*. Man played pinball machine throughout the play. And just before the final curtain, he hit and the pinball machine lit up the whole stage. Worked for him. I figured it would work for me."

•

"Take everything you think of and twist it to fit your own ends."

•

"The best promotions occur almost spontaneously. They come from something else. The plotted ones get tired: like Bat Day, Hat Day, Ball Day, Cap Day, Shirt Day, Jacket Day. Idea: When you give away a jacket—for a game—fine. But, at the end of the season, anyone who wears the jacket—gets in free!"

•

"People like to identify with swashbucklers. Who wants to identify with a .210 hitting second baseman? You identify with the guy you want to be: The one who hits the ball out of the ball park; the one who doesn't conform to the rules; the one who's exciting; the one *you* want to be, the non-conformist. 'Gee, that's who I'd really like to be . . .'"

•

"Don't accept what has been done before as the *only* way to do anything. Invariably it's the wrong way. It was done at a time when tradition was being established. Don't let tradition become a stinking, dead albatross around the neck of PROGRESS."

•

"Gags can backfire. YOU MUST BE CAREFUL. One time in St. Louis we had a night for the Teamsters. Harold Gibbons, head of the Teamsters, gave away sponge rubber baseballs. Imagine, now, 8,000 young people in the upper deck with the rubber baseballs. First man up hit the ball to right field. Now the stands wanted to make sure that ball was not caught. So, all of a sudden, there were 4,000 baseballs in the air. One thing for the right fielder, though—he caught *one* of them . . .''

●

His epitaph for the midget story: "He helped the Little Man."

Update

Bill Veeck died in 1985.

We did some research to find out exactly how he kept himself busy his last years. Here's his thoughts:

On keeping busy: "I wander around the country speaking here and there. Do a few pieces, covered the World Series '83 for USA Today, review a book or so a month, see maybe 50 ballgames sitting in Wrigley Field with my shirt off, drink a few cans of beer, tell a lot of lies. . . ."

Causes: "Then, of course, we spend a lot of time on what I call our lost causes, the ones we have not yet won: ERA, Handgun Control and Anti-Nuclear. And add to that the Cubs and you have four non-winners so far. I don't know why we can't be attracted to one shoo-in but I suppose that would spoil the whole pattern."

Baseball and Ownership: "I traded in my Easton, Maryland home for a small piece of Center Field in Comisky Park. And then I got the small piece of center field back again when we sold the White Sox and now we have our Atrium house in Chicago—on the South side, of course."

Life according to Veeck:
"It's a kind of a Shakespeare busyness I presume, much ado about nothing, nonetheless I do feel we are getting something done here and there. Today, for instance, I'm going to have a very difficult day: we're going to go down to the beach and swim. It's a strain on all of us."

Frank Gravatt: The Quiet Legend

IT IS 1897.

The slight, sandy-haired seven-year-old spreads newspapers over the floor of one of the rooms in the Seaside Hotel in Atlantic City, New Jersey, overlooking the Atlantic Ocean. He works ahead of his father, a carpet layer, who is in a neighboring room. The newspapers serve as padding for the carpet.

Since he is working ahead, the young boy decides to wait. He walks over to the hotel window to look at the ocean below. Workmen are putting together metal beams to an amusement pier extending out to the sea which they call "The Steel Pier."

His eyes travel down the expanse of beach, and he sees small rooming houses and a wooden boardwalk laid parallel to the ocean as far as he can see.

In a few short years, many new high-rise hotels will dominate the sand dunes facing the ocean. Their names will be Traymore, Royal Palace, Esplanade, President, Ritz-Carlton, Shelburne, Ambassador, Lafayette, Chelsea, Colonial, St. Charles . . .

And the seven-year-old boy looking through the window will not only own them all but also the pier below him and the hotel in which he turns to continue helping his father lay the carpet . . .

Frank Gravatt was a quiet legend. Neither he nor his name appeared in the spotlight like most of the promoters and salesmen mentioned in this book. This was true throughout his life with one exception, his pet project: the Steel Pier. There, under the large sign welcoming everyone to the world-famous amusement attraction, you would see, in much smaller letters, "Under the direction of Frank Gravatt."

He could be excused for that one venture in the open. For "to play the pier" was the goal of all the great entertainers of this country. And the reason for the pier's prominence and mystique was . . . Frank Gravatt.

The Gravatt story is an inspiration, and perhaps one day will be a book. It is a story of one man's dedication to the city with which he carried on a life-long love affair, Atlantic City.

More than any other one person, he gave Atlantic City the aura and excitement it held in its heyday: the thirties through the fifties. He prophesied the coming of the casinos long before anyone else, though he never believed his community needed anything else but the God-given values of beach, ocean, and fresh air.

Every promotion he assembled was conceived with one goal in mind: to have people say good things about Atlantic City. And to come and share the good times with him.

It was difficult for reporters to put together a history of what-he-did through the years because he was a quiet man. In his later years he consented to have us tape record many hours of never-before-told stories on his promotions. His request they never be made public in his lifetime was honored. He died, in 1980, at the age of eighty-eight.

Here, for the first time, are some of his recollections of the exciting and marvelous Ideas that made him famous and wealthy in his own time. He lived through the era of Dr. Russell Conwell's inspiring classic speech about opportunity, "Acres of Diamonds," whose theme was all men and women can discover success and happiness in their lives right where they live. (See "Expectations Vs. Reality.") Frank Gravatt did just that. He even paraphrased the "Acres of Diamonds" to mean the sun's reflections on the many prismed particles of sand on his admired Atlantic City beaches.

We have selected and condensed some of the stories of his early life, dwelling largely on his purchase and development of the Steel Pier. He built and promoted it to a world-wide attraction during his twenty-year tenure as "The Salt Water Barnum."

Many of his techniques were simply copying and improving upon the success and ideas of others. For Idea men use similar tracks to arrive at their destination. Some blow their horns loudly to tell you they are on their way . . . or have arrived. Others chug quietly into the station and you never know they made the trip. Until it's over . . .

Frank Gravatt was a quiet one.

Like many top men of his generation, Frank Gravatt had very little formal education. From his early job of helping his father put down the carpet in the Seaside Hotel, he was a careful, conscientious worker. Owner-Governor Charles Evans was so impressed with the work of the seven-year-old, he gave young Frank five cents—his first bonus. The young boy promptly spent it all in a Boardwalk soft drink concession stand with the sign, "All you can drink for a nickel." He filled his stomach but was left with empty pockets.

He learned Lesson Number One: Don't spend all your money in one place at one time.

From that day on, he put aside a portion of everything he earned . . .

As a young teenager, he delivered newspapers morning, noon, and night. His four routes each paid him $1.50. Total week's take: $6.00.

He left for a grocery store job where he (1) took care of the horse (2) put out the produce (3) waited on customers (4) made up the orders (5) delivered them and, after work, (6) drove the wagon as a bus.

Since he was in a resort town, he saw the need for ice cream cones. He quit his job and with money saved from the grocery store and newspaper routes, he bought equipment to make ice cream cones. Looking for a place to work, he found a pool hall on Atlantic City's main street with a large curtain covering the big front window so no one could see inside.

He persuaded the owner to push the curtain back a few feet and rent him the space directly in back of the window. Passers-by would stop and watch young Frank Gravatt make ice cream cones before their very eyes. Showmanship. And Sales. He discovered that one followed the other.

Lesson Number Two: Showmanship gets you sales.

He took the profits from the ice cream cones and bought a horse and wagon to sell ice cream in Atlantic City. His main competition was a man called "Ice Cream Johnny." But young Frank felt because he had the newer wagon, all he had to do was go up and down the street and customers would come and buy his ice cream. He did not bother putting his name on HIS ice cream truck because he did not think it necessary to tell anyone who he was. Wrong.

Wherever young Frank would take his horse and wagon, Ice Cream Johnny had preceded him and sold the crowd. Everyone knew Ice Cream Johnny. His name was splashed in big letters all over his truck. He yelled and told everyone he was on his way.

Young Frank quickly learned *Lesson Number Three: You Have To Gain The Attention of Your Customer* which was quickly followed by *Lesson Number Four: If you want people to know what you have: Advertise!*

By the time he learned THOSE lessons, he was broke.

He sold the horse and wagon to pay his bills and went to work as a door-to-door coffee salesman. Again, putting aside a portion of his earnings for the future.

Then, as now, young men liked bicycles. With another man, Alvah Hall, he opened "Hall and Gravatt," a motorcycle and bicycle shop.

World War I had just begun and something called "automobiles" appeared on the dirt roads of Atlantic City alongside horse and buggies. Hall and Gravatt expanded and opened a small Buick agency. They brought the cars to Atlantic City. They went to Detroit . . . and drove them back! His sales increased and soon he had a group of young men making steady round trips to Detroit bringing new Buicks to Atlantic City.

He stationed a car outside his showroom on the street and installed a loudspeaker. Since he knew most of the businessmen in town, he would wait till they walked by, and suddenly the car "talked" to the potential customer, inviting him by name to get in and test drive the new Buick. The businessman, at first startled, then inquisitive, then amused would sometimes start to carry on a conversation with the car—and more often, he took the "car" up on its offer to test drive it. And buy it.

(Years later Allan Funt of "Candid Camera" fame would cause laughter in TV households with his famous "Talking Mailbox." But Gravatt's "Talking Buick" preceded Funt by fifty years.)

Soon his agency grew to one of the largest in the country. Gravatt, remembering his early soda-drinking experience, continued to save a portion of his earnings . . .

One day a customer came into the auto agency and asked if Gravatt knew anyone who wanted to buy three apartment houses. The price seemed reasonable to Gravatt, who approached partner Hall and suggested they buy the buildings. No, said Hall, he was in the automobile business, not the real estate business.

Gravatt thought about that and then invested his savings to buy the buildings. Within thirty days he sold them and made $3,000 profit. He brought the check to his partner and offered to share the income since they WERE partners. Hall refused. He said Gravatt had made the investment and should keep the profit.

Gravatt began to think maybe there was something in this real estate business . . .

The 1920s were heady times for land speculation in Atlantic City. People stood in line for thirty-six hours to buy empty lots on nearby islands. Gravatt would place a small deposit on a building or piece of ground and then resell the property at a profit—often before he made final settlement himself!

One time he had difficulty selling a group of buildings. He contacted the best real estate salesman in town and said, "If you use all your efforts to sell this property, and nothing else for the next two weeks, I will double your commission." The real estate man sold the houses in ten days.

Lesson Number Five: Spend Money To Make Money.

Soon Gravatt was making so many real estate deals he would be in and out of the bank completing as many as four transactions in one day!

The Chelsea Bank was so impressed with this dynamic young real estate person they made him a director. His buying and selling continued at such a rapid pace, a group of his fellow directors asked him to put together a large deal and they would be his partners.

Gravatt knew the famous Steel Pier was up for sale. And he also knew he did not have the necessary cash. Now, with all these new partners, he went to pier owner Louis Burk, well-known wealthy Philadelphia wholesale sausage distributor. Burk agreed to sell. His price: $2 million with a down payment of $500,000 payable within six months. Plus one condition. The attorneys for Burk insisted on their client not paying more than 12 percent in the newly proposed capital gains tax law, about which little was known, on the total deal. Anything over that would be picked up by the buyers. Gravatt agreed and put up $50,000 of his own money as a good faith deposit with the $450,000 balance due in six months.

He returned to Atlantic City and told his new partners the deal. The attorney for the group, Walter Gill, was astonished. He argued *against* going through with the transaction. He asked who-would-know-how-much the overage of twelve percent would amount to? Gravatt had bought a pig in a poke. And he, for one, was out. And so were the remaining ten partners.

Gravatt remembers he was so nervous he could not stand up until everyone had left the room.

He had invested $50,000 of his own money. Now he was faced with two choices: Lose the $50,000. Or take the entire deal himself.

Lesson Number Six: Don't Have Partners.

But where would he find nearly half a million dollars needed for settlement?

After the meeting he went down and talked to the cashier of the Chelsea Bank, Phil Besser, and told him his story. Besser put his arm around Gravatt and said, "You can buy it, Frank. All you have to do is get rid of all the real estate you have. With the market the way it is, you'll have the money in six months."

And he did.

And he bought the Steel Pier.

And now comes the O. Henry twist. Gravatt's attorney, Walter Hansteen, met with some bright accountants. Together they researched this new Federal Capital Gains Tax Law. They came to the conclusion the MOST Burk could pay in capital gains was . . . twelve percent. That was the MAXIMUM under the law.

Some of the original partners heard the decision and asked to come back into the deal. Gravatt's answer was what you-would-expect. "Thank you, but—"

QUESTION: What did this unsuccessful ice cream peddler, successful automobile dealer and real estate entrepreneur know about show business?

ANSWER: Nothing.

So he went out and bought copies of *Billboard* and *Variety* magazines, the show business bibles. He looked for the biggest grossing attractions in the country. If he was to be successful, why not bring in the winners?

The year was 1925. For the next twenty years he did just that—brought the most successful acts and made the Steel Pier second in fame and reputation only to the Palace Theater in New York City as the pinnacle for show business performers.

It took time. Gravatt had bought an open air pavilion populated by ladies in rocking chairs who paid ten cents apiece to listen to oompah bands or take afternoon naps to the sound of the ocean.

For his first headliner, he signed the March King, John Philip Sousa, to a "lifetime contract."

As he began his first year with his big-name attraction, Gravatt began to believe his original partners knew something he did not, because it rained eleven of the thirteen weekends that all-important first summer!

Atlantic City and the Steel Peer, the hotels and the hot dog stands, and the rooming houses and the bath houses—all depended on the weather, in the pre-gambling days. The weekend sun and temperature determined if the crowds from sixty-mile distant Philadelphia would—or would not—pack the Boardwalk. Summer was the season in Atlantic City. The success (profit or loss) was in direct proportion to the degree of heat and days of sunshine. The hotter the better. Rain not only kept customers from coming but encouraged those arrived to leave.

Sousa, playing to half-filled and often near-empty auditoriums, looked at the skies and called himself "The Rain God." Gravatt began to call himself "The Sap," wondering what happened to all the fun and profit he once had buying and selling real estate. But he didn't quit.

It took two years for Gravatt to come up with the Formula For Success. It was two-fold: Low Admission and Lots of Attractions.

Wondering how to attract huge crowds to his pier, Gravatt noticed Woolworth's five and dime on the Boardwalk attracted huge crowds to their store by a mixture of low prices and offering something for every taste.

If it worked for Woolworth's, would it work for the pier?

Why not? (Steal Ideas. The XIth Commandment.)

He rented huge billboards on all the roads leading into Atlantic City and advertised the Steel Pier with one sentence: "A five dollar show for fifty cents."

In later years Gravatt would say of this decision, "I see where the food stores and appliance stores are going "discount" today and they think it's something new. It's not. I went discount on the pier nearly fifty years ago . . ."

Lesson Number Seven: Find Out What The Customer Wants . . . And Give It To Them.

The success of this one price for everything policy was seen in attendance figures: More than one million paid admissions a year! In their top year, they hit nearly *two* million.

Gravatt continually sought new attractions. He was determined to have so much to see and do that customers would leave knowing they had to come back to simply get it all in. And they would tell others. And the name and fame of the pier spread . . .

In an article written for *Collier's* on July 30, 1938, columnist Lyle Crichton wrote it would take at least seventeen hours on the pier simply to "see two motion pictures, a minstrel show, a performance of opera in English, a complete vaudeville show starring Willie and Eugene Howard and Helen Morgan, dance in the ballroom to the music of Benny Goodman, sit through a complete set of circus acts including diving Hawaiians and a diving horse, listen to two Hawaiian-Filipino orchestras. Then browse through 'Laughland,' tremble through the 'Haunted Castle,' and have hours of entertainment still left."

All this for fifty cents.

In the beginning, Gravatt would watch the thousands of hungry and thirsty people march through his pier daily, all wanting to drink and eat. But he was unable to offer food because of a city ordinance prohibiting the sale of merchandise on the ocean side of the Boardwalk.

He rose to the challenge. Soon there were food and drink stands all over the Steel Pier. When the constabulary arrived, Gravatt pointed to the signs made for the occasion. They explained the food and drink were . . . free. But he was, uh, *renting* the containers that held the food and drinks to the customers for a small fee . . . (Get out of the Box!)

Eventually the ordinance was repealed. But Gravatt learned *Lesson Number Eight: Every Problem Is An Opportunity In Disguise*.

Through the years, anecdote piled atop anecdote all contributing to the history of the pier and the mystique of Gravatt the Showman. Among the more memorable:

● *The Seventy-Ton Whale:* Gravatt would travel to Europe and throughout North America to book acts for the pier. One day at a fair in Toronto he saw the longest line was waiting to get in to see an exhibit for a seventy-ton whale.

He bought a ticket, stood in line and saw the display. He spoke to the exhibitors and convinced them to sell him the whale. The agreed on price: $15,000. Fine. Now . . . how do you transport the 140,000 pounds of whale from Toronto, Canada, to Atlantic City?

Gravatt hired a flat bed freight car out of Toronto. Eventually, eighty men working 3,000 hours brought the whale to Atlantic City. Now . . . how do you move the mammal from the railroad station to the pier?

While he was thinking about that, everyone in town knew the whale had arrived. Not from the publicity. From the smell. The whale was full of formaldehyde, all seventy tons. The odor permeated the city. Gravatt worked fast, making contracts with housemovers to bring their combined equipment to the railroad station to transport the whale. By now, one of the property owners on the route of travel contacted City Hall and told the mayor, "I don't want that stinking whale coming down my street!"

Gravatt met with the mayor and asked for twenty-four hours to move the whale to an air-conditioned building on the pier.

The mayor did not have much of a choice. On one hand he had the original air-polluter at the railroad station. On the other hand he had Frank Gravatt's word the problem would be solved in one day. He agreed. And the crowds watched the slow-moving procession with fingers holding noses.

Millions came to see the whale. The attraction was one of the most-attended in the history of the pier.

● *The General Motors Display:* Gravatt was still active in the automobile business. He watched the crowds go through his new pier and thought there must be some major corporation that would rent space to show off their wares to millions of potential customers. Why not his friends in General Motors?

He went to Detroit and offered a display area for GM cars. He pointed out for about nineteen cents a person, General Motors could have prospective customers touch, feel, and sit in one of their cars. Where the nineteen cents figure? Gravatt simply divided the number of people who came to the pier by the rent he wanted. Result: nineteen cents.

GM agreed. IF . . . Gravatt would build an exhibit hall for them. He did. At a cost of half a million dollars. But his lease was for $156,000 rent a year. Four years later he had his investment back and the tenant was still paying the rent . . .

Now he had a car company. Why not an oil company? He contacted the Texaco people and offered to build them a sign atop the ballroom a half mile out at sea. Not only would the sixteen million visitors to Atlantic City see the sign but so would all the ships at sea.

Texaco rented the sign. For $80,000 a year.

● *Zoo's Who:* Gravatt had a zoo on the pier complete with camels; chimpanzees; Goliath, a 6,000 pound sea lion ("the largest sea lion in the world"); a gorilla, Gargantua ("the largest gorilla in the world") before it went to Ringling Brothers. Leo, the MGM lion, and Elsie, the Borden cow, both made appearances on the pier.

● Abe Lyman, the band conductor brought part of his band into a cage with a live tiger. The photograph made all the news services.

● And then there was the diving horse . . .

Gravatt bought the act from an agent in California. When the horse and diver arrived, the horse would not jump into the ocean. The agent was 3,000 miles away and suddenly not answering his phone. Gravatt simply built a huge addition at the end of the Steel Pier creating a large swimming pool.

The horse "dived."

● And then there was the boxing kangaroo who had an exhibition match with heavyweight champ Primo Carnera (no record of who won).

While he searched the world for animal acts, he knew the big draws were the name entertainers. Some he discovered—like Bud Abbott and Lou Costello. Others he showcased at their peak. A list of performers playing the pier during Gravatt's tenure would be a history of American show business filling many pages this size. Among the bands were Harry James, Sammy Kaye, Guy Lombardo, Rudy Vallee, Benny Goodman, Tommy and Jimmy Dorsey, Eddy Duchin, Paul Whiteman, Glenn Miller, Gene Krupa, Xavier Cugat, and literally hundreds more. Among the entertainers were Bob Hope, Milton Berle, George Burns and Gracie Allen, the Andrews Sisters, the Ink Spots, the Mills Brothers, Perry Como, Kate Smith, Edgar Bergen and Charlie McCarthy, George Jessel, Eddie Cantor, Sophie Tucker, Ed Sullivan, The Three Stooges, W. C. Fields, Dinah Shore, Red Skelton, and Amos 'n' Andy.

Through the years, Gravatt played to millions of people. He spent nearly 2 million for expansions and new theaters and new attractions. He installed a full sprinkler system because of his concern for safety. And he insisted on cleanliness. ("Not only did we keep the pier morally clean with wholesome entertainment for the entire family but also physically clean," said Gravatt). Full time clean-up crews worked day and night for, like Bill Veeck and Walt Disney, Gravatt knew a good show could be ruined by a dirty rest room.

Soon his whole life revolved around the pier. Every waking—and often sleeping—moment was tied in directly or indirectly to its operation. Gravatt worried not only about having the best attractions in the world but also topping himself, constantly improving.

The pressures began to show up on his other businesses and on his family. And so, reluctantly, almost twenty years after the day he had purchased it, he agreed to sell the Steel Pier. He felt he had reached the pinnacle and wanted to rest and relax before taking on new challenges.

His only concern was the pier not be sold to his competitor, George Hamid, owner of Hamid's Million Dollar Pier (also in Atlantic City) with whom he carried on a running promotion battle. In the beginning, Hamid, a former circus acrobat, agreed to run circus acts and Gravatt would run bands and celebrities. But soon the two overlapped. One time Hamid booked in Glenn Miller's band. Gravatt, furious, booked a Glenn Miller movie and then rented nearly every billboard coming into Atlantic City. All the public could read on the signs were "Glenn Miller" . . . and . . . "Steel Pier." The pier pulled in the crowds. It was one of the few times the Glenn Miller band did not draw sold-out crowds. The traffic was down the block watching the Glenn Miller . . . movie.

Hamid made overtures to buy the pier and though Gravatt wanted to sell, he would not sell to Hamid.

He ran ads in *Variety* and was contacted by Abe Ellis, the hat-check king who financed night clubs in New York City with revenues from hat and coat checking stands. Gravatt sold to Ellis. After the sale, one of the managers of the pier came to see Gravatt and asked, "Do you know who bought the Steel Pier?"

"Yes," said Gravatt, "Abe Ellis."

"No," said the manager, "it is George Hamid."

It was true. Hamid had persuaded Ellis to act as front man to buy the pier, and Hamid gave him the concessions in return.

Lesson Number Nine: Don't Underestimate Your Competition.

Gravatt shrugged. It was time to pay attention to his family. And his other businesses. In future years he would build the first escalator in town, the first air-conditioned hotel, begin the career of the Tisch brothers (now owners of the famed Loew's corporation), predict the coming of casinos (while claiming Atlantic City never really needed them), revive the Miss America Pageant, and have more than 2,000 people on his payroll.

But first he would rest after twenty years with the Steel Pier.

Then . . . he would go out and set new records, create more legends for people to talk about and ask, "How did he do that?" The challenges were all out there waiting.

Lesson Number Ten: Once You Achieve Your Goal—Make A New One.

Frank Gravatt died January 28, 1980. He was 88. There was a story in the local PRESS. No mention since. No placques, awards, memorials for the man who created a strong positive Image of Atlantic City past. Atlantic City present is casinos and gaming. Different story. Different image. Different town. Sic transit gloria.

Reese Palley, Bill Veeck, Frank Gravatt . . . what is the formula that made them Winners?

Author Edwin P. Hoyt in his book *America's Top Salesmen* concluded each of them had the following ten characteristics:

1. Work hard.
2. Self confident.
3. Self disciplined.
4. Perserverance.
5. Flexibility.
6. Goals *other than money.*
7. Respect for the buyer's good sense.
8. Willingness to learn from others.
9. Ability to make big money.
10. They are perfectionists.

Can ANYONE do this ten-point formula for success?

Yes. It begins with . . . IDENTIFICATION.

Part
Two

2 Identification

SOMEONE ONCE questioned Stanley Marcus, the founding genius of Neiman-Marcus as we know it today. "What about your store and Saks Fifth Avenue?" he was asked. "Aren't they both department stores carrying the same fine merchandise? How can you say you are different?"

His answer: "There are many ways of playing any part on the stage. Five different actresses and you get five different renditions. I often feel running a store is very much like running a newspaper. Newspapers all have access to the same news. But one comes out like the New York *Times* and one comes out like the *Daily News*. They all have the same basic material but one editor likes sex on the front page and the other wants international stories."

What's *your* story?
How will you tell it?

Nearly 10,000 firms go out of business every year in the United States. So how come you're still around?

And will you be here next year when the mortality roll is called on that great Dun and Bradstreet roster in the sky?

What causes one business to die and another, newly-born, to succeed? What does one do the other does not?

Ask yourself these four questions:
1. Who are you?
2. What's your name?
3. Does anybody know?
4. Does anybody care?

Businesses are like people. They must have a reason for being. Another paint store is simply . . . another paint store. But put your name in front of the store and it now has an identity.

Most new-born children look alike. Only when they are given a name and begin to develop their very personal characteristics do we begin to know, understand, and identify them as individuals.

And so it is with you. And your business.

What pops into the minds of customers when they hear your company's name? How would someone describe your business to a newly-arrived resident? If you listen carefully, you will hear all the adjectives describing another "person."

"They're friendly. Nice. They care about you."

Or: "They're cold, unfeeling, uninterested. Snobbish."

Comments may include your offering a particular service they cannot have elsewhere. Or your personnel being so service-oriented the customer is spoiled and simply "won't shop anywhere else." Or, the most damning of all, "It's just another store . . ." And to be a replica of someone else is to be a mirror image of your competition.

Jim Mahler owns a furniture store in Washington, D.C. He asked for help in advertising. At our first meeting, he pulled out a scrapbook of ads from his competitor saying, "Here's what my competition does. I save his ads. I see what he does and then try to top him."

But didn't this make Jim's store (and advertising) a carbon copy of someone else?

He was finally persuaded to tell his *own* story. He created his own individual identity, turning the tables on his competitor who began to open the daily paper and say, "Look at that! How can we top what Mahler's doing?" Once Jim adopted this philosophy his business soared.

There are those who protest saying, "I own a hardware store. The guy down the street owns a hardware store. We buy from the same suppliers. How can I be different?"

Begin with the time-worn word, "Image."

But in order to have an "image" you must first have a "look."

What does the name of your business "look" like?

Does it look like half a dozen other businesses? Or, worse, like your competition?

It begins with the kind of type face you use. Type faces, like people, have names and can convey strong images and moods.

When teaching Identification in our seminars, we clip the food ads from several newspapers. (It works as well with bank ads or clothing store ads or others.)

We cut off the stores' names and post the ads at the front of the room. We list the names of the businesses separately and ask everyone to match the nameless ad to the store.

The correct ad-with-store-match is rare, because so many ads look just like their competitor. You can take the signature, mix and match with any other ad and someone in the class will say, "That's right. That name belongs with that ad."

Unfortunately, it does not.

If we do not take the time to give ourselves our own identification, how can we expect the customer to identify us and know who we are?

Side story: When the Gordon and Raphel families joined forces in a small children's wear store in Atlantic City in 1949, they called it "Gordon's" and, together, did $18,000 a year total volume. Through the years the business grew and prospered to its present complex of thirty-five stores and restaurants with a multimillion dollar volume and an appreciative city renaming the street through their complex in their honor: Gordon's Alley.

All this was done using the Bumblebee Theory.

Bright folks like M.I.T. engineers will tell you the weight of a bumblebee's body cannot be supported by its tiny fragile wingspan. But someone forgot to tell the bumblebees—so they continue to fly.

No one told Gordon's there was a science to direct mail, copywriting, advertising, merchandising. So they simply started flying—making a lot of mistakes and learning what worked and, as important, what did NOT WORK.

One of the very first moves they made was to create their own "look" in their own name. Like this:

$$Gordon's$$

Which, in turn, was adapted to the present name like this:

$$Gordon's\ Alley$$

More than ten years ago they decided to run a rather small ad every day in the same position in the local daily paper. (Important: consistency and position). The ad has a distinctive style of art, type face, and the special Gordon's signature.

Murray tells a story: Once upon a time . . . we ran an ad for men's jackets on sale. The original price was $29.95. The sale price was $19.99. The ad said so. With all the right copy.

When the newspaper ran the ad only one item was missing: our store's name and address.

In effect, the ad could have been anyone's ad.

That day we sold seventeen men's jackets. Hmmmmmmm.

As each person came in to see the jackets on sale we asked, "How did you know about the sale?"

And each, slightly startled, said, "We saw your ad in the paper this morning."

We thought that amazing. Later in the day we asked one woman the same puzzling question. She answered, "In the paper—where else?" We then took a copy of the newspaper, turned to our ad, and, pointing to it, said, "But look, they left our name out of the ad. How could you possibly have known it was our store that had the sale on jackets?"

She studied the ad very carefully, then looked up and said, "In my paper at home . . . they have your name in the ad."

She saw the ad and knew it was from our store.

If the paper left your name off your next ad, would your customer know it was *your* ad?

YOUR "LOGO"

People recognize you and the product you sell by your "logo"—your personal signature. It can be your name (Coca-Cola) or it can be a picture (the distinctive shape of the Coke bottle).

It all begins when you first learn to read. The child in school receives a reading book. The word is placed next to a picture of the word. D-O-G next to a picture of a dog. H-O-U-S-E next to a picture of a house. When you see the word you also see the picture. One associates with the other from the very beginning.

The three-year-old child driving with her parents down the highway points to the billboard and says, "Look, mom, Coca-Cola!" The mother beams and says, "Karen can read." Well . . . not really. The child immediately associates the shape of the Coca-Cola signature with the name she sees on the bottle. The picture associates the product.

When someone says your or your company's name in your community, are you immediately identified with the product you sell? If not, why not? Certain pictures leap into your mind when someone says "Sears" or "IBM" or "Xerox." If K mart's is one picture, then Macy's is another and Bergdorf-Goodman still another. How about your name? What does it "say"?

Suggestion: unless you are a giant corporation or a group of banks, food stores, or a chain operation—use your own name. Avoid the fun and game names like Little Shop On The Corner. If you move, or there's a redevelopment in your section of town, that name could be a problem. Do not become this year's vogue like the many shops that became "Guys and Dolls" when the Damon Runyon based musical first appeared. Or the faddish, look-how-clever-I-am names like "Up Against the Wall" or "Down by the Tracks" or "Middle of the Road." What names do customers call these stores?

We find it difficult convincing people going into business that the best name is their own. They are uncomfortable. It is like looking at yourself in a movie. Or hearing your own voice on tape for the first time. Or writing your own introduction for a speech. You tend to be too modest, aww-shucks, underestimate yourself . . . and your name.

May we remind you—the easiest remembered stores carry names of the founders: Lord and Taylor, Bergdorf Goodman, Neiman-Marcus, Macy's, Saks, I. Magnin, Gimbels. And . . . Rich's, Bloomingdale's, Henry Bendel, Hecht's, Belk's*—the list is as long as there are major cities in this country. If stores are like people, and if stores have per-sonalities and traits like people, shouldn't stores have names like people?

Yes.

WHAT DO PEOPLE CALL YOU?

Listen to what your customers call your store or business. You have partners and use all the names; consumers shorten the title to what *they* want to say.

Sears Roebuck becomes "Sears" and Montgomery Ward, "Ward's." And it took many years before Coca-Cola copyrighted "Coke," finally listened to the generations of teenagers pushing up to their local drugstore counter and asking for their favorite drink by their shortened name, "Coke."

Merrill Lynch Pierce Fenner and Smith, becomes "Merrill Lynch." On the incoming side, the many named legal firms counted the minutes wasted by the operator reciting the litany of partners, and the operator now simply answers, "Law offices."

"Identification"—associating the merchandise you stock with the name of your store—is a basic step toward the success of your business. When your customer sees your name in a newspaper ad, hears it on the radio, or quickly glances at it on your direct mail piece, does a picture flash through her mind of the merchandise you have in your store? It should. That is your ultimate, final, looked-forward-to goal: that your name becomes part of the English language—at least in your home town.

Example: We once did a critique of the advertising of one of Washington's finer department stores, Woodward and Lothrop. We

---

*Stores *can* grow without newspaper advertising (talk about nontraditional thinking). Belk's, a major retailing chain in the South built their volume to more than $2 billion with *no* advertising.

What they *did* do: Put up the money to build churches in every community in which they had a store. As you walked up the path to the church there was a simple metal identification sign saying, "This church built by William Henry Belk." And as you left you saw an identi-cal sign on the inside of the church. Belk created perhaps the earliest "billboard" advertising in the South.

wrote complimentary phrases about the quality of the advertising and asked the question, "But why don't they call themselves what everybody else in Washington call them: Woodies. Did you ever try saying 'Woodward and Lothrop' three times fast?"

A short time later we received a rather indignant note from the advertising manager. She wrote she appreciated the kind words about the ads but we were wrong in our statement about what the customers called the store. "Everyone calls us Woodward and Lothrop" she wrote, "because that is our name."

We wrote back and thanked her for her comments. And included a note from her secretary mailed with the original copies of ads. The secretary ended *her* note with, "Thank you for thinking of us at Woodies . . ."

PS: We told this story at seminars for months. One day a lady stood in the audience and said, "That's a true story." She identified herself as the advertising manager of the store and displayed a new ad that commented on the store's remodeling. At the botton of the ad was the traditional Woodward and Lothrop signature. And, beneath it, in parenthesis was the simple phrase, "Or, as our friends like to call us . . . Woodies."

Another: A recent ad from Johnson and Johnson was headlined, "Nobody makes Band Aids." Really? Did they go out of business? Should we run to the nearest drug store and stock up on competitor Curad?

As we read further, the ad explained the correct name of the product was "Band Aid," not "Band Aid*s*." We promptly wrote Johnson and Johnson and asked if that meant there was only one in every box . . .

No one answered.

Since seventy-five percent of the people read the headlines and only twenty-five percent keep on reading, make sure your headline tells an accurate story in one quick flash.

Our philosophy ties in more closely with the TV comedian who says, "You can call me Ray. Or you can call me Jay. Or you can call me . . ." Whatever you want. As long as you buy my product or services.

Other firms spend thousands of dollars to teach consumers how to pronounce their name! They give language lessons rather than benefits and reasons-to-buy.

And so we read that Noilly Prat is pronounced "New-lee Prawt" and Opici is really "o-peachy," Dewars Scotch is "Doo-Wars," and Kamchatka breaks their name into syllables: "Kam-Chat-Ka." Russe vodka says it "rhymes with juice." But not why we should choose Russe over Kam-chat-ka.

The only problem we see in the "sound" of a product's name is when the company make different products with the same name. Scott Paper Products controls about forty percent of the total consumer paper products market. But they gave such similar names to each individual product, the consumer became confused between Scot Tissue, Scotties, Scottkins, and even Babyscott. Into this void jumped marketing experts Proctor and Gamble and Mr. Whipple who tearfully pleaded with mythical TV supermarket cutomers, "Please don't squeeze the Charmin." Which soon squeezed the leadership away from Scott in the paper towel business.

A BRIEF SPLASH OF COLOR*

Hospitals discovered years ago soft green on the walls is more restful than antiseptic white. Colors convey emotions and feelings. Blue is cold. Red is hot. Purple is exciting. Earth tones are warm.

If you sell ice cream, use bright cheerful colors. Not dark tones. The feelings are contradictory.

Now all this probably sounds picayune, tacky, and too detailed. If, at this point, you are about to throw up you hands in exasperation and cry "I have fourteen salesmen on the road spending money and nothing to ship" or, "The new government regulations will cripple our production forecast," or, "If our computer doesn't get straightened out soon. . ." "—and you're talking about what color our company logo is. Are you kidding?"

You're right. First things first. Each priority in its place. Don't worry about "the paint" when the house is on fire.

But there comes a time when thinking about your business and its image becomes as important as those perennial fires you are always running to put out. When that time comes (and make it come) pin up all your printed materials on a wall: Your ads, letterheads, memo sheets, shipping labels, photos of signs, return business envelopes, *everything* that leaves your place of business with your name.

You may be unpleasantly shocked at the variance of graphics and your image. Don't worry about it. The time has come for a reckoning— graphically.

Many who attend our Great Brain Robbery seminars mail us, in advance, samples of their advertising, printed materials, letterheads, and even their business calling cards. The people who send the materials are jolted when during the seminar they look at the three large screens and see their company name in three or four different versions, and several totally

---

*Color does not mean extra dollars for advertising. It simply means "Identification." *Example:* our local independent insurance agent uses bright orange for his envelopes. When the mail arrives and there is a touch of orange in the pile, you say, "There's a letter from Batzer Insurance." *Example:* A stationery salesman in Cambridge, Mass., had one color of shirts: blue. If you could not remember his name you said, "You know— the guy with the blue shirt."

different type faces; and. . .colors ranging from pale to wild; and. . .signs on buildings different from letterheads; and. . .mailing labels that have little or no reference to the engraved company letterhead. . .and calling cards! A totally separate kettle of graphic fish.

CALLING CARDS

> *If they say, "Can I keep this?," You win.*

We call calling cards "miniature billboards" because. . .that's what they are.

The problem: most calling cards, like the ads we mentioned previously, look alike. Perhaps because so many fast printers make calling cards ready for you for a special-for-100 price. All looking exactly like the last special they printed. The only things changed are the name and the company. But the color, the type faces, the layout, the "look"—all the same.

Should not be. Because calling cards are an extension of. . .you.

Test questions: Are you the same as every other person? Is your company the same as the competition? Are you different or the same as? One sure way to tell: your calling card.

Note: We are convinced the people who design and print business calling cards are from a different world, trained in tombstone dullness, and, from the size of the type and phone numbers, in league with the opticians of the world. Business cards are seldom interesting or intriguing or worth keeping and rarely have anything to do with any of the other expenditures for corporate image.

Here are some questions to ask yourself:

Does it look like you (or your firm)?: The same type faces, the same color combination. KEEP THE IDENTIFICATION CONSTANT. Some retail shops design their card to show off the front of their store. Instant identification. It can REALLY look like you if your name signifies an object. Like Rose. Or Carr. Shade. Ivy.

Does it show your product?: If it can, it should. When you open our calling card, up pops a mini typewriter (and says: "Am I the type writer you're looking for?") Because. . .we write. A salesman for a paper supply company has his calling card tucked into a. . .right—miniature paper bag. A lumber yard prints their cards on thin-shaved balsa wood. Our glassman's card is on see-through vinyl. (Love the one from a shop in New York named "Clips." Their card has their name printed on a see-through plastic bag that holds. . .ah, yes, different color paper clips.)

And our salesman from Poland Brothers (who make paperbags and boxes) has a mini-mini box for a calling card. The card is die-cut on the edges so he can carry it flat. Just before he comes to see you, he tucks in the corners and hands over his box-shaped calling card.

Gerry Ewing is an audio visual specialist in Florida. His calling card is his name on a piece of film invisibly glued to a regulation-size card.

Is the shape unusual? Author Considine also has a marketing agency and knows secretaries take business cards and retype them on Rolodex file cards. So his card is a Rolodex card, with holes punched in the bottom that make it automatically fit into your file. One more difference: his card is printed on blue stock. Next time you flip through your Rolodex card file, there's only one blue one: Considine.

Milt Smolier from Names Unlimited has his firm's cards die-cut so they have an extended tab in the upper right hand corner—much like a file folder. On the tab: the salesman's name (and yes, it means it sticks up a quarter-inch higher that the OTHER cards). (We tried to persuade Milt to add the phrase "Our name stands out above the rest." But never succeeded.)

Is the texture different? One banker has his calling cards printed on check stock—looks just like a check from the bank in a mini-mini size. Another banker had a calling card that looked exactly like the folded edge of a five-dollar bill. He left them wherever he went. Oh yes, people grabbed them and read them. . .and remembered.

Sillcocks-Miler make plastic products. Their calling card is made of. . .right. The man who makes our leather bags and belts has a calling card of. . .leather. An aluminum salesman has his calling cards made of wafer-thin aluminum. So when the customer takes your card, a simple touch or feel, and they know who you are and who you represent.

Other possibilities: A picture of you, your store or your business. A card that has four sides instead of two (folds over with your store name on the outside and all other information inside). Why not use the *back* of your card? Watch someone the next time they take your card. They read it. And turn it over! And there is nothing on the back. Why not? Our most recent calling card has the front of our store on the front of the card. And the back entrance of the store on the back of the calling card.

Again—the acid test to tell if your calling card works: Next time you hand your card to someone and they ask, "Can I keep this?"

Can they keep it? Of course. That's why you had them printed. And, now, it has become something special. And to be remembered.

THE CLASH OF SYMBOLS

Somewhere in this country there is a group of designers who work in triangles, squares, and circles. They are paid, literally, thousands of dollars by companies who ask them to pick the right triangle, square, or circle to represent THEIR company.

CRAZY.

Example: The American Broadcasting Company's radio section has four divisions: American Contemporary Radio Network, American FM Radio Network, American Information Radio Network, and American Entertainment Radio Network. Here are the symbols for each (but not in the same order):

OK, students, which symbol belongs to which division?

It would make much more sense for the ABC radio network to have ONE major corporate identity. And each division would carry this same identity with their individual trademark.

To find examples of symbols which need advertising to make their meaning clear, simply let your fingers do the walking through your nearby yellow pages. You will come up with graphic symbols like this one:

This is a company that (check one)

A. Makes ropes.

B. Makes chain link fencing.

C. Makes knitwear.

If you guessed "C" you guessed right. Why does a firm have a symbol that could mean many things—instead of one thing?

Is that possible? Sure. Here are a few:

Everybody knows those symbols. No confusing. No guessing. No wonder they have Instant Identification.

Enough with the surrealistic art. For if this symbol represents the Rita Richard Personnel system:

R

And this symbol represents Jeep products from American Motors:

And *this* represents Kinney National Service. . .

K

Or do I have them mixed up?

Which is precisely the problem. For no matter how much you spend to promote circles, triangles, and straight lines, or in what combination you put them, they symbolize little or nothing about who or what you really are.

It is easy to see how a giant corporation can lose perspective. Wrapped up in the womb of their structure, they see their symbol as a decal on the front plate glass entrance, atop each sheet of stationery and interoffice memo* and tucked into the corner of each and every expensive ad in national trade magazines. Why, *everyone* knows the circle and the dot in the middle means ABC Electronics.

Hmmmmmmmmmmm.

Ah yes, in our modern world most names have ceased to be names. While there are those among us who cry we are turning into computer numbers, there are others who claim we are turning into corporate symbols.

THE BEST SYMBOL

The best symbol is simply one that tells the story of your business. The picture of the "bell" works marvellously for Bell Telephone. The picture of the leaping deer for John Deere farm equipment. The picture of the sailing ship Mayflower for the moving people. And the picture of the greyhound for you-know-who.

---

*A good spot to remind you to stop printing those memos "From the desk of . . . ." Who wants to hear from your desk? *I* want to hear from *you*. Put your name up there. Even your picture. Why not?

If you publicize a symbol often enough, the customer will accept your design. Which is why "owning a piece of the rock" is buying insurance from Prudential.

Animals are symbols. Choose a Republican elephant or Democratic donkey. Or the U.S. Forest Service's Smokey the Bear.

And you really do not drive a car. You drive a Mustang, Cougar, Pinto, or Rabbit (unless Hugh Hefner is in the car business).

Morris the Cat meows about Nine Lives cat food—or did until his ninth life ran out recently. Charlie the Tuna is still angling to get on board with Starkist. If you're interested in the stock market you can choose either a lion (Dreyfuss) or a herd of cattle (Merrill Lynch.)

Sometimes, like movie stars, animals sell too many products. You become confused about whom they really represent. Does Tony the Tiger sell Frosted Flakes or Exxon gas?

So whether you choose from animal or vegetable (Green Giant) or mineral (Prudential's rock) be sure the symbol is yours and not another's in similar or—worse—competitive fields. In THAT case, you wind up with the horrible cacophony brought on by the clash of symbols.

After all this, consider the fact if your business is for real, why play make-believe?

Use your name. That means identification. Or your initials. Clear and readable (IBM, RCA). Now, that's distinctive! Now, that's Identification.

Down with silly signs, fuzzy symbols, and nutty numbers. Especially numbers! Everyone wants to be number one. Except Avis.

Let us stop straining to be known as AAA Shoe Repair just to be first in the telephone book. It rarely works. In the Manhattan phone book, there are fifty-nine firms that begin their name with AAA. Someone soon reasoned if they had four As, THEY would be first. And then there was the one who said, "Gee, if I have FIVE As . . ." Today, there is one firm beginning the parade with NINE As.

Funny fact: Everyone seems to have forgotten that just *one* "A" will precede the others. And the first one in the Manhattan phone book is simply "A" with main offices at 5 Beekman Place. Whoever THEY are.

Well, you could be untraditional and be the *last* in the phone book ("Last in the phone book, but first in cleaning rugs . . .") But be careful. There already is a Budd ZZZyp.

3 *Positioning*

Is there anybody out there?
Is there anybody listening?
—*1776*, a stage play

How many brands of toothpaste are there?
Name them. The first few come easy. Then you uh . . . let's see . . .
Now . . . think of a few more. Uh . . . and you start repeating names.
Then you give up after naming half a dozen.

And yet there are *several dozen* brands of toothpaste.

The average supermarket carries 10,000 different items.
How many can you name? Ten percent? Five percent? Not likely.

This year you will see, hear, or read more than half a million advertising messages. All the tumult and excitement and yelling tries to capture
the consumer's attention as each product screams out "Buy me!"

We once had a friend who lived in the city. We visited him one evening
and, through his open window, we could hear the sounds of the city: am-
bulances, police cars, horns, shouting voices. We said to him, "How do
you stand the noise?"

And he said, "What noise?"

His mind had automatically edited out the sounds, so they all blended
into an even tonal quality not quite heard by his conscious mind.

This presents a problem for all of us selling, advertising, promoting.
We feel *our* message is THE message. And so does our competitor. The
half-a-million "making noise in the street."

How then do we have the customer listen and hear *us*. How do we
convince the customer, to paraphrase McLuhan, that *our* message is the
medium by which they can lead a better life, or become a better person?

This way: we have to *position** ourselves and/or our product so it fills
a need for the customer. We have to show customers and prospects that
what we offer is better-than or superior-to or an alternative-from what
they are using/doing/working with . . . today.

*We highly recommend ordering POSITIONING: THE BATTLE FOR YOUR MIND, Al Reis/
Jack Trout, $17.95, McGraw-Hill Book Company, 1221 Avenue of the Americas, New
York, N.Y. 10020.

Look at it this way: You sell children's clothes. If someone in your town says to their neighbor, "Where can I buy children's clothes?" does the neighbor name *your* store? It's the "association" game we talked about in the previous chapter on Identification.

But it's also "Positioning." Positioning yourself in the market place so that you and your store become automatically and unconsciously associated with the product or service you sell.

You're an insurance agent. If someone asks, "Who should I buy my insurance from?" is the automatic response *your* name?

You're a dentist. If someone moves into town and asks, "Where can I get my tooth filled?" does that someone get *your* name as a reaction, Doctor?

Just because a retail slogan says, "Our store is the best" doesn't make that so. The customer probably says, "All stores are the same." (Or, "all salesmen are the same.") Or worse, "I think there's *one good* store" and then they name your competition.

Should we mention our competition?

Why the sudden recent rush to spend our budgets to advertise the competition? David Ogilvy (who is not a beginner at this game) is at a loss to explain why advertisers and agencies spend any money at all to even MENTION the competition. One possible whiplash result: Some viewers and readers recall the competitor's name—and not the product or service we advertised! Consumers forget who made which claim about what. But they remember a name . . . some name. The wrong name?

Franklin Delano Roosevelt never mentioned his political opposition by name. He would, in his famous sing-song cadence intone phrases like, "worthy opponent" or "some people are fond of saying . . ." but never the name. The only name he wanted to appear in the newspaper the next day . . . was his.

And since his reelection record was good enough to get him inaugurated four times, there certainly must be something there we all can use from the Brain Robbery philosophy. If a technique works, repeat it.

Sometimes you can position yourself in the market place by swimming *against* the current. Taking the opposite stand. Supermarkets are now offering services like courteous baggers and box men, check-cashing, neatly stocked shelves with everything clearly priced. Along come "warehouse stores" which instruct *you* to mark the food prices yourself and *you* carry the items out in the original cardboard shipping cartons. Oh yes, you will save a lot of money because you are doing some of the work yourself. Fine. Makes sense. And if price is the prime consideration, I become your customer—and mark and carry. OK. I KNOW where I stand. And, as important, I understand what you are asking and offering. And I agree to that. When some neatly-stacked, price-marking supermarket points out the disadvantages of my buying from your pick-it-and-take-it warehouse, they are simply reinforcing the *advantages* (and savings) you offer for a slight inconvenience (to which I have already agreed).

If each automobile is more beautiful than the next and I can't tell one model from another, what if one car says it is uglier than all the rest? The "Against" position at work. The tradition-breaking Doyle Dane Bernbach campaign forever established the "Bug," "Beetle," and "Lemon" as classics in success for . . . Volkswagen, of course.

And so if you mention any name in your copy, sales presentation, or advertisement—make it your own. And in your slogans . . . no confusion, please. Can I take your slogan and make it work for me as well as you? I can? You've got the wrong slogan. Badly blurred positioning. Not unique.

"The one beer to have when you're having more than one" is a great slogan for Schmidt's. (Or is it Schlitz?) Or is it . . .? We forget. One we *do* remember: "When you say Bud, you've said it all." Gee, I guess you have. Bartender!

And why does Good*rich* advertise Good*year* blimps? Crazy. Confusing. Not creative. If I were Goodyear I'd cut my advertising budget in half. And let my competition do the work for me.

If every airline "makes noise" about champagne breakfasts and gourmet menus, what would happen if one said, "We'll give you just a sandwich—and only if you pay for it. Oh, by the way travelers, our fare is the cheapest to and from Europe." And for a while, Freddie Laker and People's Express flew that route.

Even your name positions you in the customer's mind. If your name is Eastern, do you only fly in the East? If your name is Allegheny, do you fly only over the Allegheny Mountains? People might think so. (Maybe that's why they changed their name to USAir.)

Or take the case of Alpha Beta supermarket food chain in California. They decided to take a different position and not fight on the traditional food advertising battleground with full page newspaper ads. They cut that medium and poured their dollars into TV.

Their genial, friendly spokesman was Allen Hamil, who "visits neighbors", cooks barbeques, recommends recipes, and constantly invited viewers to "Tell a Friend." Since then, Alpha Beta has gone back to heavy newspaper ads but made a strong impact when they first switched to TV: Non-traditional. They "got out of the box."

Different markets, different names. If you are trying to sectionalize and separate markets within the same industry, try a totally different label on the same products. Hallmark cards are available at Hallmark stores. *Ambassador* cards are available at . . . your local supermarket. Both are very successful divisions for Hallmark.

Positioning is seeing a need—and then filling it. When the tornadoes struck and destroyed a good part of Wichita Falls, Texas, a firm making prefabricated homes, Connell Manufacturing Company in distant Austin,

Texas, reacted. They hoisted some of their prebuilt structures onto flatbed trucks, hauled them up to Wichita, rented some ground, and started selling houses immediately. The market shifts. The wind blows. The reaction of smart marketing people is to instantly *position* themselves and grab the opportunity.

Can the small store or just-starting-out salesperson compete with the Biggies? Sure. "We are small. We all know each other. It's an intimate kind of service," the little ones can say—which is a heck of a different shot from being Number One, the Giant, First, slow-moving, "sorry-we-can't-find-you-in-the-computer." Don't claim to be what you can't be. Stay believable. Once your "unbelievable" claim is exposed as unreal—goodbye.

But you can Try Harder, truly Be Eager, Do More—if indeed you do. Doesn't Believable come down to *Performable?*

One mistake people and firms make is to stake out a position already occupied. Trying to sell your newspapers on somebody else's corner starts fist fights, name calling, and giving money to lawyers. Not to mention the confusion to the customer (who will probably keep buying from the original source as long as it performs).

IBM had the market cornered on computers. Then RCA announced, "We are going to corner the market." The consumer was puzzled. "How can that be? Doesn't RCA make records and tapes and TV sets?" Yes. RCA was positioned as a home-entertainment company. Now, if RCA could figure a way to make computers tie-in with home entertainment—like computerized video games, TV programs on disc, *that* might work. But large-scale office equipment? RCA? Wrong position. They entered the arena, lost, and left.

And so along comes Singer sewing machines and says THEY will make computers. Oh? And, to add confusion to confusion, Singer tried to stitch the slogan of their sewing machines, "Touch and Sew," to their new computers as "Touch and Know." Huh? So the housewife tells her husband she's taking her sewing machine to the local Singer store to have it converted into a computer. They entered the arena, lost, and left.

But wait, here comes Xerox. So strongly positioned in the copying market the name becomes the generic term.* "Xerox this for me" means "make me a copy . . . on anybody's machine!" THEY decide to go into the computer business. And take full page ads in magazines showing a machine that looks like their copying machine. The headline: "This Xerox machine doesn't make copies." What's that mean? Are they OUT of the copying machine business? Have their machines all broken down—What?

---

*An enviable accomplishment—to have your product name describe the entire field. Examples: Frigidaire for *all* refrigerators. Kleenex for all pop-up tissue.

And the ad goes on to say: Xerox is making computers AS WELL as copying machines.

Sorry, folks, can't deal with that. They entered the arena, lost, and left.

And then comes along GE to enter, lose, and leave the computer business. And another TV commercial says "NCR means computers." Sorry, folks, I'm programmed. In *my* memory bank IBM means computers.

The stories continue and you might think someone would be learning from all this. (And doesn't this make you feel better—knowing the big companies DO make mistakes?) Thousands of health and beauty products (with big healthy ad budgets) fail every year because they have not "positioned" the appeal correctly so that the customer wants to buy that item.

The Edsel failed, and, conversely, the Mustang succeeded. From the same company! Edsel was reputed to be the result of a massive research on "what the American public wanted in a midsize car." The Mustang made it because the country, the youth, and the I-want-to-be-youth market was ready for the sporty, sleek, two door, bucket-seated pseudo sports car and Lee Iacocca was a hero. The Mustang is a classic. Edsel was a tragedy.

Does that mean if one company has the business no other company can get into the business? Of course not. But not by attacking the incumbent head on. Present yourself as a viable alternative ("The UN-Cola," and 7-Up. "We're Number Two, but We try harder," says Avis). Or an added feature. Or a different price point. Or a compact, easy-to-move-around size. Or immediate availability of service. Or . . . anything that positions you and/or your product to do the same job as the competition but ALSO filling another need.

If you do NOT do this, if you do not come up with your own special slot, then the consumer takes your advertising or sales message and identifies what you say with your competition! Where's the difference?

Positioning is also a *Point-of-View*.

How you were brought up, what your parents did, how your teachers taught, what your textbooks said . . . all this, and more, contributes to how you think, believe, act as a salesperson. Once you recognize that everyone in the whole world did NOT have the same set of parents, teachers, and working superiors . . . you will begin to understand other people's *positions*—which helps you understand how *they* think, talk, and make decisions.

You were both born in the North. You read all the history books on the Civil War. You learned later in life that the victors wrote the history books . . . but you knew all about Lincoln and the fight to save the Union and you had your feelings about the South and the slaves. You were preconditioned. You had been "positioned" to think and act in the "northern'' manner when the words ''Civil War'' came into the conversation. Suppose one day, while doing a show in Austin, Texas, you took a walk in the center of town, up Commerce Street to the statue of Jefferson Davis in front of the state capitol.

There, inscribed on the side of the base were these words:

D I E D

For states' rights guaranteed under the Constitution. The people of the South animated by the Spirit of '76 to preserve their rights, withdrew from the Federal compact in 1861. The North resorted to coercion. The South, against overwhelming numbers and resources fought until exhausted. Number of men enlisted: Confederate: 600,000. Federal: 2,859,132. Losses: Confederate; 437,000. Federal: 485,216.

Wow. Until that moment you had been positioned to believe the South were the bad guys. But this inscription said they died for ''states' rights'' and withdrew from the Union because of the ''Spirit of '76'' and ''to preserve their rights.'' Sounds pretty logical to us . . .

Point of view.

Only by understanding the other person's point of view, the customer's ''position,'' can we make our cause known and appreciated.

Every product you sell (yes, including yourself) must have achieved its own ''position'' to succeed. Rosser Reeves, advertising genius, once referred to this special place as USP—Unique Selling Position. What makes yours or you different from all the rest?

Too often we tend to take our jobs and our product for granted. Only the professional salesperson and actor understands there is always excitement in selling his merchandise again and again. Each sale is a thrill. The actor goes on stage for the thousandth time in the long-running play and it is like opening night all over again. The audience is new. They present a challenge. Particularly if you ARE successful. The audience develops a ''show me'' attitude. This has happened to you when the critics and your friends rave about a new movie comedy. You finally agree to go and your attitude often is, ''OK, make me laugh. Go ahead. I dare you . . .''

And so, we must approach each day with the knowledge we will succeed only by selling the unique positioning we and our products occupy in the marketplace.

HOW CAN YOU POSITION YOURSELF?

1. *Know who you are.* Not who you ''think'' you are. Or would ''like to be.'' But who-you-are-today. We once did a survey for a bank on the

West Coast to find out who their "typical" customer was. We asked the chief executive officer for a description of his "typical" customer.

He said, "They're about 60 or so. Upper income. Community leaders." Really?

We asked the middle-management and they said, "About forty or so. Children about grown. On the way up. Good solid citizens." Interesting.

We asked the tellers and they said, "In their twenties and thirties. Newly married. Just starting out. Lots of energy and drive."

What had happened? Every group questioned *in* the bank had identified the "typical" customer outside as . . . about their age, about the same family status, about the same income. Not so.

The actual statistical survey revealed that bank's average customer was mid thirties, married a few years, two children, one and a half cars (must be the new subcompact models) and an income in the $20,000 range. Once the bank heard that, the marketing directions were changed to meet the profile of who *really* was their customer.

2. *Know Who You Want To Be.* If what you are doing is working, keep on doing it. (Winners repeat.) If you are starting out, wondering what the route to Success is, pick a model.

We have a friend in the retail field. His business is not very large, but he is ambitious. Salesmen and merchandise people are constantly coming in with Ideas, urging him to "buy," or "this one is a winner," or "Can't miss—one of my big sellers."

The medium size retailer is confronted with pressures. He needs a system to position himself and to guard against being oversold. With each supersales presentation, he asks himself one question: would Saks Fifth Avenue do this? If the item or Idea isn't in keeping with his "model," he doesn't buy (although he is often threatened with having made "a terrible mistake"). He is growing nicely thank you.

Knowing Who You Want To Be is one thing. Getting there is entirely another. We hope the chapter on Goal Setting helps. The shorthand of that chapter is Steps and Checkpoints. It doesn't hurt to repeat it here.

Hugh Redhead, one of the great early men of marketing in banking and later president of Campbell-Ewald agency for Chevrolet and other major national clients, said in a speech once in Los Angeles, "If it isn't on paper, you haven't got a plan. Talking about what you want to do is like a New Year's resolution: It's all verbal, makes you feel good and nothing ever happens." Put it on paper. And check the progress. Are you becoming Who You Want To Be. We hope so.

3. *Is What You Are Doing Matching What You Want To Be?* Here is one of the largest and worst traps in positioning. A clever Idea pops up. Why not try it? Question: Does it fit and support what we decided we are trying to be? If not, put it in a drawer for a later time . . . or never.

Someone brings you a nifty Idea on an elephant promotion. "It worked for another client. Great traffic builder." Does the elephant fit what you want to "look like"? Is that the image you have chosen? Would your mentor do that?

Deviation from what you *said* you were going to be is the worst sin against positioning. Al Reis in a speech on his positioning theories said trying to keep a planned position is like commanding an aircraft carrier: if you react to every wave that slaps the side of your ship, by the time you turn about (a) you're off course (b) the wave you worried about has long since disappeared into the sea. Good advice. Stay on course, captain.

4. *Know When To Turn Off Course*. Like the captain we just mentioned, you are in command. Look to the seas. There are times (and you knew there would be exceptions to the Rules of Positioning), when you get a once-in-a-great-while sudden opportunity. Case: Connell Homes. Tornadoes. New market. Be alert and MOVE. But do not lose sight of where your REAL course is.

Shoals, reefs, and submarines (translated as business dips and threatening moves by competitors) may *shift* but not change your true course. During the Depression (why is the word capitalized?) Neiman-Marcus, led by the master merchant, stood their ground for top quality . . . and survived.

The phone company is an example of *staying on course*. A monopoly, why should they advertise? But what about Touch-Tone, Princess phones, extensions, new services? A constant barrage of Ideas to make you "think more telephones." And when their monopoly was cracked, the telephone utilities were and are still the major force.

5. *Remember To Do What You Did To Become Successful*. In all of the Great Brain Robbery seminars, we stress the Basics—personal P.R., personal notes, personal contacts. Too many businesses, when they get "big" (which is a very relative term), forget to do what they "used to do."

Salesmen who "used to" write notes to paying clients "don't have time any more." No time for the people who are paying you?

Hotels who do "selected surveys" and misspell current guests names would do well to look into doing what they used to do well—when they were smaller.

Banks with clever machine-printed notices slyly tell us, "Unless you make your payment, we will have to tell our computer on you." What positioning genius thought that one up?

Airlines. There used to be a wonderful guy at American. Jack Mullins. He had a mind-blowing system for answering "orchid letters," the kind of notes we sometimes write to commend people in flight who are exceptional. Jack was exceptional. Somehow you would get a *short* personal note which specifically related to exactly what you wrote. After receiving several of these, we desisted. Two years later on a flight from Dallas, we were so impressed with one stewardess's handling of an unruly passenger, we zapped off a quick compliment. The note from Mullins was a classic: "We haven't heard from you for a long time. We are very pleased you are still flying American and cared enough to write. Thanks. Jack." And for our next flight, we would choose . . . which airline?

How do they do that?

The good guys do. They keep the touch that put them where they are. Positioning is doing just that—even after you "arrive."

4 Communication

"If we all speak the same language, how
come we don't understand
one another?"

THE QUESTION WAS: "Shall the community spend $12 million to build a new
high school?" Everyone in town was pretty much convinced. The school
was overcrowded. And old. And deteriorating. Everyone, of course, had
his *own* solution on how to do it.

Solution: have a mass meeting. Invite everyone. Parents, teachers,
administrators. Explain the problem. Offer the solutions, communicate
and . . . start building. The night of the meeting, everyone showed up.
The opening speaker was an educator/planner chosen because he "had
the facts" and would "persuade the people."

These are *verbatim* excerpts from his speech:

"Heterogeneity will be reduced by social innovations peripheral to major
modification of certification requirements. . . . The concepts are
generalized and incorporated into the educational mainstream. . . . There
are intrinsic protectives of vested interests . . . and generally regressive fac-
tors and deteriorating conditions to the microstructure of achievement and
learning."

There he was, in front of this wanting-to-be-convinced audience. And
he was speaking in a foreign language.

Following his speech discussion groups had been planned. Nobody
stayed. Everyone went home. There was muttering, "What did he say?"
And . . . nothing happened. The old high school still stands. And no one,
to this day, quite remembers or understands what-exactly-went-wrong.
What-went-wrong was very simple—a lack of communication.

"The communicator," says author Leo Rosten, "is the person who
can make himself clear to himself . . . first!"

Try out your next selling speech on a friend. A close customer. A member of the family. Ask: Does it "sound" good? Does it make sense? Most of all, did I make my point? (What was my point?) In brief, was I communicating?

"Communication," says Professor Wendell Johnson, is "a two-way thing. A completed circuit." Good definition. It means (1) I say something; (2) you listen; (3) you understand what I say.

How does a Boston accent talk to a Southern drawl? (Answer: slowly.) Each has his own set of words and phrases peculiar to his background, part of the country, everyday living. And if you meet someone from a different country—one where "English" is also the language—watch out. The words may simply not mean the same thing. To an Englishman the "underground" is a subway. To an American it is a clandestine group. A "flat" to you and me is what happens to our tires in the middle of nowhere. To an Englishman it is simply the apartment where he lives. "Lift" means to "pick something up." Here. Over there, it means "elevator." And if someone talks to you about a "chemist," you picture the laboratory with test tubes. The Briton pictures his neighborhood druggist.

In some foreign markets, automobiles with interiors marked "Body by Fisher" were being advertised as having "Corpses by Fisher." The Americans in charge of marketing didn't understand the language of the host country well enough to catch the distortion. Or this one: when Pepsi was introduced to Taiwan, the slogan "Come Alive" became in Chinese a sacrilegious message: "Pepsi brings your ancestors back from the grave." Ah, the nuance of language.

Even in our own country the same word has a different meaning in different parts of the country. The sandwich in the long, skinny roll filled with delicious cold cuts is named "Hero" in New York, "Hoagy" in Philadelphia, "Sub" in Washington, and "Poor Boy" on the West Coast.

In your conversation, in what you write, the choice of the "right" word is most important. For words form the language to communicate with one another. And since language reflects place, time, age, sex, and circumstance . . . so must the words we choose.

Here is a classic example of how different words affect different people. Heinz was fighting the near-monopoly of the market by giant Campbell Soups and needed a blockbuster ad to make their point. Here it is: The setting was a restaurant. The illustration showed a pretty waitress in an all-white uniform, and she was formed quite well. A businessman was being served a cup of steaming hot soup by the attractive waitress. The headline said: "What she knows about your husband that *you* don't know." Obviously (it was supposed by the writers) that he enjoys Heinz soup served in restaurants.

The ad pulled well; had good readership. The agency decided to run the same ad in *MacClean's* magazine for the Canadian market. That magazine refused. "The headline copy is too suggestive," they said. The agency protested, quarreled, and lost. A new headline was created and accepted. This one: "He gets it downtown—why not give it to him at home?" Why not, indeed!

Harold Ross, editor, mentor, and fiery director-general of the *New Yorker* magazine, waged an endless war against wishy-washy words and fuzzy phrases. Against pronouns which the reader couldn't "relate where they related to." He ranted, pounded, and preached—clarity . . . clarity . . . clarity.

Ross became very ill and was dispatched (how he'd love that slip!) to a New England hospital. A young reporter was put "on watch" to monitor and report back to New York on Ross's condition. After days and nights of corridor-pacing, waiting, and standing by, there was a crisis and the young reporter filed his two-word report: "It's over."

The operation was completed? Ross is dead? The worst is over? What???

Ross had died—and this final, inept report of his death was what he spent his journalistic life fighting against.

What says Professor Johnson about a story like the one above? Here's a quote: "The degree to which there is communication depends precisely upon the degree to which the words represent the same thing for the receiver or the reader as they do for the sender or writer. The degree to which they do is an index of the clarity of the communication of the written statement."

What's that mean? This: If I say something, shouldn't everyone understand what I'm saying? Answer: They should—but do they? Larger answer: They might *not* unless you make yourself clear.

What are the ingredients of communication? Three behaviorists (Borden, Gregg, and Grove) say there are four:

1. THE SOURCE

The person who is equipped with the skills of communication (hopefully), a set of attitudes, a bank of knowledge, all within the pattern of the social system and culture in which he or she operates.

People communicate differently in different cultures. If an American child misbehaves, the mother says, "Be good"—which implies of course the child is being bad. The French mother corrects her child, "Be wise." The Scandinavian mother says, "Be friendly." The German murmurs, "Be in line." And the Hopi Indian mother says it best with: "That is not the Hopi way."

So the source is the sender.

2. THE MESSAGE

The communicator has to get it all together—the verbal, the physical, and the vocal. If the attitude of the speaker tells one thing verbally and another physically, the meaning and the message are distorted. Would you trust an accountant or a banker who plays the expert financial adviser and in front of you makes basic, bumbling arithmetic mistakes? Hardly. And the same is true for the confidence the listener perceives if the message deliverer shows nervousness while claiming expertise, or when the body language, licking the lips, stroking the perspiring forehead, and fumbling with objects distinctly tell the watcher that what is being said is not so.

The message must be clean and true.

3. THE CHANNEL

Marshall McLuhan claims the medium or channel IS the message and all other considerations are subordinate to the medium itself.

"It's printed, so it's a fact." "I saw it on television." That makes it true. "The New York *Times* said . . ." Or, for some, "It's in the Bible." Authority. Slides and audio-visual presentations make a much stronger impact than the spoken word.

The strong, visual effect of the medium (television) is one thing. The participation or lack of it is the other. McLuhan is correct (and he doesn't need us to tell him this), but TV gives the receiver nothing to do, no need to respond. The Source says Sit-back-and-watch. We will entertain you. You do nothing . . . but supply the ratings (which sell products and which mysteriously decide which show will live or die).

Maximum participation; maximum medium. But change the medium and you change the need for participation. Change the medium to personal selling, negotiating, purchasing pitches or persuasion. Now you have maximum medium *and* maximum participation.

Does your medium elicit response? Or just observation? Involvement or ennui? We should be aware this third step in the communications chain can vitally affect whether or not *we* will have a response. Beware, great creative presenters. Your slaved-over visual medium may please you as the creators but lull your TV-movie-trained audiences into sleeping through "just another light show" . . . with their eyes open. The same applies to too many flip charts, overheads, and over-emphasized show-and-tell trinkets.

The medium can be the message . . . and murder you.

4. RECEIVER

That's us, folks. We, the audience. Them the audience. Are they responding? If not, why not? Let's see what blocks this final link in our Source-Message-Medium-Reception?

Well, for one, the encoding and the decoding. That's the way the sages phrase it. Encoding is the manner and the method the speaker uses to deliver the message. Decoding is the listener—hearing, sorting, checking, comparing, contrasting what he/she hears with what he/she believes.

The speakers are sure of what they are saying—encoding—from *their* point of view, from their experience/intentions/culture/age/background. This is not necessarily true for the listeners going through the decoding process. Dr. Morris Massey tells us: *"You are what you were when."* Which means . . . you believe what you are "sending out." But whether that matches what the audience believes will depend on whether *your* values match their values/age/background/beliefs. If the receiver-audience *shares* those same values to a fairly high degree, the communication is right on. If not, there is a conflict of values (disbelief or rejection) and communication is blocked.

People judge events from their own points of view (background/training/interests).

For example, an automobile accident is observed by four witnesses—a doctor, lawyer, clergyman, and mechanic. The result will be widely different reactions to the same accident. The doctor will focus on the medical injuries and condition of the injured. The lawyer will note the position of the victims, the car, the cause, and the possibilities of liability and legal judgments. The clergy view will be concern for the well-being physically and spiritually of the participants. And the mechanic's eyes would be roving, assessing the cost of repairs as he goes forward with his calling card listing his body-shop services—different "body shop" repairs than the clergyman, attorney, or doctor plan to offer.

The Curse of Assumption, alluded to in another section, strikes hard at the core of this car-collision situation. Same accident. Same physical positioning of the elements and the people. Totally different, instant analysis. Wildly varied reaction.

The same is true with the reactions of receivers in an audience of many or one.

There is a story in one of the Paul Bowles books which makes the point. A professor is traveling with three Buddhist monks on a bus trip to a very remote city, Ayudhaya. In the back of the rickety bus is a native of the area who is "either crazy or drunk." He shouts, screams, howls constantly throughout the trip. The native passengers are totally serene, unheeding and uncomplaining.

The yelling and wailing finally are too much for the westerner. "Why don't they throw that man off?" he demands. His seat partner turns calmly and comments that the rest of the passengers don't even hear the dreadful din. The westerner shakes his head, "The poor man back there! It's incredible!"

"Yes," says the native, "but he is very busy." Busy? "He is working very hard," is the quiet explanation. "He is telling the driver 'go into second gear,' 'we are coming to a bridge,' or, 'be careful of the people on the road.' Yes . . . he is very busy." And the bus rolls on.

Then the reverse. The native begins a polite question as to the significance of neckties in the western dress code. He wants to know the meaning of the various properties of neckties. Some are long and narrow. Others are fat. Some have matching lengths. Some are longer on the front side than the back . . .

The westerner has no explanation, insists there is no significance. "Absolutely none," he states. The statement is unacceptable to the questioner, whose facial expression and reserved attitude tell that he knows he is being kept from some secret, subtle significance.

Point of view. Culture, background. Values. Encoding. Decoding. Sometimes, ver-ee difficult.

Some large American companies have started new courses in management for their employees. Nothing new about that? In this case—yes. The courses: How to listen.

If we could *really* hear what the other person was saying, we would be able to better understand. If we didn't "take a position" (our values vs. theirs), what the other person was telling us might come through (rather than being blocked at the doorway of our personal prejudices). If we stopped thinking about what *we* were thinking about, there *might* be some room in our brains to accept the message from the sender.

One of the foremost proponents of listening is John McKinven, president of the Communications Workshop in Chicago. This former advertising executive (Fuller, Smith and Ross) became fascinated and frustrated in the continuous conferences and business meetings which went on and on . . . mainly because the people involved didn't listen. He observes (most correctly): "Many people hardly ever listen. Their apparatus is on *Transmit* and in worst cases, they are incapable of switching to *Receive*."

Right. Reason: Tests show that people listen *less than half the time*. The rest of the time they are either nodding their heads to show they are concerned (but are not), and are somewhere else-in-their-head. (The most prevalent form of Two Timing.) When the speaker is speaking they are not listening; they are planning what they are going to be saying as soon as the speaker stops speaking. Ego. Self. Fear.

Fear? People don't listen because of fear? One might think that they would listen closely out of self defense, or to be able to join the speaker at just the right moment politically, emotionally, or even romantically.

Dr. Lewis Thomas in his brilliant book, *The Medusa and the Snail,* calls the deep-rooted concern in most of us "selfness." And he notes we each are furiously and constantly attempting to establish our uniqueness. "The markers of self," he says, "are conventionally regarded as mechanisms for maintaining individuality for its own sake, enabling one kind of a creature to defend and protect itself against all the rest." Although he is cellular-scientist-biologist, the doctor must have been in a lot of committee meetings in his time!

Back to John McKinven. After a long and successful (and highly creative) career in advertising, this curious and introspective man pondered: How to get people to listen? Company figures show that its people spend eighty percent of their time talking. Face-to-face, on the telephone, in meetings. And if they listened more than they talked—as good executives should—half of the time they were receiving salaries for was wasted. Because they simply were NOT listening.

The technique is intriguing. We went up to see it in action. The setting is a living room-conference room. Corporations retain the workshop, come in and actually hold a real meeting there. The environment is comfortable and "wired." There are small, unobtrusive video cameras set up in the corners of the walls. There are microphones and a one-way view wall (all with the knowledge and approval of these far-seeing client companies).

The day we were there, a well-known national company (no names, please, but instantly recognizable) was about to hold a meeting. Although we were not permitted to attend, the procedure was explained like this: The executives would assemble, and meet. The cameras would run. The tape recorders tape. Then there would be critiques—pointing out on tape the facial expressions which say, "I can't agree with that." Or head motions with agreement (uh-huh) and disagreement (uh-uh). Arm-folding and all the often talked of but barely recorded proofs of non-listening. Evidence.

Another nontraditional exercise of the workshop lets the speakers speak and suddenly over the intercom comes a voice: "Would you please stop? And at this point would the person to the right of the speaker now present the views of the speaker . . . to the rest of the group . . . *to the speaker's satisfaction?*"

The key is the phrase "to the speaker's satisfaction." Can you imagine what would happen the first time this startling interruption was directed to you, as the person "to the right of the speaker?" You would probably leap in mental panic, recover, and look up brightly, perhaps smile and say as smoothly as you could, "I'm sorry. I missed his last point," or, "Ha ha

. . . you really caught me when I was thinking of something else . . .''

But beyond your consternation as the one challenged, can you picture how many polite arguments would then roll out between the original speaker and the one who is trying to accurately present the original point of view? "No. No. That isn't *exactly* what I said, Tom . . . you didn't get it quite right—or perhaps I didn't spell it out as I should have . . ." And then the original speaker re-explains "what he meant" or "what he had intended" to say.

McKinven has a phrase we are very fond of and we use in our Great Brain Robbery seminars all the time: "Most people are too busy running their own tapes inside their heads to hear what anybody outside is saying."

Been to a cocktail party lately? Step back and scrutinize the cross-wired conversation in your group. Who's listening? Probably nobody. Just you. They are all running their own tapes and standing there, smiling, showing their well-capped teeth, nodding. Just waiting for the other prattle to stop so THEY can tell this "absolutely fascinating thing that happened yesterday."

So part of the listening process is being interested IN, concentrating ON, what the other person is saying, rather than getting ready "to defend and protect" yourself against the rest.

"Suspend your own agenda" is the best shorthand to begin to learn to listen. Put *your* mental agenda aside . . . at least until proven that the other speaker has nothing of interest or value for you. And the harder you listen, the sooner you will know whether you want to be a part of or participate in this conversation. (That's the propitious moment at the cocktail party, when you hoist your empty glass—little body language there—smile and murmur, "Think I'll freshen this up, excuse me," and depart.)

Story: A manufacturing plant had a serious quality control problem. It took months and many thousands of dollars to solve. Later, one of the younger employees mentioned he had known what was wrong from the beginning. He did? Why didn't he say something? Said the young man, "I tried to tell the foreman and the plant engineer but they wouldn't listen. They made me feel like a jerk."

As old Samuel Butler observed: "It takes two people to say something—the sayer and the sayee. One is just as essential as the other."

None of us has the problem of being the "sayer." But how many of us listen—really listen to the person talking to us? Or are we "running the tapes" again—our own nicely centered, selfish, wait-till-I-tell-you tapes? Developing the skill takes *lots* of practice. It is rarely perfected. How can you completely stop "two-timing" your listener? Tough.

It's called the Art of Active Listening. It's the super mental concentration that keeps "tracking" with the speaker, saying with a mind clear-of-

opposing thoughts, "Go ahead. I'm with you. Yes . . . yes? I *hear* you."
It's very complimentary.

But don't always be taken in by close attention from every listener.
There is another species afoot. Some people may listen very intently at
times but not necessarily for understanding. Manipulators, persuaders,
negotiators often listen well, but are constantly screening everything you
say for flaws, weak points, errors. They are ready to jump on you at first
flaw. Aha! they say (loudly or softly), and then turn your point to their
advantage.

This form of "manipulative listening" is accepted in marriage, business, and in other forms of interpersonal warfare. Manipulators are often
as involved in detecting your errors they only hear part of your story—the
part they are readying to attack. We call it "lawyer listening."

Then, in this most complex warfare of human communication, there is
the anti-stance, when the speaker suspects that the alert listener is collecting ammunition for a counterattack. So what happens? So the speaker
doesn't really open up. It's like two karate opponents circling for an opening.

This is the time for confrontation. You know what that means: speaking up and saying, "Hey, I think we have a problem." And then getting it
out. Why not? We both know as experienced warriors of words that this
encounter isn't going right; that there is a threatening, blocking atmosphere building up. And *instinctively* you both know something isn't right.

Is there a way to find out how large a problem this is between two
people? Yes. Here is a suggestion: "On a scale of one to ten . . . how
important is this to you?" That can mean leaving papers, smoking cigars,
emptying the trash, not wringing out wash cloths, taking the lead in every
meeting . . . you name it. "It's" bothering *you*.

On a scale of one to ten . . . gives you both a chance to *measure* how
far apart (or together) you are.

"Was I taking the lead in every meeting? I didn't realize that. I'm
sorry. How do you want to handle it?" On a scale of one to ten, how
important? "About a nine."

If you are the person bothered by this decision, and you have the same
"high nines" feeling on the other side of the issue, you'd better start mar-
shalling your best persuasive forces. You've got a problem.

Or no problem if the reply is, "Well, let's talk about it. It's not that
important to me."

That's what happens when you Get It Out.

Sure we all think we are constantly and politically getting our partners,
associates, and acquaintances to "understand" how we feel. The risk taking is saying it. And saying it will force a decision.

If we have been listening . . . actively.

And who better than a salesman should develop this fine art of active listening? There aren't many courses listed on sales training curricula for listening either. Maybe you ought to put one into your company or organization.

Full listening, if you like that phrase, is done without making judgments. John McKinven suggests you "hang loose and put all your energies into simply hearing what the speaker is saying, *thinking about it from his point of view.*"

You put yourself in the speaker's position. This is not easy. Listening usually can be done only by very secure people. Most everybody approaches the world with an overload of conditioning, parental injunctions, ought-to's, biases, prejudices, fears, defenses, and the strong need to justify themselves and to defend their position.

In short, the full listeners have few or no hang-ups. Or they have the ability to "turn off" their position, their identity. They are able to suspend their own agendas, at least momentarily. After all, you can always reaccess your own mental computer and at the right time, present another "program," another view of the problem. As salesmen,* like our brothers the attorneys, we have *plenty* of information about "presenting our case." The trick is to present the right point at the right moment. The clincher. The one that gets the verdict we want.**

Listening like any other skill is learned and takes practice. Much like writing. Or shooting baskets in basketball. Or selling. And since there aren't enough sales listening schools, you'll probably have to do it yourself.

How can you begin practice? By concentrating on what the other person is actually saying. Practice ignoring the telephone, voices floating in from the outside, people walking in and out of your range of view. Nothing is more distracting to a speaker than having the eyes of the listener darting here and there to check up on what's going on, who's going by. The speaker *knows* you are not hearing.

People have a tendency to be distracted when they are sitting at their own desks. The "territory" is so familiar. There are so many things there

---

*Very recently at a speech we gave to the Professional Sales Association in Los Angeles, the gathering afterward was a protest-questioning-debate from the attending competent successful selling women. "You keep saying *salesman*. Where do we come in?" they complained. Some of the men countered with, "It's a category, it's accepted. Understood. Do you want to be called 'saleswoman'?" NO! chorused the lady peddlers. "Well, what *do* you want to be called?" One of the young women snapped, "I go in and say: *I'm in Sales*. Damn it! I don't want to be separate and lib or any of that stuff. I want to be respected for what I am: in Sales." YEAAA! was the answering cheer. Super-speaker, Dr. Marty Cohen handles it this way: "I will use 'his' and 'him' as a pronoun . . . being perfectly aware this audience is made up of macho and machettes!" The response is always a roar of approval.

**This section, thanks to a generous John McKinven's *Notes on Listening*.

to be done. As you are talking to them, their eyes are shifting about while they mouth Uh Huhs, vague Yes's.

We call this the Curse of Assumption. It works like this:

My neighborhood druggist has a salesman who comes for an order every week. He is polite, courteous, and always asks the proper questions about family, health, and business. The druggist felt the words were perfunctory, automatic—that the salesman said them out of rote and not out of concern.

The next time the salesman called and asked, "Hi. How's everything?" the druggist answered in a calm, unemotional voice.

"Well, our house burned down, my grandmother died last night and our children have been missing for three days."

And the salesman smiled and said, "Gee, That's interesting. Glad to hear everything's OK," and then, "Let me show you our newest products."

He had not heard a word. He was so busy listening to what he was selling, he simply assumed his customer answered as usual.

There is a new bank building in center city Philadelphia. When you step into the elevator on the ground floor, know where you are going before the doors close. Otherwise you are faced with a list of buttons to push that say (reading from the bottom up) P1, P2, C, 1, LM, UM, Alarm. (Guess which button we wanted to push?)

One person, out of frustration, used a Dyno lable to spell out "lobby" and Scotch-taped it next to the appropriate button. It soon was pulled off. The reason: who wanted an unsightly looking label inside an expensive elevator?

The architect was so busy listening to what he knew made sense he simply assumed the customer knew as well.

A bank recently sent out a letter to their customers offering special programs for IRAs.

I asked the bank officer, "What's an IRA?"

"Don't you know?" he said answering my question with a question.

"Of course," I said. "It means Irish Republican Army."

"What?" he asked, shocked.

"Uh . . . it means, my uncle Ira in Vermont?"

He shook his head and said, "It means Individual Retirement Account," adding, "Everyone knows that."

Really? I suggested he stop ten people on the street and ask.

The banker, the architect, the salesman all suffer from a highly communicable disease reaching epidemic proportions. Its name: The Curse of Assumption.

The symptoms: People in business talk to one another in their own language and assume everyone else knows what they're talking about.

The cure: Put yourself in the position of the person talked to. And listen!

A client called the other day on a mailing piece we sent. "Why don't you have your phone number in your ad?" she asked. "Why do I have to look it up to call you to spend my money in your store?"

Uhhhhhhhhh, why we just assumed she knew our number. After all she is a customer. Don't all our customers have our store's number right next to the phone with the doctor, dentist, police, fire, and ambulance numbers?

Hardly.

A recent survey revealed eight out of ten business letterheads were not doing their primary job: identifying their company. They simply assumed everyone knew who they were.

What an indictment. Can you hear the man who buys the envelopes saying, "Well everyone knows who 'our' company is." He does. And his wife and family and anyone else working for the company directly or indirectly. But is that everyone who receives the mail? You rarely see the major corporations forgetting who they are. They continue to spend millions of dollars advertising because they never assume everyone knows who they are.

A week does not go by without a new customer coming in our store and asking, "My, this is a nice store. How long have you been here?" And we softly answer, "Forty years."

One out of five people move every year. Why assume everyone knows who you are, where you are, and what you are doing?

During World War II, Ford Motor Company spent millions of dollars advertising automobiles almost impossible to buy. When asked why they spent the money they wisely replied, "The war will end some day. Then people will want to buy cars. We think it's important to keep on reminding them who we are and what we do."

No Curse of Assumption here. They knew the importance of repeating and repeating and repeating the same basic facts over and over and over . . . again.

The lesson today: Assume Not, Want Not. Face each sale with basics firmly in hand. Do not assume everyone knows what you do. It simply ain't true.

There is a famous advertisement from McGraw-Hill Magazines showing a dour-faced, heavy-set man glaring from the page at the imaginary just-arrived salesman. The copy says:

"I don't know who you are.

I don't know your company.

I don't know your company's product.

I don't know what your company stands for.

I don't know your company's customers.

I don't know your company's record.

I don't know your company's reputation.

Now—what was it you wanted to sell me?"

Picture the dour-faced, heavy-set man as a new customer tomorrow morning. Have you answered the questions? Or have you simply made a request to buy without telling who/what/why you are. After all why do that? If you know, doesn't everybody?

If you believe that, you are plagued with the Curse of Assumption.

One superb insurance pension salesman has several ground level techniques which are prescriptions against the curse. He shared them with an audience of Allstate Insurance salesmen. "I have three moves I make all the time," he said. "I never carry a pencil or pen. I never let the client sit at his own desk. I never *sell* him anything."

Alan J. Setlin is a multimillion producer, owns his own agency, has Las Vegas real estate holdings. How does he do THAT?

"First things first," he said. "I walk in. No social nonsense. I get the client involved. First thing I want to do is get the guy away from behind his desk. That wouldn't be easy with the kind of clients I call on. So, I never have more than one copy of my proposal, even though we have about thirty-seven secretaries. I suggest he come around and sit with me so we can go over this idea."

Next, he borrows the executive's pen. "You'd be amazed," he says, "how carefully an executive will watch you and pay strict attention when you are drawing with his favorite personal solid-gold pen." Basic human nature at work.

Next, borrowing a sheet of paper, he draws a series of three crude little boxes in a row. The first is full of dollar signs. "I point to the dollar signs and suggest that his company is probably generating a sizable amount of money every year. He'll agree with a nod. I jump to the second little box marked TAXES, 'and you pay the government most of what you earned.' And then quickly to the third box, 'and this is what you have left at the end of the year—NET.'

"Now," he says, "here is a fourth little box, down here, underneath this first box with the dollar signs." And he marks it PENSION as he draws an arrow down from the dollar signs. "How would you like to enter into a legal conspiracy to take those earned dollars and put them down here *before* you pay taxes to the Government?"

And he immediately adds this case-clincher: "You *know* if you give the money to the government they are not going to give it back to you. No chance. None. If you invest in a Pension Trust Plan, you have a good chance of getting it back. What do you think?"

No wonder he's one of the best in his business. He has solved how to keep the attention of a client. (And, oh yes, he does return the gold pen, after all he has a drawer full of his own gold pens back at the office.)

People *talk* at the rate of about 125 words a minute. But the same person can listen *four times as fast*. That means there is a lot of extra brain time available for the listener to be distracted, look around, away-from, and even think of something else at the same time you are talking.

You know this from being at a seminar or meeting where a boring speaker goes on and on in a dull unmodulated tone. Or drones on about a subject of very little interest. The audience quickly shuts out the source, the message, *and* the medium. We tune out the speaker's words and barely hear the hum of the voice sound in the background. Wrong.

It is said of achievers (winners) that the highest rate of return is reserved for those who "recognize they are there." Odd phrase. But let's have a look at it. The ones who get the most out of any activity are those who *come to get*. They are determined to profit for the time they have committed to spend.

The achievers are not turned off because the speaker has a paunch or a hairpiece, or looks like an unfavorite member of the family, or is so good looking "how could she possibly know anything?"

No, the rule of the seekers is "there has to be a good idea in here somewhere." And they get past all the prejudice and dig it out. "One Good Idea" has always been the justification for spending the time and the money to go to a meeting, a seminar, a clinic. Where is it?

Before he became California's unorthodox tam-wearing senator, S. I. Hayakawa wrote these words of advice in *Language in Thought and Action:*

> Listening means trying to see the problem the way the speaker sees it—which means not *sympathy,* which is feeling for him, but empathy, which is *experiencing* with him. . . . All too often, we tend to listen to a speaker and his speech in terms of generalizations: "Oh, he's just another of those progressive educators . . ." Once we classify a speech in this way, we stop listening, because, as we say, "We've heard that stuff before."

In Conway, Arkansas (It ain't the end of the world . . . but you can see it from there!: old speaker joke), at an FMC sales rally we did, there was a big frowning Boston Italian fellow. He sat right up front. He didn't laugh. He didn't react. All the while the rest of the jolly FMC fellows were "falling about" in enjoyment of the entertainment-education. We had been warned "this guy from Boston never responds." At the end of the session, up lumbered the large unsmiling menacing man. There was a moment of anxiety. Was he going to strike, criticize, complain? He growled, "Everything you said, I knew." (Well, we thought, you can't win 'em all . . .)

Suddenly he stuck out his huge ham of a hand and with what passed for a smile, he said, "But I listened, and half of the things you said I haven't been doing lately. So I got something out of it." And he spun away.

A strange but rewarding compliment for a speaker. He had been *experiencing with*. It just hadn't shown.

Force yourself to listen. A phrase, a fact may suddenly make sense to you. And you can use it at some future date. Or even a gesture, a stance, a pause. The way speakers handle their bodies is a "language" by itself and communicates sometimes better than spoken words. All of this may come in handy when it's your turn to be the speaker.

As speakers/persuaders/presenters we all occasionally fall headlong into this trap. We have been on the "bored" side at a seminar or meeting when some speaker drones on in a dull monotone and you as a member of the audience tune-out not only the source and the message, but the medium—you barely hear the hum of the voice as a background. (Are we guilty of "humming" the audience when we are the speaker?)

Look people *in the eyes*. Nothing will ever replace *seeing* what your audience is thinking.

Involve the audience, the speakers. "Do you agree?" (Get heads nodding.) "Would you say we're on the right track?" (Yeses.) "I think we've covered that. Shall we move on now?" (Signaling to your audience that this is the end of a section.)

"Work" your entire audience. Too many speakers and presenters concentrate on one or an 'up front' portion of their audience. Remember, everybody here paid the same price in time, money, and effort to attend. They are *all* customers.

Don't favor a friend or a familiar or friendly face. The rest of the audience resents being left out.

Invent imaginative, exciting, or intriguing titles. Some of the dullest and most predictable titles are of sermons. Here are some dandies that would bring the flock flocking in:

"The Wages of Sins Is Aaaughh!"

"God Is Where the Action Is."

"Freeway Faith."

"Will the Real God Please Step Forward."

"How to Sin and Enjoy It."

We don't know if they all originate in the church, but if they do, we'll bet there's a problem parking when this series hits the congregation. Imagination. Don't be afraid of outrageous titles.*

Above all, the words. Select them. Slave over them. Steal them from other speakers. Listen and learn. Don't overestimate the amount of knowledge or information your audience has.

Each word is important. Each tells its own story. Each triggers a reaction in the mind of your customer, your listener, your audience.

*Sermon quotes from *An Introduction to Contemporary Preaching*, Daniel Baumann, Baker Book House, Grand Rapids, Michigan, p. 129.

There are two halves to communication: the sending and the receiving. To fully listen—you must listen fully . . . without judgment. Not yet. Hear it out. Sometimes the solution is revealed to the speaker, as he or she speaks. Sometimes the solution is divined by the listener. Sometimes they agree.

At other times, there must be confrontation to resolve the conflict. And a method of establishing how far apart you are . . . perhaps on a scale of one to ten.

And as John McKinven sums it up, "In any case, both the speaker and listener run the risk of being changed by the process of full listening." And we presume he intends that to mean on *both* sides.

Talk and write with care.

That's exactly what the March Hare told Alice in Wonderland.

To which Alice hastily replied, "I do. At least I mean what I say— that's the same thing, you know."

"Not the same at all," said the Hatter. "Why you might just as well say 'I see what I eat' is the same thing as 'I eat what I see.'"

5 Goal Setting

"Make no little plans. There is nothing in little plans to stir men's blood. Make big plans."
—DANIEL BURNHAM, *Chicago Planning Commission*

A VIENNESE PSYCHIATRIST once studied the lives of 200 famous men and women. While each of them led different lives, had different drives, and different approaches to success, there WAS one constant theme: *Every single one had a self-selected goal that directed all their energies.*

Paul J. Meyer was an insurance salesman. And a millionaire. At age twenty-six! He once listed his steps toward success. Here was the first one: *Establish a goal.*

How do YOU become the one person out of every 1,000 taxpayers who is a millionaire in America?

We once watched a TV talk show with host Merv Griffin. His guests that day were several "new" millionaires, including the man who made the Lear jet, the developer of Kentucky Fried Chicken, and other self-made individuals.

"What was your goal," asked Griffin, "to make money?"

Each of the guests shook their heads "no." Each answered, in a similar way they merely wanted to "do" something. That they had a dream. A Goal. (And money "just happened.")

Each, in turn, merely repeated what Andrew Carnegie said years earlier, "No one has been known to succeed without applying the principle of definiteness of purpose. All riches and all material things anyone acquires through self effort begin in the form of a clear, concise mental picture of the thing one seeks."

Earl Nightingale said there are three goals to become rich:

1. Make up your mind you can get the money you want.
2. Decide how much you want to earn and by what time.
3. Find a need . . . and fill it.

We all know people who feel life is not worth living. Or whose conversation centers around food or television programs to the total exclusion of everything else. They watch the world go by. They exist only because they are. They do not contribute to the world, nor, in a greater tragedy, to themselves. A great philosopher once said, "There is not much to do but bury a man when the last of his dreams is dead . . ."

The Apostle Paul recorded his goal in Philippians 3:13, "This one thing I do, forgetting those things which are behind, and reaching forth unto those things which are before, I press toward the mark . . ." Paul had a commitment to spread the word and his faith. His goal.

We once met a busy executive and discussed goal setting. He said, "I've always wanted to set a goal to read more. But I just don't have the time. I'm too . . . well, busy."

We suggested we could give him eleven days—eight hours a day— every year, of free time, just to read. Would he like that?

"Great. But impossible," he said, "I just don't have the eleven days available."

We asked if he had fifteen minutes a day he could set aside for reading? The *same* fifteen minutes every day.

Certainly. He was well organized. He could do that.

Fine, we said and then, "Fifteen mintues a day is eleven eight-hour days a year. Add it up."

He pulled out a small calculator, punched in the numbers, smiled and said, "You're right. I'm starting today . . ."

We reminded him that to make such a plan work he must pick the time which best suited his busy schedule, and do it comfortably. He had to shut down the phone and close himself off. A few moments in the morning, after lunch, before dinner or before going to bed—he had to be comfortable, isolated, and free to concentrate. If he was to accomplish his goal, he had to insure that the conditions were right, that they were constant, and that his concentration was uninterrupted.

Dr. William C. Menninger, world famous psychiatrist from Kansas once wrote: "Do you know whether you are going in the right direction? And, most of all, where you *want* to go? Not just in your business but in the atmosphere in your home, your relationship with members of your family, your own feeling of status, dignity, and your own integrity?"

Only if you have goals.

Why set up goals?

Because we should be masters of our fate. To decide what will happens to us, what achievements, what results, what satisfactions. None of this can happen unless we begin by setting up goals.

Goals are not constant, good for the rest of our lives. Goals are ever-changing. They need to be reviewed, looked-at down the line. But they ARE important because they:

1. Set a specific target to reach.
2. Are measurable so we can see how much we can do and how often we can do it.
3. Tie into a definite time period.

Once having set a goal, you must commit yourself to working at it steadily. You must not give up too easily. Thomas Edison said, "The trouble with most people is they quit before they start."*

Gee, what happens if you accomplish all you set out to do. Can you handle it? Emotionally? Psychologically? Physically?

A ten-year study by General Motors Research Institute revealed that as men received promotions and increased responsibilities, their mental and emotional capacity increased proportionately. It's called Stretch.

Well now that we know you can handle success . . . how do you achieve it? Most people fail to achieve their goals for three reasons.

1. *Their goals are too general.*

If someone says, "I wish I had more money." We would ask, "How *much* more?"

They rarely know. They just wish they had more.

If we ask, "What do you want the money for?" We find out: "new dining room furniture" or "a good second car" or perhaps "a boat."

"When do you want to have your boat?" Usually they hem and haw and then pick a date.

We then ask, "Exactly how much is your boat going to cost?"

When we have the answers to those questions, the original *general* goal "I wish I had more money" sounds more like, "I need $3,000 to buy a boat with an outboard motor and trailer by June first, one year from now." That's a goal!

2. *Their goals are not measurable.*

The goals are not broken down into small enough Action Steps. The smaller the size of the Action Steps, the better are your chances of accomplishing them. Each step is simple; it's small; it's a "bite at a time." Each step means measurable progress. Most people don't set down definite starting dates and completion dates for each of those Action Steps. They don't commit themselves to *writing a plan*. They are content to make general lists of wishes.

You need a plan, start dates, check dates, and completion dates.

The check-point date is very important. It permits you to see whether you were too optimistic about your plan, your progress, or completion date.

---

*Or the first time they fail.

3. *They abandon the goal with "first failure."*

It's easy to rationalize abandoning a personal goal. "I wanted to learn racquetball but it was too much of a hassle to get the equipment, join the club, find someone to play with." Yet, the same person will say, "Gee, I wish I had time to play racquetball." The goal never gets beyond the "wish and want" stage. Why not start again?

Or on weight control, "I lost three or four pounds but I love desserts too much!" Why not adjust your weight-loss goal rather than abandon it? How about two pounds a month—with a six-month program on paper? Why abandon it?

Personal development. "I want to read more. I'd like to study psychology. I've heard *est* is good. I'd like to change enough in six months so that I wouldn't worry about other people's approval, so that I become stronger and feel better about myself." Next: Take a lesson from business. Each company sets a monthly goal, a forecast. It's called Profit and Loss.

How often does business hit its goals or surpass them? When they do— wonderful. But more often than not, they miss in one way or another. Do they abandon the business, close up, or shrug off a failure? No. They readjust. Set a more reasonable figure. Check into costs or—extend the time needed to accomplish a goal.

Why don't we do that with *personal* goals? They're too general, not written down, and who will know when we let them slide away? Let's take an example. Remember our friend who wanted $3,000 for a boat? Let's say that the goal is to get the money in one year. First thing to do: create units of time and divide them into dollars. $3,000 divided by twelve months is $250 per month. Now we can further clarify our goal and say it is "to earn an additional $250 per month for the next twelve months."

How do we do that?

The first thing we have to do is take an inventory of our skills. It's pretty obvious that unless we get a sudden increase of $250 per month in our present job, we are going to have to cut into our reserve of leisure time. Or we must supplement our present income. What are we good at, what can we learn that will make us money?

Reaching your goals involves what we call "trade-offs." Earning $250 per month means about $60 a week average. If you're prepared to "trade off" three nights a week, you'll want to earn about $20 a night. If it's only two nights you want to give up, that's $30 a night. And one night a week is $60 a night.

Many people look at their evening leisure time and say, "I can't give up bowling on Tuesday nights." Or, "Are you suggesting I break up the bridge club by not playing on Wednesdays?" Well, what we're suggesting is this: if you're not prepared to trade off enough of those evenings, and to give up some of your leisure time, then perhaps you'd better settle for a rowboat and a pair of oars.

Do an inventory of your skills. What are you good at? In addition to your present job, how can you make extra income?

Could you learn to be a bartender? Work in a gas station?

A lot of people don't want to get involved in those occupations. Some people thrive on them. But many people have what we call "Give-Away" skills—skills they are good at and they can start charging for; the same skills they used to give away. We all have them. Think about yours. What have you been doing for so long with no pay? Working for charities? Cooking for parties? Doing accounting for the church? Typing for your club?

How many of you are handy around the house with tools of any kind? Carpentry, cabinetry, electricity, plumbing. How many times have you helped a neighbor build shelves in his house or garage? Or wired his living room for stereo, or fixed his plumbing? And for free? Well, now you say, "Fred, I've got myself a goal for the next twelve months. I am going to get me a boat and motor and trailer, and I'm going to do all the fishing I've always wanted to do, and so I have to charge you now for those new cupboards you want. It will still be the most reasonable price you can find next to free, but I do have to charge." And Fred will know it, and Fred will pay. (And surely Fred will get to enjoy the boat he helped pay for. Added Value.)

If you have a special skill to offer don't rely just on word-of-mouth advertising. Put an ad in the Pennysaver, or the Dime-a-Line section of your local newspapers. Many daily newspapers offer *free* classifieds today. Spend fifteen dollars for business cards. Spread the word, and spread the cards. Have your wife and your family help. Your kids can tell the neighbors. Soon their dads will know what you're up to. And here is what is most important. Every one of the things we have just said is an Action Step. And every Action Step must have a start date, a check-point date, if necessary, and a completion date for certain. For example, "I will write the copy for the Pennysaver and Dime-a-Line ads on June first, and I will place them both on June second. (No check-point date necessary there.) I will begin to design my business cards on June third, and I will deliver the copy to the printer on June eighth. (No check-point date necessary there). We cannot emphasize this point too much: WRITE DOWN EVERY ACTION STEP YOU CAN IDENTIFY, AND UNDERNEATH IT, PUT THE DATE YOU WILL START TO DO IT, AND THE DATE YOU WILL COMPLETE IT.

Your check-point date should be the fifteenth of every month. Take a look and see how much you made. It is exactly at this point that many people abandon their goal. On the fifteenth of the month. They did not make the total $250 the first month, only $150. So they say, "Well, it was a great idea, and I can always use the $150."

Wrong. If business isn't meeting goals, do they abandon the whole enterprise? Of course not. They make changes in the plan, but never abandon the goal. So let's make changes in our plan, but not abandon the goal of getting that boat and motor and trailer.

Let's think about financing the boat instead of trying to pay cash. You can probably buy the whole unit, boat and trailer, for twenty-five percent down, or $750. You've already accumulated $150. Doesn't look so bad now, does it? That leaves $2250 to finance and if you decide to finance it over two years, your payments will be about $110 per month.

So now your goal is restated to read, "Earn $600 by July first." Then rewrite your plan to earn $110 a month rather than $250. Sound like a much easier task? It is. We do not advocate going into debt. Make that decision yourself.

Never abandon your goal until you have relentlessly searched out every possible alternative. Again, it's called a "trade-off." You are trading off going into debt temporarily against giving up your dream of a boat entirely.

In addition to trade-offs in your goal-setting, there is the turning of disadvantages into advantages.

When you set specific goals, obstacles will appear. Do you give up and turn back? Or make the obstacle work *for* you, instead of against you? Sometimes what appears to be a block to your goal can be merely a test of your wits, imagination, and ability to work-it-out. Here are a few:

The goal of the young boy in Decatur, Illinois, was to be a photographer. He answered a magazine ad for a book on photography. The company mixed up the request and sent him one on ventriloquism instead. He did not have the money to reorder the book. And it was too much trouble to send it back. So he read the book on ventriloquism. And studied it. And made a wooden dummy for fun. He and his dummy became known to the world as Edgar Bergen and Charlie McCarthy.

The goal of the advertising company was simple enough: do more business.

But what do you do when you run out of growing room? Metromedia's outdoor advertising division on the West Coast complained to boss Ross Barrett that they could not set goals for increasing their business. The reason: they were running out of places to put up billboards. New environmental laws and special interest groups were going to court to stop additional billboards. The company couldn't increase its prices much, because they were already at a competitive high. What could they do?

Barrett analysed the situation and in true Brain Robbery tradition "stole" a page from one of his competitors: radio. Instead of selling billboards on a per-month basis, why not sell them like radio does: on

thirteen-week contracts? This gave him an automatic four-week fre-
quency increase over the year. And increased his gross intake by thirty-
three percent.

While everyone around him was trying to figure out how to do more
business within the framework, Barrett went "outside the box" and
turned the disadvantage into an advantage.

The goal of the clothing designer Ralph Lauren was to sell "natural"
fibers. He knew some of the initial comments from consumers accus-
tomed to wrinkle-free double-knits and cotton-blend fabrics would be
about the wrinkling of all-cotton merchandise. He overcame this objec-
tion very nicely. He had woven into each label on every garment:
"*Guaranteed* to wrinkle . . ."

Carl Stokes's goal was to be elected mayor of Cleveland. He had the
ability and dedication. And one factor that made him different from any
other candidate: he was black.

Would the political system accept a black man as mayor of Cleveland?
Would the voters?

His supporters decided to bring the race issue up front. If it was being
whispered about, why not have it *talked* about? They put together a series
of ads and this was the first giant headline in the newspaper: *"Don't Vote
for a Negro."*

Everyone in Cleveland read *that* headline.

And then, in smaller type, came this copy . . .

"Vote for a man.
Vote for ability. Vote for character.
Vote for a leader. A man who can attack the problems and solve them.
A man who can rally the people of Cleveland behind him.
Vote for a man.
A man who believes. Carl Stokes."

He won.

Jim Young's goal was to sell apples. He was proud oᵢ his bright shiny,
rock-hard, juicy apples. He built a good mail order business and his customer's knew to expect the same smooth-skinned quality every year.

One year there was a hail storm just before the harvest. Almost every
apple was bruised with hail marks. There was Jim Young with thousands
of mail orders and checks. If he mailed the apples, he would have
thousands of dissatisfied customers and a ruined business. How could he
take this disadvantage and turn it into an advantage?

He knew the apples were top quality. He knew the damage was only in
how-they-looked. In fact, the taste was even better since cold weather
when apples are ripening improves their flavor.

His decision: fill the orders. But. In every carton he put this card:

"Note the hail marks which have caused minor skin blemishes on some of these apples. They are proof of their growth at a high mountain altitude where the sudden chills from hail storms help firm the flesh, develop the natural fruit sugars, and give these apples their incomparable flavor."

Not one shipment was returned.

The clincher: the following year he received orders reading, "Hail-marked apples if available. Otherwise, ship the ordinary kind . . ."

The moral: move it up front.

Goals are set throughout your life. The classic tale for each person who has gone to college happens in their first weeks of classes when the professor says, "Look to your left. Now, look to your right. Two of the three of you will not be here on graduation day."

Yet each student had the same goal: To graduate.

This same story can be told of every business on Main Street in your town. A retailing friend joined us at a nearby shopping mall and pointed out shops around us, commenting on them one by one: "That one's going bankrupt after the first of the year. That other store carries nice merchandise but doesn't have enough capital and not enough people know the store, so it can't last the winter. See that cosmetics store? It hasn't done a thing for Christmas which should be one third of its annual volume. They probably won't last too long . . ."

And so it went with an occasional, "Now *that* store is doing great. They have a product to sell . . ." Until we found ourselves back again in college looking first to the left, then to the right, wondering which of us would remain and achieve our goal.

(And yet didn't *each* of the stores have a goal? To succeed?)

What determines success? We believe there is no one reason. There are a combination of reasons which determine the success or failure of any plan.

What makes one business reach its goal and another not? If we were limited to one word, it would have to be: Attitude.

What is your attitude toward your business? Toward yourself? How well do you think of yourself? (That's how others will think of you.)

Set up definite determined criteria—goals and check points. It is drive—and attitude—which produces the business that remains for half a century on Main Street, becoming part of the tradition of the community.

It is this drive—this attitude—that motivates the people written about in the first chapter in this book—and those self-made rich men who sat around and chatted with Merv Griffin a few pages back.

It is not enough merely to insist on having your store clean at all times. It is important, but not enough. It is not enough to make sure there is sufficient stock from which the customer can choose. It is important, but not enough.

It is not enough to simply greet each and every customer who comes into your store to show you care. It is important, but not enough.

It is not enough to have the direct mail piece sent to the customer who shops your store to show the very special importance she has with you. It is important, but not enough.

It is a combination of each and every one of these actions (and perhaps forty-four more actions similar to these) which results in your business being successful and attracting crowds when other shops wonder what special attraction you have. (Which is a reminder of the frustrated small store on the town's Main Street that watched customers jamming the next door John Doe Department Store. And so he made a big sign and placed it over his shop which said, "Main Entrance to John Doe Department Store.")

But it is not enough to merely copy or to rely upon the traffic of the next-door store. Do not fall into the trap of wondering what the competition is going to do.

Your goal: Make your competition start wondering about what *you* are going to do.

No one will come—why bother?

A collection of small, quality shops in a unique, restored village shopping area near us planned an end-of-the-year clearance. Suddenly, at the last minute, the owner decided none of the shops should have a sale. His reasoning: the local discount stores ran pre-Christmas sales and therefore no one would come to shop his small specialty shops if they were looking for sales.

What sad reasoning. The owner lost sight of what he was, once he began to identify with what he was not. His story was a different story than the discount store's story. He forgot the characteristics of his main subject. His best seller became a nonpurchased item. He let his attitude be changed by the thinking of others. In his effort to become something else, he became nothing. Goal: Don't just stand there—*Do* something!

Katie's commitment

Katherine Hepburn recently spoke about commitment to completing an assigned job, saying she was taught no other way. She recalled once having accepted a certain script and then being dissatisfied once production began. The easy decision was to withdraw. But she had made a commitment. She knew she must continue till the end, giving it the best of her talents. This is her attitude toward her goal. What's yours?

Goal: I said I would and I will.

Don't be what you ain't

With unemployment at a high peak, with a heavy recession as part of economic daily life, the accepted ways of doing business and the pattern you have set may seem like they need a drastic change. Be careful. Do not become that which you ain't. Soon, no one will know who you are.
Goal: Build identity. Your own.

Hello?

Recent stories in *Advertising Age* tell about cutbacks in all kinds of retail expenses: less inventory, less personnel. But not less advertising. Every time your ad is seen at your customer's house, it reminds her you are still doing business on the same old street, at the same old stand, in the same manner that made that customer come to you the first time and return. And return. And return.
Goal: Keep keeping in front of your best customers.

Good Quality in Poor Times

Stanley Marcus, of Neiman-Marcus, tells about his store's troubles in the Depression of the 1930s, saying, "Declining sales made it necessary to curtail purchases and to institute salary reductions, first for executives, later for all employees. With prices falling at wholesale, our prices at retail reflected the changes, but at no time did we ever yield to the temptation, as did some other retailers, to lower our quality standards to bring in more sales.

"My father, burdened with a large store and a back-breaking personal bank loan, stood firm and exhorted his buyers not to succumb to the temptation of cheaper, inferior goods, just to get badly needed sales. He urged them, time and again, to maintain the standards of quality our customers had learned to expect from us."

Their goals remained firm. Time proved the success of their decision. Others failed. Neiman-Marcus continues. Moral: This too shall pass. Hang in there.

To Summarize:

Set a goal and get going!
That's the very first step. Don't fall into that awful trilogy of "I want," "I wish," "I hope." Those three expressions will do more to kill an ambition, or keep you from getting what you want than any other words in our language. Why? Because each one, "I want," "I wish," "I hope," is an

admission you don't feel you can get what you want. Have you heard yourself saying "I want . . . I wish . . . I hope"? We hope not. Because each time you hear yourself or anyone else saying those "killer" phrases you know either yourself or the other person is living for later. And it will probably never happen.

Don't live for later

How many of us are guilty of that? You see, any expression that is not NOW—is simply an excuse. Of course there are future plans, goals that are not literally obtainable at this moment, but don't fall guilty of the "all talk" someday-in-the-future fakery. If you have a friend and he or she ever says to you, "Oh, you've been saying that for as long as I've known you . . ." you're guilty as charged.

Listen

Listen—to yourself—and to others who care for you. Realize most of us keep saying things we really don't want. "I'd like to be a drummer. I should have started long ago. It's too late now. I'm too old." "I've always wanted to play the piano." (So? They're still giving lessons.) Pop Miller of Glendale Savings fame took up golf after fifty years of age, became senior champion, and I think has two holes-in-one to his credit, one of them after age eighty.

There is no such thing as a weakness. Only underdeveloped skills. "No weakness? Ha! You don't know *me*."

All right—try it this way: What you don't do well, you avoid and are probably not good at . . . yet. It isn't a weakness. It is a skill you have never developed, OK?

If you do something successfully seven times, it becomes a skill.

Is that true? Think about it . . . in telling a new story. In developing a new theme when speaking. In putting together a sales pitch. By the time you say it the seventh time, it's like learning a role in a play. Second nature.

A skill.

It ain't necessarily so

Why do we keep saying we want something and then never do anything about it but talk? Is it because we really *don't* want it? We think we should. It's so very fashionable to be lean and trim. Everybody wants to be thin. Not really. We have a friend. He has a big fat tummy. Around New Year's we visited his record store and kiddingly patted him on the stomach. "For the New Year you'll have to get rid of that." He smiled back and said, "Not really. I like it. I don't drink any more. Gave up smoking. Love to eat. (Patted his own tummy and said:) I've decided to keep this." Any questions? Noooooo . . .

If you want it: write it

Put down on paper, "This is my goal." Convince yourself you do want to attain that ambition, whatever it may be. It's yours. It's private property. Set out a Start Date as we've suggested. Nothing new about that—except doing it.

Then have a check point. How are you doing? Not well? Start again, recycle, reforecast like business does.

Completion date—when? If you want enough to write it and do it, you'll get it! This is a great way to see in fairly short time if this goal is really what you want to pursue.

If you find with a few attempts this activity is not for you, the weight lifting is a drag, or the extra nights of direct selling earning are not working out, the night school courses are nowhere near up to your Expectations, then make another decision: forget it and get another goal.

But—stop talking about it. Cancel it. Make the decision to move onto something else that will give you greater pleasure, greater fulfillment, more joy, more fun.

Because if you are not having fun, not feeling good about yourself and what you're doing . . . what's the use?

Set aside time to write down your goals today. Simply put down on paper where you want to be when. Make a couple of copies. Scotch tape it above the desk where you work (or, if you want to keep it confidential, inside your desk drawer) or in your bedroom to look at first thing when you get up in the morning. Daily reinforcement. And type a small copy to put in your wallet along with your credit cards and driver's license.

That's the first step. Deciding what you want, when.

The next move is to take the first step toward achieving that goal. Make your mind up what you will do—and do it! Now . . . print this motto in great letters and put it up on your wall for everyone to see.

$$\boxed{\text{D W Y P Y W D}}$$

When anybody stops to ask you, "What does that mean? you can honestly answer, "It means the same thing backwards and frontwards." Some will nod their heads in agreement and say, "Sure does . . ." and leave. Others will remain, look at it frontwards and backwards and then say, "Uh, it sure does . . . but what does it *mean?*"

Then, you can tell them the meaning of the phrase. And suggest they follow the rule:

Do What You Promised You Would Do.

For Yourself.

6 The Psychology of the First Person Plural

It was a February morning in New Orleans. The weather was cool and crisp and we made plans to have the fabled "Breakfast in Brennan's" at the famous restaurant on Royale Street in the French quarter.

The waiter came over, handed us the menus, and said, "My chef has prepared several interesting dishes for you gentlemen this morning." (His chef? Was he Mr. Brennan?)

He spoke of "our" baker waking up every morning at three a.m. to prepare "our" home-made rolls. He gave us the philosophy that "we believe in."

After the meal, after commenting on how good it was, we realized a major part of the enjoyment was the waiter making us believe we were in on something very special. We were made to feel at home, comfortable; and the food tasted better by his introduction of the first person plural ("we," "our") throughout his conversation.

We thought about that. And decided to check it out.

We approached a salesman we admire who constantly scores high sales ratings. He sets even-higher goals and constantly overachieves. We asked, "What is the secret of successful selling?"

Talk Personally

"I treat customers as if they were coming into my home," he said. "If you come to visit me tonight and I opened the door would I say, 'Can I help you?' No Way. I would say, 'Hello.' I would ask how you were. I would invite you in. I would offer you something to drink. We would talk about sports, politics, business. I would become involved with you in your interests."

Involved with me? That is what the waiter in New Orleans did. He made me feel as though I was invited into his home and he cared about . . . me.

Did you ever closely examine the words in the mail order catalogues that arrive in your mailbox? Almost all the pronouns are first-person plural.

From Norm Thompson's latest outdoor clothing catalogue: "The only store of its kind in the world . . . ours . . . is waiting for you at our home in Portland, Oregon. It's here we get to talk with our customers personally." The inside front page has at least two dozen "ours" and nearly as many "we's." By the time we finished reading we felt we had received a letter from an old friend.

Here is a good example of the "welcome to my home" approach: "Just pull up your favorite easy chair and relax. There is no rush. No hurry. You can take as much time as you like in making your selection."—Eddie Bauer, sporting goods, Seattle.

And another:

"We hope this catalogue provides you with lots of fun. We still have many ideas of things to come and will want to keep in touch with you more often. Write to us . . ." The Enchanted Doll House.

Involving their merchandise with you is this one:

"We think the special excitement of these hand-crafted items is that each has been individually made. No two are exactly the same. All have been chosen especially for you." The Smithsonian catalog.

There are those firms that go beyond the involvement of them-with-you. One step further: you-with-them. Like this:

"We appreciate any suggestions, comments or questions. We consider our customers a part of our organization and want you to feel free to make any criticism you see fit in regard to our merchandise or services." L. L. Bean, outdoor gear, Maine.

A recent phone call from a merchant in Mississippi complained of his inability to find someone to print a catalog for him. His mailing list was only 1,500. No one wanted to bother and the cost was too much. Our suggestion: do it yourself.

We recommended Vrest Orton's "Voice of the Mountains" catalog for a primer on how-to-do-it. His copy reads like he was in the room with you talking about his products ("We call our peanut butter home made because we make it ourselves using nothing but peanuts. It is not homogenized, not filled with other stuff, not hydrogenated and chemicalized.")

He invokes philosophy, wisdom, letters from readers, and Vermont independence throughout his catalogue. One example:

"When national advertisers introduce a novelty and advertise it in national magazines, they always list stores in the states where it can be purchased. You seldom, if ever, see the State of Vermont ever mentioned. We believe it's because innovators know darn well that Vermonters are stubborn. We don't take quickly to new fads until we prove they work."

That is believability. And reinforces every item in the catalogue as to performance and reliability. (Send Vrest twenty-five cents in Weston, Vermont 05161 and ask for a copy.) It is the best example we have on file of the me-and-thee approach that makes direct mail a powerful selling tool.

When you sell your product, your company, or yourself, the public has more confidence if you simply say "we . . ."

On a visit to Britches mens shops in Washington, D.C., we examined each store's merchandise display but were most impressed by their personnel. Each was courteous, informative, helpful—all the Boy Scout adjectives. We said, "We've never seen such consistently good sales people." And she said, "We're not good. We're the best. Because we work for the best store."

Wow. Talk about commitment . . .

Do your people feel that way about your business? (If not, read the chapter, "If You Don't Like It Here . . . Get Out! Out! Now!")

Contrast the Britches experience with this true story at the check-out counter of a major Eastern supermarket.

As the checker added up our purchases we asked why there was no Coca-Cola in the store.

She laughed and said, "When this outfit begins to pay its bills, then we'll have Coca-Cola."

Embarrassed, we sort of half-laughed and said how much we enjoyed her little joke.

"Hey," she said, "it's no joke." And, to prove her point, she yelled across the aisle to the next checker in a loud enough voice to cover half the store, "Hey, George, I just told this guy the reason we don't have any Coke is because they don't pay their bills. Isn't that right?"

And George yelled back. "That's right, mister!"

We hurried out telling our companions, "That market just ain't gonna make it."

They didn't. They went bankrupt a few months later.

Yes, bad management was a reason. Yes, bad planning was a reason. And yes, most of all, bad liaison with the people that represented them to the public was a major reason.

Most companies fall into this trap because they believe the only—or certainly the most—important category in terms of people's needs is money.

Not true.

A recent national survey covering varied fields of employment listed ten most important categories for people's needs when working. Can you put them in the right order one through ten in the little boxes?

1. Full appreciation of work done. ☐
2. Feeling "in" on things. ☐
3. Sympathetic help on personal problems. ☐
4. Job security. ☐
5. Good wages. ☐
6. Interesting work. ☐
7. Promotion and growth in company. ☐
8. Personal loyalty to workers. ☐
9. Good working conditions. ☐
10. Tactful discipline. ☐

The final results are at the bottom of this page.*

"Wages" is almost invariably the management's first rating for what employees want. They don't. "Wages" is the "I-Me" syndrome of management. But the people who work for us want to know *you know* that they are doing a good job—and are recognized for what they are contributing. And recognition and appreciation are on-going, time-consuming absolute MUSTS for management.

In one multimillion dollar direct mail agency, Leonard J. Raymond, the chairman of the board and owner of Dickie-Raymond, was constantly "out among 'em" with what the professional training teachers call Team Building and Supportive Techniques. Simple compliments. Concern about the personal and family situations of each of his employees, some of whom were seventeen, twenty-four, and thirty-eight year veterans of the company!

After his retirement and selling out to a large conglomerate, someone asked "What did L. J. do when he was here?" The answer was, "Oh—he went around telling everybody how valuable they were and how much the success of the agency depended on what they were doing . . . stuff like that." Interesting. Because the man and his company were inordinately successful, keeping accounts for an unheard of thirty-six years in a dog-eat-dog world of client-agency relationships.

Once you have the customer buying because your approach is one of personal pride and personal belief . . . once you have them involved with your product . . . once you convince them to buy because of your personal conviction and enthusiasm—chances are you have done this by working in the first person plural.

They tell the true story of the original Marshal Field who opened his first store in Chicago. It was his pleasure to walk through the store and listen to the comments of the customers.

One time he heard a little girl talking to her friend about her father who worked in the store. Her conversation was full of phrases like "my father's store" and "my father takes care of customers by doing this . . ."

* They're in the right order.

The mother suddenly noticed Mr. Field listening. Embarrassed, she went over to apologize for her daughter's conversation.

"Nonsense," said Mr. Field. "If everyone in this store used those same words and felt the same way, the success of this business would be guaranteed."

7 The 400 People

MRS. ASTOR HAD a problem.

She and her wealthy financier husband had just finished building their beautiful new home in Manhattan at the turn of the century and she wanted to have a party to show her friends what they had done.

And where better than in her new ballroom?

The problem was: space.

For even in this magnificent new building, the ballroom could only be so large. And hold only so many people.

Her architects told her that the room would comfortably hold 400.

She sat down at her writing desk. Taking pen in hand, she began to selectively invite the cream of New York society to what was to be the most sought-after affair of the year.

Word of the party soon traveled up and down Manhattan Island. Each day would-be social climbers looked anxiously into their mailboxes wondering if they were to be one of those chosen; if they were—in the words of the newspaper columnists of the day—"one of the 400 . . ."

To this day being "one of the 400" means being selected as one who has made a distinctive mark for him or herself, worthy of inclusion into a very select grouping.

This story may be apocryphal but it illustrates a concept we found works well for us: that there are, really, *only 400 people in the world!* Well, in YOUR world. You invite them to be part of your life. You ask them into your home and you ask them to participate in your social and business activity. It's a necessary step towards your success.

We first discovered this as we began to build our list of new acquaintances and old friends, the people who could get things done. Who, when *they* say, "It's taken care of," you moved on to the next problem on your agenda knowing, if they said, so, it WAS taken care of.

We once spoke of how this worked. The conversation went like this:

RAY: There are only 400 people in the world.

MURRAY: You lost count somewhere.

RAY: No. There are, at best, only 400 people. Count them.

MURRAY: Count them?

RAY: Yes. Start with listing all the people you know, do business with, can call up on short notice, tell them you have a problem and you need their help now. The Secret Word is "Now." "Now."

MURRAY: How do I begin?

RAY: By listing their names, addresses, telephone numbers, private, public, and home numbers—on a Rollodex file near your desk. You now have started to formally assemble your 400 Club. It's actually been there all the time. You just never thought of it. Now, when you have an urgent problem the answer is at your fingertips. Flip through your file and you'll find someone who has the answers, the resources or, even more important, who can tell you Where and How to get what-you-want at once. It works all the time . . .

MURRAY: I know how it works. Say I have a problem. In any field: law, politics, religion, business. I merely summon up the outstanding practitioners in that field and ask his or her advice. If someone comes into the store and offers me a great promotional idea, I pause before giving an answer. I go into my office and mentally assemble Stanley Marcus, John Wanamaker, Mr. Bergdorf and Mr. Goodman and Mr. Bloomingdale. (I admire all their philosophies and their merchandising.) "Fellows," I say, "here's the proposition I just received, what do you think?" All those fellows are members of my 400 Club, right?

RAY: Wrong. You haven't got it yet. They are members of your Invisible Cabinet. The Invisible Cabinet is made up of people of great renown, who have respectability, who have proven their wisdom through the ages. You select a handful of these heroes from various fields. They are giant models of Success, Achievement, and Judgment. You need this hand-picked cabinet for moral guidance, major policy decisions, what-do-we-do-down-the-road kind of thinking. The 400 Club is a different breed.

MURRAY: OK, try me again . . .

RAY: Your personal 400 Club is involved in the nitty-gritty. They come up with the solution TODAY. The most important key to the 400 is their *automatic* response to your call for help. If the person you call says, "When do you need it." You have a Club member. They DO NOT say anything about cost, delivery charges, trouble, inconvenience, aggravation. They simply ask, "When?"

MURRAY: Give me some examples.

RAY: You need to talk to someone who knows something about selling uniforms to waitresses. THAT name is on your 400 list. You need advice on what magazines pull best for your product through the mail. THAT name is on your list . . .

MURRAY: Aha! People that help you in your business, right?

RAY: Wrong. People who help you in your LIFE. It can be someone who solves a business problem. It can be the private number of the mechanic who fixes your air conditioner, a man you can call on weekends or nights. It can be the home number of the person in charge of shipping your most important resource. It can be your Congressman. And, just as important, his administrative aide.

MURRAY: Do you sit down one day and come up with all these names?

RAY: You can. But the 400 Club is a constant add-on list. All you have to do is make sure everybody you deal with meets the three-K criteria: Knowledge, Know-how, and Kinetics.

MURRAY: Kinetics?

RAY: Right. Kinetics is a branch of dynamics treating forces affecting motion. That means: People Who Know How To Get Things Done. NOW! Every problem is a motion going in a certain direction. If it's going fine, don't stop it. You may want some help to change its direction. You need someone with Knowledge, Know-how and . . .

MURRAY: Kinetics.

RAY: Korrect.

MURRAY: But what happens when I finally accumulate all the 400 names. How long does anyone stay on my list?

RAY: Longer than you think. Years longer than you think. You see, the same people keep popping up in your life. After months, a year, you think, Well, I'll never see that person again. But sooner or later the same name pops up or a problem comes up that only they can solve.

MURRAY: So, how do I know WHEN to drop a name from my 400 Club?

RAY: Well, there are no absolutes. Try this one: When you flip through your cards or Rollodex and come across a name of someone you haven't heard from in a year (which isn't all that long in a lifetime), drop him or her a note saying, ''What's happening? Saw your name in my 400 file and wondered how you are doing?'' It's a kind of an alert check to see if they're still responsive. You'll be amazed the wonderful full reports you get back just by ''checking in'' with them. Which is another part of the 400 Club philosophy: Keep In Touch.

MURRAY: I could send newspaper articles, a funny story, or a clipping about the business they're in.

RAY: Great. But you MUST include a personal note from you. Handwritten is fine. I try to send about 1,000 of these notes every year.

MURRAY: One thousand? That means writing about four notes a day.

RAY: Right. See how that ties-in with our Four-mula for success. All these ideas work well with one another. You should prospect on your 400 list with at least four notes a day. The form or the length doesn't matter. Just keep in touch. Multiply it yourself: 250 working days times four notes a day gives you 1,000 contacts every year with the 400 people most important to your business and personal life.

MURRAY: Sounds like it takes a lot of time. I don't know if I have the time . . .

RAY: Sure you do. Get your own shorthand communications form. One that is easy and natural for you. A postcard is fine. Friend and great speaker, Bill Gove scrawls a new joke on postcards while on airplanes, in restaurants, in lobbies. Or "Saw your friend Wade Cannon in the Atlanta airport. Hell of a guy." That's how Gove does it. Some business people keep a small pad or tablet right by their phone and they dash off impulsive two sentence handwritten messages *while they are waiting on the phone.* Or between conferences. They mail them all the end of the day.

MURRAY: I get those all the time: 'From the desk of . . .'

RAY: Ahhhhh, yes. But I really do NOT want to hear from your desk. I WOULD like to hear from YOU. Have your printer run off a couple thousand five-by-eight-inch pads with something personal printed that relates-to-you. Could be a sketch, a picture, the company logo, or a saying people associate with you. Joey Dee, from Hiram Walker, always says in response to his customers' phone calls: "You got it!" And his notes say that. With his name and *home* telephone number.

MURRAY: Well, I see one problem. How do you remember who-does-what? In most files names are alphabetical. Do I cross-file another card under "Painter" for a painter's name. Or under "H" for home phone of the air conditioner guy? Pretty soon I'll have to study up on my Dewey Decimal System for reference.

RAY: No. It's simply a case of association. We all remember things according to how the information came into our mental computers. We associate specific products or people with specific needs.

MURRAY: What happens when your list gets too big?

RAY: You just drop someone who hasn't answered your last two notes. The single requirement to stay on the list is: You must respond—both ways. Otherwise, you're out.

MURRAY: Any other rules or cautions before we close today's meeting?

RAY: Yes. One most people forget. When you have a problem and need an answer in a hurry, you reach out, riffle through your 400 deck and ask one, "HELP!" When the crisis has passed, you forget it. Wrong. Remember to "loop back."

MURRAY: What's that mean?

RAY: Go back to the person who put you on the right track. The one who told you where to go and who to call. Say, "Thanks." With a quick phone call. Or one of those four notes: "Called Paul Vaughan and he got me the lists. Thanks." That's the loop. Very important. There's an old Chinese proverb that says it best: "When you're drinking the water, don't forget who dug the well."

8 Winners and Losers

"We can't all be heroes. Somebody has
to sit on the curb and clap as they go by."
—WILL ROGERS

WHAT MAKES ONE PERSON or one business succeed and another fail?

What characteristics are common to those who come out on top . . . and those who stay at the bottom (or worse, someplace in the nothing middle)?

Analyze the success stories of history, business, or your own personal experience and you will find similar habits and patterns that reoccur so often, it's important to examine what *makes* it happen.

We call these categories: *Winners* and *Losers*.

We found the first letter of each category begins a key word that describes who belongs to which group. Read on. Which group describes . . . you?

"Winners" begins with:

W—Work

WORK: Winners work harder than other people do. It's a fact. Dr. Armand Hammer of Occidental Petroleum was asked, "What is the secret of your success?" He replied, "I work fourteen hours a day, seven days a week and you'd be amazed at all the good deals I fall into."

There are other adages: Don't Work Harder; Work Smarter. Or this one: The exceptional salesman makes a habit of doing what the ordinary salesman doesn't do (Bill Gove). They are fine but note: Each of them says simply, if you want to make it you've got to do MORE than the other guys . . . (and don't forget, they aren't asleep either!)

A company did a survey on the results of their salesmen. One salesman did three times as much business as the others. They assigned a crew to follow him, to listen, observe, and report back. Their findings: He really didn't do anything much different than any of the other salesmen. With one exception: He saw three times as many people, and, therefore, made three times as many sales.

This does *not* mean you are a slave to your business. Just the opposite. You *really* enjoy what you do! (If you don't, get out.)

Vrest Orton, the founder of the famous Original Vermont Country Store. Says Vrest, "I can't get over the fact that people pay me money for what I enjoy doing. . ." Which is an echo of Thomas Carlyle's phrase "Blessed is he who has found his work, let him ask no other blessedness." That takes a little looking, a little luck and some soul searching—at any age. And folks, you ALWAYS have the chance to change and *do what you want to do!* (See "Techniques and Tools of Change".)

Enjoy what you do. There is no greater thrill than to create something and see and touch the final results: a table crafted from a tree, the final copy version worked and reworked that becomes a powerful message which causes people to act upon your words . . . the rare compliment of perfectly delivered products . . . or the ultimate personal compliment of "where are the other people like you who care?"

Kahlil Gibran said it so well in his famous treatise, *The Prophet:* "Work is love made visible. If you cannot work with love, but only with distaste, it is better to leave your work at the gate of the temple and take alms of those who work with joy."

W—WORK
I—IDEAS

IDEAS. Winners have *Ideas*. And know how to use them better.

Author James Webb Young condensed his idea-theory into a training program for J. Walter Thompson, then the largest advertising agency in the world, and into a small book, *A Technique For Producing Ideas*. He took Pareto's* thesis that all people fall into two categories—*speculators* and *rentiers*. "The speculator," says Young, "is constantly preoccupied with the possibilities." (Note that word preoccupied.) This group recognizes that there are no *new* ideas, just novel combinations of existing facts, which, when combined, become the NEW IDEA. (Shades of Bill Veeck!)

The *rentier* group, says Young, are those who are "routine, steady-going, unimaginative, and conserving." Interesting word—"conserving." Means "don't take a chance." "Let's keep it like it is." "Don't make waves." Status quo. Keep your head down. Don't volunteer. Those familiar signals will identify the *rentiers*.

---

*Pareto was the Italian sociologist who conceived the famed 80/20 principle: 80% of all productivity is accomplished by 20% of the people. Our question: How do we get into the top of the top 20%?

The *speculators* make things happen. They are constantly working on, thinking about, and creatively combining two disparate ideas to become the New Idea.

Says Young, *"First,* gather the raw materials of your immediate problem and those which come from a constant enrichment of your store of general knowledge. (He notes there is no subject "under the sun" in which the idea person could not easily get interested—from Egyptian burial customs to modern art.)

"Second, work over these materials in your mind." He calls this the "Mental Digestion Process." He likens it to masticating food, chewing on it mentally.

"Take one fact, turn it this way and that, and look at it in different lights." Young likens this stage to holding a kaleidosope to your eye and looking at the ever-changing pieces of colored chips. See how many ways the same chips and colors combine and project just by rolling them around.

What you are *really* doing: fitting things together. Taking separate images, words, concepts and seeing if they can groove smoothly. In woodworking, professionals call this union "forty-fives," perfectly joined corners. Or mitered. There is no *obvious* junction between parts.

Like counter-sinking a nail to make the nail head *part* of the surface. Like a jigsaw puzzle. Taking several pieces away and fitting them to form one complete picture.

"Put these ideas down on paper," says Young, "and never mind how crazy or incomplete they seem."

Leo Burnett, another of the creative greats from the advertising field, used to jot down ideas on scraps of paper and throw them into a drawer. When it was time for a new campaign, out came the scraps. On went the Fitting process. Whether the precise words were there didn't matter. The germs and the worms of the idea would trigger the eventual campaign strategy for the New Idea.

"Third, Incubate," Young continued. "Let something besides your conscious mind do the work of the synthesis." We have all experienced the success of "sleeping on it," let it be, let it simmer in the cranial computer. Friend T.H. Buckingham of Fort Worth says you wake up in the morning, lie on your back, wiggle your toes, and "there isn't a problem in the world you can't solve." So T.H. does it with his eyes opened—*after* he's slept on it.

"Fourth," says Young, "the actual birth of the Idea—the 'Eureka!—I have it!' stage." It could happen while you are shaving, showering, walking, driving to work, in the elevator. Most people fail by trying to vault into this fourth and suddenly-inspired stage. Without going through the vital steps of Gathering, Kaleidosoping, Incubating. They want the Idea to happen right now. It doesn't.

"Fifth," says this idea-producing formula, "take your little idea out into the world of reality." In other words, it sounds Great, Marvelous, Terrific! Now test it. Expose it to other people. See if it flies. They might kill it or add to it. They may tell you it is impossible. (Don't falter there, Speculators.) Or, happiest of all thoughts, your sounding board people may just concur completely and reinforce the fact that your Idea *will* work!

Winners constantly create, reconstruct, and kaleidoscope images. Trying. Fitting. Examining. Asking "will it work?"

In a practical way, how *do* Ideas work for Winners?

They forever think of a new way, an option. They are not satisfied with the simple computer letter—they want it personalized. Then they want the name several times throughout the letter.

First they offer one way to renew a subscription. Then they give a choice of two. Then a choice of several.

If an idea works, it is not enough. They must improve, find another way to solve the problem, "create the traffic," have the customer respond.

Ideas are all around you.* Simply train your mind to be alert. How does someone else sell their product successfully? Now, how can that idea work for me? There are more ideas around you than you can use. Pick and sort and select and choose and adopt and adapt and decide which idea fits your own particular needs at your particular moment. Be open to accept or reject an idea. If it does not work, forget it, find another. The philosopher Alain wrote, "Nothing is more dangerous than an idea . . . when it's the only one we have."

Ideas do not normally come to groups of people any more than leadership functions well in the hands of a committee. Winners create ideas all by themselves. Then they work with copywriters and photographers and artists to create the final concept. But it begins with one person. With one idea.

W—WORK
I—IDEAS
N—NOW

NOW. Winners do things *NOW*. They do not procrastinate, equivocate, wait-til-the-time-is-right. They cringe at the final scene in *Gone with*

---

*Ed Finkelstein, CEO of Macy's New York City department store, draws a half a million dollar salary and tells how he got the idea for the revolutionary concept of The Cellar, Macy's must-see revitalized, redesigned, remarkable retailing renaissance: "I picked up ideas from the Crate and Barrel in Chicago, the Pottery Barn, Harrod's of London, a gourmet soap emporium in a Palo Alto shopping mall, and from a little shop in Paris that sells stationery paper by the pound." An official welcome to the Brain Robbers Club, Ed!

the Wind when Scarlett says she will change things "tomorrow." The *mañana* syndrome. The "let's do it later" philosophy. (See "Losers.")

Winner's know today's mail automatically replenishes with tomorrow's. Clear it. Handle it once. Make the decision Now. It takes the same amount of time. They decide what color paper to use, what paper stock to order, what message to write, whether to mail first class or bulk, stamp or no stamp. They start, they go, they finish. And leap to the next problem.

Winners remember the simple sentence from the Bible in Corinthians: "Now is the accepted time."

Reams can be written and have been on this single three-letter word, N-O-W.

DO IT NOW says the wall plaque and the desk paperweight. But how many heed that challenge sitting right before their very eyes? Few. The Saying and the Doing are two separate planets.

Here is an exercise you might try if N-O-W appeals to you.

When tasks and chores pile up (see there on the edge of the desk, on the cabinet, on the floor, in the corner, in the neatly marked DO IT NOW file folders stacking up), *make a decision every time you are asked a question.*

Aha! There is a challenge for you, friends.

Get ready. Brace yourself mentally. Go on full Brain Alert.

Next time anyone asks you a question, *answer it.* Give the decision you were asked for. Now.

The movie that launched Ernest Borgnine's career was *Marty* (we told you we were crazy about movies). In that flick, the bachelor characters do a constant see-saw ask-with-no-answer routine. "Whattaya wanna do tonight, Marty?" "I don't know, whatta *you* wanna do?" And back and forth they go with the "I dunno." Answer, a too-real dramatization of every day nondecision-making conversations.

Winners *know* what they want to do, *what* they want to accomplish, *where* they'd prefer to eat dinner, *whether* the color ought to be orange or yellow. They are *used to* and practice making decisions *all the time.*

"Practice makes perfect" is a groaning old adage, but—you *can* practice making decisions, small and large, every minute, every time someone asks you for an opinion or a choice.

It's an interesting exercise. Arduous at first. You have to regear your mind *from* what you are thinking about *to* what you are being asked. Now.

John McKinven who teaches people How-to-Listen in his Chicago Communications Workshop says a terribly high percentage of people are so busy constantly "running their own tapes, they can't hear anyone outside themselves. Suspend your own agenda," John says, "and listen." Good hard usable advice.

W—WORK
I—IDEAS
N—NOW
N—NATURAL

NATURAL. Winners are *Natural*. They are predictable. There are no two faces for Winners. You know if they are tough, genial, fair, arbitrary, impatient, ferocious, honest, dependable . . . because that's the way they always are.

They perform their craft with a skill and an ease that makes the observer react in one of two ways:

1. "How did he or she do that?"
2. "Anyone can do that. Look how easy it was."

Winners make work look easy.

The world of sports is filled with old-time legends like Red Grange in football or Jim McMahon today; Willie Mays or Reggie Jackson; Larry Byrd (the magician of the Boston Celtics) or the acrobatic, incredible Dr. J, who has perfected "hanging in the air." Try that, next time you shoot a basket. It's easy. Watch Dr. J.

Smooth, easy, natural. These are the words announcers apply to the champions of sports skill, or the critics use in awe to describe the soaring, bounding, gazelle-like leaps of Mikhail Baryshnikov.

We cannot all aspire to these physical heights. But we *can* take the Sundance Kid technique and apply it to the models of management or sales, promotion and persuasion.

The problem is most of us *think in a tunnel:* ours. Too seldom do we peer over the fence to see what's going on in the next yard of activity.

Watch a super salesperson in a retail store. One who is—are you ready?—*Natural*. Say to yourself, "How did she do that?" Analyze the selling moves that pro made. Ask yourself, "How can I do that?" And, "How can I transfer that into my business?"

Reruns. That's what the major football teams do every Monday. So do the hockey, basketball, ski, and tennis professionals. They study the easy, fluid moves of their opponents and themselves.

What are they looking for? Naturalness. Quickness. Good strategies. Smooth moves.

Those who write successful direct mail and print copy have the readers saying, "The words are so natural. It's as though someone were sitting next to me, talking to me."

Looks easy. Try it. It is not.

The training, experience, and dedication (key word) that make up the learning of that talent never appears on the surface. Skill is never obvious. That's why Winners acquire that Natural presence.

La Rochefoucauld said, "Nothing prevents our being natural so much as a desire to be so." So even *being natural* has to become natural for you.

Winners walk a one-way street. Their decision-making is simple, never schizophrenic. Recently, a client of Gary Blasiar of Alert Answering Service in California heard a suggestion that a certain time management form be printed in a limited quantity to "see if it would work." Gary shook his head emphatically and disagreed: "Let's do it right . . . now . . . and make it work!"

Interesting, too, that Winners behave and react the same in their business and personal lives. The same dependable, never-fail resources (members of your 400 Club, no doubt) will be as prompt for a dinner engagement and will have made reservations (if that was part of their commitment.) And, being Winners, probably arranged for you and your party to sit down as soon as you arrive.

They will have the correct bottle of wine pre-ordered as an added value. And they will learn or already know the captain or the waiter's name, even though this is their first time at the restaurant.*

It all seems so natural and effortless . . . for them. Contrasted to the endless scuffling, waiting, using the too late, too loud techniques that the boisterous ones use.

Winners know how to do the job. They think through the up-coming situation. Through experience they know that the preparation works and "off the cuff," seat-of-the-pants odds aren't good enough to assure things will go smoothly.

They apply techniques they have read about, observed, and analyzed. Seeing what has worked will work again whether its in a restaurant, a hotel reservation, a sales meeting, a birthday party, or a national sales campaign.

Doing all this without evidence of effort results in the finished work of Winners appearing to be . . . natural.

W—WORK
I—IDEAS
N—NOW
N—NATURAL
E—ENERGY

*One of the people we know travels frequently across the United States. Whenever he hears of a "really good" restaurant in a city he plans to visit, he gets the address of the restaurant, takes out his calendar, plans which night he'll be there and mails off a short note: "My wife and I plan to be in (city) on (date) and would like to have dinner in your fine restaurant. I have enclosed ten dollars cash for our reservation and we would like to eat at nine o'clock."

NEVER has a reservation been refused! NEVER has the money disappeared! Usually upon arrival and identification, our friend is royally greeted (who else *writes* for reservations with a deposit?), shown to a table, and fussed over the entire meal. And the ten dollars has ALWAYS been credited to the dinner bill.

Winners have ENERGY. They love what they do and they can't wait to "get at it."

Their energy is often simply organization. From Alan Lakein's A-B-C list of what-must-be-done-first to the quick brush-away of energy-sapping irrelevance or petty complaints, they go to the heart of today's problems and work to its conclusion.

They thrive on the joy of Getting Things Done, closing that chapter, and saying exultantly, "Next?" and they are ready to charge into the problem that follows.

Then there are the others . . . tired, groaning like galley slaves chained below decks, every motion an effort. Their work is lackluster. They *don't have any fun.* They let the day slip by, then the week, and a lifetime, while they are bogged down and buried in what Lakein calls "C" categories. Those items which would evaporate eventually anyway. That's how unimportant so-called "priority Cs" are. These people live a "C" life, barely a passing grade.

Recognize "C" people in your surroundings. "As soon as I get a few of these small things out of the way, I'll be ready to start." Never happens.

Jack Thayer, a Winner, vice-president and general manger of WNEW, Metromedia's flagship TV station in New York, has a grand trilogy of cautions for all of us. It goes like this . . .

Ask yourself these three vital questions:
1. If I Don't Do It, *Who* Will?
2. If I Don't Do It Now, *When* Will It Get Done?
3. If I Don't Do It *At All,* What Will Happen?

Try this test. If you are a victim of question one (If I Don't Do It, Who Will?), look to thy delegation fears, baby. "I can do it so much better, I'll take care of it." Uh huh. And no one else can do like you, right? So there is little hope of your ever getting away from *that* responsibility. Or, "I can do it myself faster." Hmm. OK. You shall forever be stuck with doing that, too.

Let Go!

So, "they" don't do as well as you do . . . Charles Schwab, President of U.S. Steel, used to be rated the best technician in the steel business. He could work faster and better than anyone on the floor. Only one trouble: they couldn't afford to have him there. At any production rate. He was just too valuable.

What is your production rate? What are you worth per hour? Does it pay your company to have you do what is "easy" for you—or are you costing them and yourself money just because you won't *let go?* WHO will do it? Somebody else. Anybody else! Not you. Winners know how to delegate.

If I Don't Do It Now, WHEN Will It Get Done?

Biggest trap in time management is the compulsion to "get things done." That is *not* the answer. The answer is to get the RIGHT things done. It's called the activity trap by those bright folks who have studied us all. The great and burning urge to be Doing.

To be Doing . . . Anything!

WRONG.

Have a look at the list the way the Winners do. And note, there is a very fine line between procrastination ("we'll do that later"), and the management skill of selecting what is NOT important enough to do now.

Salesmen, the traveling type, are enormously guilty and constantly falling into this trap. Errand here. Quick stop there. Just one quick phone call and then go . . . and all the while with the greatest of Intentions.*

People go into offices and drop into this WHEN trapdoor. "What's in the mail today, Joan?" They let the incoming mail control the direction of their day.

One friend has an interesting switch on this. He said he was going to withhold all the mail and force his staff to come up with something they should be doing, instead of waiting and *reacting* to what the mailman brings. (Of course, you could always shoot the mailman.)

But a lot of us are guilty of waiting to "see what the day brings." Like good friend and speaker Gunther Klaus says about Planning: "Most people's idea of long-range planning is—what shall we do after lunch?" All too accurate.

So we avoid the Activity Trap. Let's US decide what needs doing. WE pick what will be done. Bob Townsend in his book *Up The Organization* said he had a printed challenge right in front of him on his desk: IS WHAT I AM ABOUT TO DO GOING TO TAKE ME ONE STEP NEARER MY GOAL?

Wow. Lots of the "B" and "C" priorities on To-Do lists would fail to meet the Urgency requirements of that commandment!

If I Can't Get It Done Now . . . let it come up on another A-B-C priority list another day. See if it qualifies then. Winners can ignore the social

---

*The Master, Bill Gove, tells this old but wonderful chestnut: Guy gets up in the morning, puts on his Earl Nightingale tape, shouts in the shower, peers into the mirror while he's shaving muttering, "Man! Look at those eyes, that determination," and keeps saying to himself, "You can do it! You can do it!" Only trouble is, he never gets out of the house till noon!

and peer pressure "to do." They know it's doing the RIGHT thing—and that only which will win the game.*

Thayer's third question: If I Don't Do It At All . . . What Will Happen? The answer to that is Nothing—in a great many cases. For example . . . there are signals. Every time you feel pressure (read: nervousness, tightness, mounting anger, frustration), chances are YOU are doing something wrong—in terms of judgment.

"I've GOT to get this done!" is the anguished cry. "WHY?" says Thayer's Law. "Because . . ." Because you had it on a list. (Take it off.)

Every time you feel the walls closing in—back off, review Thayer's principles. Put them under the glass on your desk. Put them in the right-hand desk drawer for a quick peek. At the first signal of panic—how can I get all this done?—see if you are violating number one (Can you delegate it?); number two (Is your next action moving toward your real goal, or is it another Activity Trap?); number three (What is the *worst* thing that can happen if you don't do it at all?)

Winners establish goals. They list where-they-want-to-be-when, and tack them up on the wall, print them on memo pads and review them constantly.

David Ogilvy, the advertising expert, tells of the day he opened his office in 1948. He made up a list of the five clients he wanted most: General Foods, Bristol Myers, Campbell Soup, Lever Brothers, and Shell. He says of this goal-setting list, "To pick such blue chip targets was an act of mad presumption. But all five of them are now clients of Ogilvy, Benson and Mather."

W—WORK
I—IDEAS
N—NOW
N—NATURAL
E—ENERGY
R—REPEAT

Winners REPEAT. Winners know what works. And they do it again. Maybe with a variation. Change a sentence, phrase, headline, approach, but if it worked once, they will do it again.

---

*Gunther Klaus again on rattlesnakes, fires, and crises. "Too many people," he says, in his guttural Germanic tone, "are far too busy killing rattlesnakes, putting out fires, and solving minor crises to get anything Big done." Then he tells the tale of the three entrepreneurs who passed a prime real estate site in Los Angeles and each said "Wow! What a place for a hotel, right in the middle of everything." One went back to his office only to be told that he would have to leave immediately to fire some incompetent in Seattle. (Rattlesnake.) The second returned to find his president had made reservations to leave that night for Dallas. Some problem. (A Fire.) The third guy, according to Gunther, went directly back to his office, closed the door, called the real estate adviser, his lawyer, and the financial man, and starting making plans to buy the ground and erect the hotel. And then Gunther smiles that satanic smile, looks at his audience, and says, "Which one are you?"

Change is evolution, not revolution. Dickie-Raymond's famous direct mail headline for the Kiplinger Letter decades ago, "Are you ready for the boom years ahead?" continues to sell that fine business service letter with minor variations.

Winners know how generations grow up who never saw the original successful sales message of yesterday. Winners dust it off, brush it up, trot it out, and watch it win again.

W—WORK
I—IDEAS
N—NOW
N—NATURAL
E—ENERGY
R—REPEAT
S—SELL

Winners all know as Red Motley was famed for saying, "Nothing happens 'til somebody sells something." You can design it, produce it, warehouse it, advertise it, but nothing happens 'til somebody sells it!

One of the worse faults is The Curse of Assumption (see "Communications"). We expect people to know what we're selling, what business we're in, and where we are. *We* know. Shouldn't everyone else?

Not really.

Try this sometime. Ask one of your golfing, tennis, social friends, "Do you know what I do for a living?"—and hold on to your hat (if you happen to be wearing one), they won't all know!

A banker friend took this advice to heart. He started asking all his customers, "Need any money today?" At first, taken aback, they replied, "Uh. . .no. . .not today." "OK," the sales-minded banker would say, "when you do, call me." The second encounter, they were a trifle amused. The third time, the customer joined in with the question. Then at a later time, they would call on the phone and ask, "Is that offer for money still on?" That banker does a *lot* of loan business he would not have without telling what he is selling.

Winners are always selling their products and services. The calling card (we call them "miniature billboards") will do it more often than you believe.

Walter W. Bittner, vice-president of the First State Bank of Miami, Florida, selectively hands out a small plastic card which contains his official bank business card on one side and a real silver dollar on the other. "Isn't that awfully expensive?" he is constantly asked. "Not to get the appointment to talk about thousands of dollars," says Walter.

Winners sell emotions, safety, security, health, happiness, comfort. The winning travel agent doesn't sell standing in lines at airline counters, but the romance and the charm of a vacation to a distant land. The good tire salesman ignores the chemical compounds of rubber and talks about the safety of "your wife and family" in the car. The super insurance salesperson doesn't talk premiums. Growing kids in college, mortgage paid for, peace of mind, cash values are the lead subjects in his sales presentation. The direct mail writer knows the first question a reader asks is "What's in it for me?" and answers that question as he begins his selling letter. Never mind the age of the company, its assets, and the pride of the board of directors. We're not selling them. We're selling "What's in it for me, the buyer?"

Winners are always selling. But they are thinking with their *YOU* head. And they are always, always putting themselves and their company second. First is *YOU* and the answer you want to hear: "What's in it for me?"

Winners never forget that.

WHAT ABOUT THE LOSERS?

The important thing is learning how to instantly identify the Losers.

Our favorite is the story about the man who was told to "go to the back of the line." He went and returned with this gem: "There's somebody already there."

That's a loser!

Or the company faced with a novel advertising campaign and a director asks "If it's good, how come nobody else has done it?"

That's a loser.

The world is made up of Winners and Losers, as seen in the daily standings of the sporting news and the company standings in the *Wall Street Journal*. From the winners of the best Campaign, the Most Outstanding Success in Retailing, down to the cynic who says, "We tried it once and it didn't work."

What makes a loser? Here are some of the clues:

L—LATER

LATER. Losers do things "Later."

"I've got a problem and can you help me?" The answer: "Leave it here, I'll take care of it later." Uh huh. Sure . . . It's too much of a problem to think of now. Maybe if it's ignored, it will go away. Or, "It's pretty close to lunch," and, "maybe this afternoon there'll be time"

Wanna bet?

Losers procrastinate. They find reasons *not* to act. It is dangerous to decide now what should be done. What if I make a mistake? Or a wrong decision?

In the great tradition of political leaders, it's safer to react than act. Cal Coolidge had some advice, "If you don't say anything, you won't be called upon to repeat it." Dandy. Do nothing. You can't be criticized that way. Let it get lost in the mail shuffle; bury it in the "pending report" pile; mark it "for further action."

The business world (and some of our home projects) are rife with this clue to losers. Listen for the "Later" and look for the Losers in your organization. Mark them for departure. Soon.

L—LATER
O—OVERWORKED

Losers are always *Overworked*. Right from the beginning. How did that happen? They never got started! The world is constantly ahead of them. Yet they are always "so busy."

Remember the axiom, "If you want something done, give it to a busy person?" That works with Winners because they are organizers. They accept problems, establish a priority, set a time frame, and finish it. "Next."

Losers are continually confused. What to do first? There is so much to do! They are easily identified by a low moaning sound as ordinary assignments come in. "But I just got all these *other* things to do," they complain. Vary the priority from one regular chore and hear the groaning chorus commence. They were "all prepared" to do the regular routine and now . . .

Have you ever been called on by a salesman who has obviously rehearsed his sales presentation so carefully and so automatically the least variation throws him completely off stride? One was a children's pajama rep. "Programmed" might describe him. Just after he began his intoned pitch, the buyer interrupted with a pointed question about the fabric construction of the garment.

The salesman stopped, puzzled, at a loss how to answer this upsetting interruption; then he solved the problem by beginning his sales pitch right from the beginning, word for word.

Or the bank salesman who was drilled about the five key points of selling household checking account promotions. In the presence of the banker, he started brightly along his path of perfected presentation, halted suddenly, turned to his sales manager who was with him and bluntly demanded, "What the hell was the third reason?" Loser.

And losers complain. "They asked me to do another job and I'm not finished with this one." That does a lot of good. But losers do have one outstanding talent. They can take almost any job and make it fill the time available. They know if they finish, somebody will give them more to do.

And they have one consuming conviction: no matter how hard you work, you won't get ahead unless you "know somebody at the top." So why try harder?

L—LATER
O—OVERWORKED
S—SO-SO

SO-SO: How is that proposal coming? Is it finished? "So-So." They'll kill you. Nothing is ever totally their fault. It's not their job. Somebody else ought to check it. That's the trouble with Losers: you cannot depend on them. Never totally.

Admiral Rickover, fabled father of the atomic submarine and trainer of Navy leaders, asked one question over and over, "Did you do your best?"

That goes right to the core. Because if a person says "yes," he is faced with being judged that what he did *was* the best he could do. Not settling for second best. Losers settle for less. They excuse. The inexact registration from the printer is "good enough"; after all, he's a friend. (For whom?) They "understand" if someone forgets an extension cord for an important audio-visual presentation. They shrug when asked why the window still squeals when eighteen dollars was paid for its repair.

We had a floor salesman once who made signs for shirts on sale. It was immediately pointed out one of the brand names was misspelled. His answer: "Who will notice besides you?"

So-So

To settle for mediocrity is to lower the estimation not only of your job but yourself.

Shakespeare summed up the phrase well in *As You Like It* when Touchstone says, "So-so is good, very good, very excellent, good—and yet it is not. It is but . . . so-so."

L—LATER
O—OVERWORKED
S—SO-SO
E—EVADE

Losers EVADE. They are marvelously talented at this skill. Remember the story about the customer in the restaurant who asks the passing waiter what time it is?

"Sorry," says the waiter, "you're not my table."

Have you tried lately in a department store to offer money, real cash, to a clerk and beg her to take it? "Sorry, not my department."

And they all wonder why the world passes them by and why other people are promoted. They operate on the "It's all who you know" theory instead of the more profitable: "It's all what you do" theory.

Where are the Rare ones who say, "It's not really my counter (aisle, area, table, division), but let me get you an answer." Where are the Upcomers, the Bright Eyes, the ones Having Fun who say, "Hey, a little out of my line, but I can handle that!" I CAN HANDLE THAT. What a wonderful phrase. Like a bell sounding upon thine ears. But where are they? (Answer: back a few pages with the "Winners" column.)

Losers always have excuses. Rarely answers. The skill is expert evasion. An infinite variety of versions of "not my job" and being adept through their years of thinking up reasons why it won't work. (See "Added Value (Reprise . . .)" for a collection of these.)

And so with their practiced skills, the evaders have climbed to the top of the category known as . . . losers (small "l").

L—LATER
O—OVERWORKED
S—SO-SO
E—EVADE
R—RETIRE

RETIRE: Losers are anxious to retire.

An applicant once came into our office for a job. (True story.)

His first words were, "My name is Hiram Walker," (not true) "and I'd like to know about your retirement plan." There he was, twenty-three years old and ready to retire.

We were quick to respond. We smiled and said, "Now *that's* something you won't have to worry about, because you won't be here when that time comes. Goodbye."

There are two kinds of people who want to retire. Those who have put in their time and deserve to, and those who just came to work and want to.

Losers are the main body of these familiar clubs: TGIF—Thank God It's Friday (two days lay-off); the Blue Monday Gang, ("Whatta you expect, it's Monday."); the Two Days To Paycheck Pack ("All this crummy work for this lousy little bit of money."); and the What-did-you-do-last-night? crew (that ought to take up the morning 'til coffee break).

Recognize them? Sound familiar? Of course! Our world is populated with them. They are not bad people. They are just content to spend most of their life on the lower rungs of life's ladder. They stay in the herd where it's "safe." They don't make waves, they don't like to be near anyone who does. They don't *think* like Winners.

They go through life whining and complaining as Archie Bunker. "It's no use trying, because THEY control everything anyway." When pressed to identify who THEY were, Archie sadly shakes his head and says, "You know . . ."

Which, typically, is no answer, but when you think about it, you *DO* know who he means. "*They*" are . . . the Winners.

> L—LATER
> O—OVERWORKED
> S—SO-SO
> E—EVADE
> R—RETIRE
> S. . .

"S" stands for—nothing.
Because Losers never finish.

9 *Four-mula for Success*

A BANKER IN NEBRASKA tried this formula and made an $800,000 sale.

A small retail store tried this formula and did an extra $5,000 in business at a cost of $100.

Another banker made a phone call and sold a $100,000 certificate of deposit during the coffee break of a Great Brain Robbery seminar.

All these stories are true.

They are the direct result of a concept we call "Four-mula for Success," a four step, easy-to-follow *guaranteed* way of increasing business.

How do we know they succeed? We explain how they work in our advertising seminars to thousands of people throughout the United States. Within a few weeks of each seminar we receive calls and letters from sales and marketing people who say, "I tried it. It works." (One even tried it while the meeting was still going on. More on that later . . .)

The Four-mula for Success requires only that you set aside part of your day to contact customers.

To begin, you must agree that it IS important to set aside a certain portion of each day for new business. Spend the rest of the day with usual routine matters involving keeping your present customers happy. If you agree to set aside less than half an hour each day, the formula will work for you.

There are four different ways. You can do one from each category, four from one or ANY combination of four. The result is always the same: more business. Here's how:

1. FOUR NOTES

This is different from your notes to your 400 Club. Write four notes a day to customers. *To customers.* Those you already have. You can do this while reading through a computer print-out reminding you who received what from you or your company. A short "thank you" will not only be appreciated, it will be passed around to friends until the letter frays at the edges.*

Example: (from a bank) "Just a short note to say 'thanks' for coming to see us for your loan. We are pleased and excited to help you with your new plans for your business (or career, education goals, or travel plans or . . .)"

That's what you write. But what the customer READS is something else. He translates your note in HIS mind to something like, "Boy, are we lucky to have a customer like you to whom we can lend money. We are fortunate because your credit rating is terrific!"

You enhance his reputation and increase his prestige. And all he does is talk about you and your bank to everyone he knows!

Remember, a personal, positive letter or note to a customer—whether it's from an automobile agency, a mail order company, a department store, a bank, or insurance agent—represents power, strength, and prestige. Recognition on a personal basis in this age of numbers and computerized forms is a special acknowledgement.

Your note/letter is quickly opened and read. Personal mail is almost unique. Fine. You can ride on the weakness of "the other guys."

Most people receive letters and notices for NEGATIVE reasons.

"Your check bounced." (Banks have a nicer way of saying that.) "Please pay. Your account is overdrawn." "We have no record of payment from you . . ."

Ninety-nine percent of form letters are . . . negative.

What is the percentage of *positive* letters mailed by your company each day? One in ten? If more, it is rare . . .

But each of the four notes leaving *your* desk are *positive*.

What does a man say to his wife when he comes home from work? Let's listen in . . .

"Hi, honey. How'd the day go?" Then, "How're the kids?" Then, "Where's the mail?"

If there was a threatening-looking notice in a window envelope (or worse, one of those new wrap-round "pull this tab out here" forms) your wife undoubtedly opened it quickly *expecting bad* news. More often than not, telegrams and window enveloped business letters mean bad news to most people. Perhaps one reason they are quickly ripped open is to symbolize the beheading of the King's messenger who brought the bad news.

But your note is *good* news.

"Thanks." "Congratulations." " Come see us." "Saw you in the news." A careful scanning of the day's paper can give you MORE than

*Joe Girard, "The World's Greatest Salesman," mails 12,000 a *month!*

the necessary material to write four notes to your customers. Four *positive* notes.

If this is too general for you, make four notes more specific and sales oriented.

For your customers over sixty-five years old, a short note on your stationery saying, "Thought you'd be interested in the enclosed. Please call me at my private number . . ." and include a brochure describing your services for senior citizens.

Or write to your customers who have one type of account with you and who could use another. Encourage them to shop by phone. Use their credit card. Simple cross-selling to *your own* customers who are after all, your prime contacts.

The avenues are many, long, unending. They direct the customer to return to you and your business, for another helping of your services or for some new products you offer.

2. FOUR TELEPHONE CALLS

This is the same as the four notes. Only on the phone. You will be amazed at the positive reactions. Ask anyone you know, when was the last time they received a *positive* phone call from anyone they did business with.

Rarely. And if they did, it was for a negative reason.

Now, imagine the reaction when you call, give your name, your company's name, and, "Is this Mrs. Jones? Good morning. I'm calling to say thank you for doing business with us. We appreciate your business and want you to know if there is any other way we can help you in the future, I would appreciate your calling me . . ."

She will probably call back to see if you really work there or if it was a practical joke. I mean who ever heard of a company calling to say *thank you?*

Boy, will you shake up your community.

Have three-by-five-inch cards made up of your personal customers. Call them a month *before* the last payment is due (after checking to see if the payment schedule was met). Would they like to buy something else? "We have some interesting new . . . (pick one: dresses, jackets, insurance coverage, direct mail lists . . .)

A friend in California told us this story about Argentina looking around to buy some airplanes. Many companies throughout the world bid for their business. One of the bidders was Boeing.

While this was going on, Argentina won the World Cup for soccer. One of the friends of Boeing Chairman T. A. Wilson suggested he contact

General Jorge Videllya, the president of Argentina, and offer his congratulations.

"The World Cup for soccer" said the friend, "is something like the same team winning the Super Bowl, the World Series, and the NBA championship on the same day. Only bigger . . ."

Wilson followed the advice and called General Videllya and offered his congratulations.

Videylla was visibly moved by the phone call and sincerely thanked the Boeing chairman.

Shortly thereafter Boeing received the contract from Argentina for their planes. And they have been selling them there ever since.

Because of the phone call? Perhaps. As they say in Brooklyn, "It certainly didn't hoit . . ."

A banker in a small town in Nebraska heard us explain this technique. He immediately started a system calling four business accounts every day. He would go through the "loans approved" list, pick up the phone, call, and thank the account for doing business with the bank.

One day he called to thank the owner of a business who had borrowed a substantial amount of money. The owner, in conference, was called away by a secretary who assumed ANY call from the bank was urgent.

The businessman's reaction was astonishment. The only reason the banker was calling him was to *thank* him for the loan? He assumed the bank had reconsidered and decided NOT to give him the money!

He was reassured but needed reconvincing the phone call was nothing more than a "thank you." He asked the banker to hold the phone for a minute. He returned with this message, "This is your lucky day. The meeting I'm in is with a new business coming to town. I just told him about this phone call. He said that's the kind of bank he wants to deal with. Send a messenger over for his check for $800,000."

The loan officer nearly fainted.

A few months ago, in an advertising conference in Texas, we told this story. Following the morning coffee break, a young banker asked if he could address the group. We gave him the microphone and he said, "I just want everyone here to know this system really works. I just walked into the lobby and I saw these golf shorts in a store window. Now I've got a customer who just loves to play golf. So I called him on the phone and I said I was at this conference and I saw these shorts and what size waist was he? He thought I was kidding and I said I just wanted to say thanks for all the business he gives our bank. He laughed, gave me his waist size . . . and then he told me to stop by tomorrow to pick up a check for $100,000 certificate of deposit."

It took us several hours to convince the audience it happened as he said it did.

3. FOUR PERSONAL CONTACTS

Most salespeople receive a box of 500 calling cards when they come to work. They tuck them into their desk and the box remains half filled one year later.

One sales manager we know uses a new box every month!

Wherever he goes, he leaves his card. He goes to dinner, leaves a tip AND his card for the waiter/waitress. Someone introduces him to a new person, he says his name and hands over his card. He goes out of town—for whatever reason—and tells every new person if they ever come to his town—or know someone who will—well, here's his card.

Your calling card should be "different" from others because *you* are different from other sales people.

Perhaps it has your picture on the card. Or the picture of your building or store. Whatever. Are you willing to pick up the extra cost for an unusual calling card for yourself? If you do, someone is going to want to know why all those people are lined up waiting for you every day while the other salesman are waiting, or are out drinking coffee.

Karl Bach, another great insurance salesman, once took a new young recruit aside. "I notice you were kind enough to ask me if I wanted to go and have coffee with you and the other salesman. Here, give them this $5.00, and you come into my office."

He sat young Mort Utley down and said, "They all go down for what they say is five minutes. It is really fifteen minutes. And the same thing will happen again for fifteen minutes this afternoon."

He took out a pencil and paper and started writing down the numbers saying, "fifteen and fifteen are thirty minutes a day . . . times 200 selling days a year . . . that comes to . . . twenty-two days!"

He looked at the new young salesman and said, "Now you know the secret, why I'm the number one salesman in this company. I have an extra twenty-two days a year—a whole month more selling time than they do . . ."

And so have you given away FOUR of your calling cards today? Only two? Quick—write two notes! Or make two more phone calls!

4. FOUR SALES

My father used to say every time two people meet, a sale is made. True. But only if one person knows it.

A banker in a large southern New Jersey town played golf every Saturday for years with one of the community's largest builders. One day the president of the bank said to the builder, "Tom, we've been playing golf together every Saturday for four years. How come you've never put any money in my bank?''

And Tom answered, "How come you never asked me?"

Successful people in the community rarely meet you when they are just starting out. A mutual friend introduces you at a meeting, a conference, a party. You have similar tastes. You go out once or twice. But because habits are made, your new friend tends to think of you as his "social" friend rather than his "banker" friend. And when a friend buys what you have to sell from someone else, you ain't got a friend!

That is really what being a salesperson is all about: making a sale. The greeting, the talking to, and the contacting of a minimum number of people every day to make four sales is NOT difficult. What makes it a bit more challenging? Each of the four sales brings you closer to your sales goal for the day. Set your sales goals. And you will achieve them.

Summary

The entire purpose of the Four-mula is to build a *network* of people close enough to you so that when you need something—information, a favor, some help in business, a recommendation, or just a friend—you'll have access to it. Many of the people who come to our seminars list "Making new friends" as a goal. Or they put it this way: "Keep in better touch with the people who are important to me." This "Four-mula for Success" chapter will do all of those things, plus if you are in business, it will help you tie-in tighter with those business contacts who are or will be important to you.

Notes: First, you must have some small type of stationery, note pads, note paper, or a post card with you at all times. Why do we emphasize "at all times"? Because it's during those odd moments—while you are waiting or being kept waiting (both unexpected)—that you use the time to "keep in touch."

A good example: our friend and national speaker Bill Gove. No one gets a letter from Bill Gove. They get a double post card stapled together. On the front of the card is a cartoon of Bill rushing to catch a plane (he spends his life on planes).

The following incident is typical. Bill was in Los Angeles speaking before an association meeting. He had to leave for Florida right after his speech. He had two tickets for the Jack Jones show that night. He left us the tickets. We wrote and said, "Thanks . . ." Within days we received his double-post card, hand-written note back: "Glad you got the tickets. Hope you enjoyed the show. Bill." Buttoned up. Finished. Wrapped. Complete. Staying in touch.

We really recommend this post card technique to everybody—a personal friend or a business associate. It keeps you in touch in a way other people never think of—because it's so simple. All you need are your cards, addresses, postage stamps, and a pen, and you have solved the keep-in-touch problem. You can't telephone everybody you think about. You can't visit everybody you like (wouldn't that be fun?), but you can write notes.

Can you imagine the effect of writing four notes a day? If you are in business 250 days a year, that is 1,000 extra contacts, "second sales calls" as one executive described these notes, spreading out into your business and personal world!

And what is the difference between the Business and Personal Category of friends? Isn't it length of time, or the chemistry created between two people, or a closeness that results from more intimate contact? We think so. With four notes a day you can create friendships from business, simply by taking the ninety seconds necessary to write down a thought, two sentences that say to someone you know: "I was thinking about you"—and I think enough about you as a friend to take the time to tell you. It's worth it—and this idea works.

Phone calls: These are made impulsively. We know you are busy. We know you're managing your time well. You have a list of Things For Today, but in between there are flashes, a name that appears on the page of a phone index, a familiar name in the Rollodex file while you are looking for someone else. If the name that flashes into your mind hits a mental computer button that says "Action"—make a call right then, fast, react!

And when you do call, tell the truth: "I was going through my file, saw your name, and said to myself, it's been too long since I called you, so I dialed your number. Are things going okay?" You will be amazed at the response. Most people are startled and answer, "You must have ESP! I was thinking of you just the other day," or, "I'll tell you something funny . . . Wednesday, no it was Tuesday, one of the guys called me about you, and I told him I'd have to give you a call. Gee, I'm glad you called . . ." YOU CALLED. That's the difference.

Keep your calls short. Two short calls are better than one long one.

Isn't it funny how many people you call impulsively were "just about to get in touch with you"? Um huh. But by using this impulsive technique you become the Source. You are generating the Communication, and you are building your network of people.

Personal contacts: Most of us do not sufficiently use the people we know for business purposes. Does everyone who knows you, really know what you do for a living? Do they know well enough to immediately call you when they need the product or service you are selling?

In all communications, sales, and management, there is a key word that distinguishes One from the many: Individuality. It's a sign of instant recognition, "Oh yes, she is the lady who is in the United Way," or, "He is the one who is an engineer for the Portland Cement Company in Riverside." How do you build that identity, the Individuality?

By making sure the people you know socially know what you do. Don't be backward about doing business with friends, or asking for business from acquaintances.

"Maybe's" don't count. "It looks good" doesn't count. The only business is the business you have booked, locked, and are ready to bill.

That is the four-mula: phone calls, notes, personal contacts, and sales. Four a day. You do not have to do every one every day. If you take just one category you are far ahead of your nearest competitor. If you do more than one category, you will soon be so busy you will not be able to handle the traffic.

And your competition will wonder, "How do they do that much business? I wonder what *is* the secret formula?"

Only give them a hint to the answer: They are spelling the word formula . . . wrong. It's spelled Four-mula (for Success).

10 Secret Selling Sentences

ONE EVENING the after-dinner conversation centered on the subject, "The greatest salesman I ever met was . . ." Our guest that evening was a young salesman who had just returned from a trip to France. "This is a true story," he said, "it actually happened to me just last month in Paris. And it involves one of the best salesmen I ever met."

He then told the story.

He was shopping along the Rue St. Honore, home of designer shops. Admiring a sport jacket in one of the windows, he decided to go into the store and check out the merchandise.

He hesitated, however, knowing he would be approached and given a sales pitch. (Don't we all?) After all, that is what *he* would do if he was the inside salesman.

How then could he go into the store and not be button-holed? One simple way: He would tell the salesperson he was "only looking" and would call for help if needed.

He stood outside the door of the shop, still looking at the jacket in the window and carefully rehearsing his performance: He would walk in the store, and as the salesman approached him and routinely smiled, "May I help you?" (don't they all?) he would say, "Thanks, I'm just looking . . ." And he would browse.

He knew his lines. He knew his plan. He opened the door.

On schedule, the salesman approached him.

He opened his mouth to say the well-rehearsed line, but the salesman spoke first, "Ah, good to see you," said the salesman, "we have your jacket waiting for you." And the salesman promptly turned and headed back into the store.

What jacket? How could it be his? Why would it be waiting for him? Our friend finally figured the salesman had him mixed up with someone else, and he would certainly correct this when the salesman returned. Indeed!

A moment later the salesman appeared with the *same* jacket our friend had admired in the window and said, "Here it is. Try this on. See how it fits . . ."

Our friend, confused but following directions (don't we all?), tried on the jacket—which fit perfectly. He felt the salesman gently lead him to the mirror; heard him quietly describe the fabric, the fit, the fine points of tailoring. Soon he was looking at matching pants, shirts, and a tie.

Within a half hour our friend had found himself (a) at the front wrapping counter, (b) watching a handsome set of clothing being expertly bundled up, and (c) parting with almost $500. All this from "having a look around."

He then asked the salesman, "Tell me. Why did you say 'I have your jacket for you' as soon as I walked in the door? You had never seen me before."

The salesman smiled and said, "I saw you outside the window admiring the jacket. I knew by looking at your build what size you were. It was only natural that I should greet you by offering you what you wanted: the jacket in the window."

Other people in the shop smiled and the salesman continued, "To be honest—that's how I learned the first basic rule in selling: Find out what the customer wants . . . and give it to him."

At Neiman-Marcus you learn how to sell by NOT asking the "May I help You?" phrase. Instead, NM salespeople are encouraged to start talking about the merchandise in the area where the customer is browsing.

Or: "Hello. I'm Mariann Gibson and I'll be glad to help you as soon as you find something that interests you . . ."

Being natural is one of, if not *the,* greatest of all selling secrets.

But that doesn't mean you shouldn't prepare or shouldn't use the proven formulas. When we began our Great Brain Robbery seminars, we used a clutch of warm-up jokes, stories, and crowd-settling vignettes. After three or four successful performances we worried: where were the new stories? Answer: there aren't any.

Bill Gove, a venerable and excellent platform performer for thirty-plus years, had told us that. "The good stories work forever," he said. "Use 'em! The audiences change—the stories don't."

And even if some of them sitting there have heard the stories before, they will nudge their neighbor knowingly and whisper, "Wait 'til you hear this one. I heard them do it in Dallas. Great!"

And top salesmen, super promoters know this secret. What works, works. WINNERS repeat (see chapter eight). Aren't the magicians still fanning decks of cards, holding them out to you, and purring, "Pick a card, any card"—and don't you still reach for a card, knowing they know now? Of course.

THE THREE SECRET SELLING SENTENCES

Secret Selling Sentence Number One: "I have a problem and . . ."

Murray learned it from his father and both he and Ray use it daily. The nine-word magic formula begins like this: "I have a problem . . ."

When you're thirteen years old it's very important to see the Albany Senators play their opening baseball game of the season.

The Senators were in the Eastern League (a few steps below AAA ball and a few seasons away from the majors—but in Albany, New York, it was OUR professional team).

The problem was: opening day was a school day. If I went to the principal and asked to have the day off, I knew he would surely say "no." If I simply took the day off, I knew there would be massive explanations at home.

Frustrated, I explained the problem to my father and told him my plan, which was for him to write an excuse to the principal.

"No," he said, "I won't do that. It's time you handled these problems yourself."

"But I don't know how," I complained.

"Well," Dad said, "I guess it's about time I taught you the magic formula."

"The magic what?" I asked, wide-eyed, which reflected my full thirteen years.

"The magic formula for getting things done," he said. "Once you learn the formula you can have anything you want."

"Really?" I was impressed.

And I love magic. Dad could take a half-dollar, clench his fist, open it, and the money disappeared, and then he would take it out of his ear. Could this new formula be as successful as the wonderful half-dollar disappearing trick?

"What's the formula, Dad?" I asked.

"It's really very simple," he said. "It is only nine words. Memorize them and you can have anything you want in life. Works every time. Guaranteed!"

"Tell me, Dad, What is the magic phrase?"

"OK. Here it is." And he paused and then said, very carefully and slowly, "I have a problem and I need your help."

A few silent moments passed. Then I said "That's it?"

"That's it," he answered.

I repeated the phrase slowly, word by word. "I have a problem and I need your help."

"You've got it!" he said brightly.

"Is there something else that goes with it?" I asked. "Gee, Dad, it sounds so . . . well, simple."

"You'll find out the most difficult things in life are really very simple, once you analyze them carefully," he said. "People complicate problems by being emotionally involved. To someone else who is objective, your problem is simple. And this phrase *works*."

"Every time?" I asked, still not quite believing.

"Every time," he said, "but, of course, there *is* one thing."

Aha, I knew there was something else. "Yes, what's that?"

"You must be very sincere when you say the words. Otherwise it won't work."

That was fine. I was very good at being sincere. I could do it. The next morning I went to see the principal of the school. He looked up, greeted me, and asked me what I wanted.

"Mr. Stahlman," I began, and then, a little too quickly said, "I-have-a-problem-and-I-need-your-help."

He peered at me over the top of his Ben Franklin glasses, waited a moment or two, and then said, "There's no problem that can't be solved once you talk it over. Sit down. Tell me what the problem is."

I sat down. I told him. He thought for a while and then said, "Fine." I could be excused for the ball game! And then, as an afterthought, he added, "Oh, please have your father write an excuse for our records . . ."

What was he REALLY saying to me?

This: "I have a problem and I need your help. In case someone on the board ever wants to know why you had the day off, I'll have an excuse on file."

But it worked. And works. To this day.

The main reason, of course, is you are appealing to someone else's ego. You are admitting you cannot find the answer to a problem and have sought them out because you KNOW they will have the answer.

The person you direct the question to invariably has the decision-making capacity to deliver what you want. Instead of asking directly, you phrase the request in terms of a problem to be solved rather than a favor to be given.

We have used the magic nine-word formula to receive goods from a manufacturer when there was supposedly nothing in the warehouse. We have used it when there were no rooms at a hotel. We have used it to receive cooperative money to pay for advertising when the company had no cooperative advertising policy. Each time, wherever and whenever We used it . . . it has worked!

Secret Selling Sentence Number Two: "You get . . . me."

What Herb Chavis knows about automobiles can be printed on one small page in very large type: not very much. But Herb knows people and he sells automobiles!

He would arrive at an agency and within a month become the number one salesman. It made no difference if the product was a Ford, a Volvo, or a Chevrolet (and he sold all three). Within a short period of time the other salesmen would see the newly-arrived man at the top of the "new cars sold" list—winning the prizes, the premium money, and having everyone wonder, "How did he do that?"

There are many kinds of salesmen. There are the flamboyant, effervescent, evangelical salesmen. There are the facts and figures salesmen, whose information of their product fills their selling speech until you are overwhelmed with statistics and product knowledge.

And then there are the quiet, observant, watching-for-the-right-moment salesmen, who wait until the customer talks. And *then* answer. Herb Chavis is this type of salesman.

We once asked him, "When do you know if a sale is made or lost?" And he answered, "It depends on which one of us talks first."

What did that mean?

"Simple," he said. "After you outline the presentation to the customer and you tell him the dollars you can give him for a trade-in and what accessories he has on the car he wants, you sit and wait. If you keep on talking, you will probably lose the sale. If the customer talks first, you win."

We said many salesmen did not have the confidence for that kind of wait-it-out, moment-of-silence game. He admitted that was so.

"That's right," he said, "but the Great Ones do. Most salespeople mistake Silence for Surrender. It's just the opposite. When you've had the chance to say what you want about your product or service, you're in the same position as the actor ending his speech, the attorney summing up his case before the jury, the writer who feels he is finished—more words and suddenly, like a spring wound one turn too tightly, it bursts and disintegrates.

"More sales are lost by talking, when all the salesperson has to do is quit. Shut up. Wait. Let the mind of the buyer catch up with the words of the seller.

"There's another way, too," he added. And he suggested we come to his automobile showroom the next day and watch him work.

We arrived the next day as Herb was in conversation with an area businessman asking about a trade-in on his car. The businessman kept referring to a page of notes he had in his hand, and it was easy to see he was comparison-shopping.

"This is the car I want," he said, "and there's my car outside. All I want to know is how much the new car is going to cost me. Don't bother me with any figures. The bottom line is what I'm interested in."

Herb smiled, nodded, and went to his little desk to add up the total of the new car and accessories. He drove the man's present car to the appraiser. He returned with his own list of figures and gave the list to the businessman.

The man quickly compared notes and then said, "I'm sorry, you're $100 too high. I can get the same from your competition for $100 less."

"That's difficult to believe," said Herb.

"Well, here it is," said the businessman, handing Herb the sheet of paper from the competitor.

Herb took both sheets of paper, looked from one to the other, obviously comparing style numbers and "extras." He read them aloud as he went down the list, and then said, "Oh-oh. There's one thing on my list he doesn't have on his."

"Impossible," said the businessman, taking back both lists and scanning them again. "They're identical."

"I don't think so, sir," said Herb. "Look at the bottom of my list. See what's there?"

"That's your name," said the businessman.

"Right," said Herb. "That's the one thing that is on my list that is NOT on the other list. And that you can't get from the other car dealer."

"I don't understand," said the customer.

"It's called Added Value by some people," Herb said smoothly. "Let me ask you a question: Have you ever had a car that you had no trouble with whatsoever after you bought it?"

"Never," admitted the customer.

"Well, that's part of it," Herb began softly. "When you buy your car from me part of my value is I will be here when you come back . . . and I feel pretty sure you will. That's when I take over. If there is a door light to fix, you bring the car to me. I get it fixed. If there's a rattle, you bring the car to me, not to the service bay. In short, part of the price you are going to pay for this car is really paying for what happens *after* you take the car off the floor—for someone to take care of everything as long as you own the car. Is that worth $100? That's the question. You see, you're not just buying a car—*you're buying me*." The businessman looked at Herb for a long moment and then said, carefully, "I'll buy the car from you."

The same thing is true with Mort Utley, the Phoenix insurance wizard. Mort used to tell all his clients, "There are three reasons why you should buy your insurance from me: (1) I will never *sell* you; I will simply *offer* you the best policies available at this time for your situation in life, then you *choose* the policy you want; (2) I will follow your career and family; as they grow and you move up I will again offer you the policies best for your situation and you make the choice, and (3) think about this—if you buy your insurance from me you won't ever have to talk to another insurance agent as long as you live!"

That last one usually did it. Today Mort has his Arizona real estate holdings, his insurance clients, and spends half his year working with young people from the Southwest College, teaching them how to become successful—and they do!

Don't we all go back to restaurants where we are known and ask for certain waiters or waitresses? Isn't part of the personal ego trip having the bartender say, "The usual, Mr. Raphel? And what will you other gentlemen have?"

Isn't this all part of the you-get-Me syndrome? When the bartender knows you and your preferences, you couldn't possibly slide by with a submarginal tip. He is one of your regular "suppliers" and as such deserves and gets superior treatment.

Whoever we deal with regularly and recommend is special, part of the you-get-Me world. Your dentist. "He's great!" (You wouldn't go to an inept mouth man. Not you.) Your doctor. "Terrific guy!" (And who would "shop" doctor prices? You pay for the *confidence* you have in this man that he will know and cure whatever ails you.)

Whatever the product you sell, whatever the merchandise you carry, the customer knows they can buy the same or comparable goods in another store, warehouse, factory, business. The only one distinctive, individual, exclusive product you have that cannot be duplicated anywhere else is *you*.

Today's customer is so used to receiving shoddy, bad, unfinished work that he has come to regard the lack of quality as the status quo. Not from you. You are the exception. You are the reason the customer returns to buy and shop and spend. Because *you care*.

Though people may say the main reason for shopping at a bank, supermarket, or drugstore is "convenience," have someone offer a special "service" and they will drive miles out of their way to be handled as a person and not as a number.

Sell yourself. It is the most valuable selling tool you have. And exclusively yours.

Secret Selling Sentence Number Three: "Which do you like?"

A new salesman watched us greet a customer who came into the store. We discussed some clothing ideas and, within the hour, wrote up a sale for more than $1,000. He came over later and said, "I did what you told me to do. I watched you. I listened to you. But at no time did you ever ask the customer if he wanted to buy anything. I never heard him say, "Yes, I want to buy this." And yet you sold him more that $1,000 worth of clothing. How did you do that?"

We explained that we simply used one of the secret selling sentences. This was a little different, however, because it is used over and over again when selling multiple items. If summed up in a few words, it would be: *Always give a customer a choice between something and something rather than something and nothing.*

Here's how it works:

Always give a customer a choice between two items—either one of which is acceptable to you. Then, the customer "decides" which item he wants to buy. Remember Mort Utley and the "choice" of insurance policies?

If you ask a woman customer, "Do you like this blouse," and she can say a flat "No," what then? If you offer her two and ask, "Which do you like best," whichever she chooses, you win.

The "which" approach at work:

A man about to buy clothing was asked if he preferred solid-color sport jackets or patterns? When he said "solid" we asked if he preferred something in the brown family ("we have camel, chocolate, beige") or something in the blue family ("grey, navy . . . "). He chooses. Once he makes that simple choice, we offer him the choice in trousers. ("Do you prefer solids or plaids?") He prefers solids. Then we give him a choice with solids. Same with shirts. ("Do you like button-down or spread collars?") And with ties. And so on.

But, as the comedian used to say, "At no time do my fingers leave my hands." Here, at no time is the customer called on for anything except ONE simple decision: Plaid. Solid. Blue. Button-down.

"Which do you prefer?" at work:

Customer: I'm interested in a typewriter.
Salesperson: Would you prefer the standard or newer model with the automatic correction feature?

•

Customer: I'm thinking about buying a new camera.
Salesperson: For professional quality or personal, family candids?

•

Customer: I'm interested in a car.
Salesperson: Is economy or comfort your first consideration?

•

Customer: I want to buy a pair of pants.
Salesperson: Something for dress or casual?
Customer: Something casual.
Salesperson: Fine. Denim, corduroys, or brushed cottons? Here's one of
    each. Which do you prefer?

At no time does the customer have to make more than *one* choice. Step by step, you give customers the opportunity to make up their minds, and at each step they are *closing the sale for you,* by their own decisions. Which makes them very happy.

In real estate there are a few exceptional salespeople, and since women dominate that residential market, here's a story. . .

An executive moves to a new area. Pressure on from company to choose home, move family, get new branch office open and running. He visits scores of houses with dozens of lady pointer-outers, who trail him from room to room, pointing out, "This is a closet. Here is a nice bath. And look at the wonderful kitchen." More of the MayIhelpyou school.

One saleslady used the "which do you like?" approach. She stopped her car at the end of a quiet cul-de-sac street, handed over a set of house keys, smiled, and said, "One of these homes could be yours . . . "

Next thing we knew, we were walking along that street, looking wistfully at each of the eight homes and wondering, *which one* is it? The smiling saleslady indicated the house with the tile roof. We went down the walk, through the courtyard gate into our house . . . ooops! Gave the story away. But we did buy the house. Not entirely because the lady played an interesting different game with us, but an important part of the decision to buy was that she let *us* make the decision.

Remember: By having the customer not only participate in the sale, but actually make the decisions for you, you are merely breaking down the initial barriers that always are there when salesman and customer first meet.

Joe Batten, one of the best known sales speakers, in person and on film, calls that initial block between buyer and seller "the invisible shield." He uses a visual example of a TV commercial of some years ago where a toothpaste touted its protective effect as being like a transparent shield. In the commercial, a baseball pitcher throws a ball at high speed at the actor. The ball is deflected and the actor knocks his knuckles on the shield.

"Get those shields down!" urges Batten. If that example makes you aware of the unseen "wall" between you and the new customer, fine. Selling secrets are only as good as they work for you. Often visualizing the shield will remind you to carefully push down the ever-present unseen wall so the two of you can talk as friends. Not pitcher and batter.

"I like the way your company decorates your offices," says one salesperson. "There's an interesting difference in each office. This is a nice warm feeling . . . " This causes the customer to have a look around his own territory. "Yes, we like it. In fact, when they repaint I'm going to ask for the same colors again." A stranger? Hardly.

Compliments. Compliments. Real ones. Sincere ones.

Whether you are catching an airplane, getting a room in a motel, selling insurance, doing interior decorating, servicing, doing plant maintenance, or raising funds for a charity, use these selling sentences—for your product or yourself:

1. "I have a problem and I need your help."
2. "When you buy my product, you also get Me."
3. "Which do you prefer?"

First, get in step, gently get those shields down, and then use compliments. They work. In all sales activity, remember you are "on stage." Say your lines carefully, naturally, realistically. Don't fake it. Be yourself. You are the best thing you've got going!

11 *Expectations vs. Reality*

"I expected you would at least have the car washed after you borrowed it."
"The way they run this company, they expect you to be a mind reader . . ."
"You charge me eight dollars for new heels—the least I'd expect was you'd shine the shoes!"

All sound familiar? With a few variations, here and there, for the product, service, situation? Sure. This is the way it is every day in shops, restaurants . . . ("Miss . . . Miss . . . is it too much to expect we could have some cream with our coffee, huh?"), service stations ("Whadya expect with five gallons of gas, a wax job?").

It might be easier to understand this every minute, every day important psychological clash if we show it to you on a graph.

Expectations . . . . .are up here at the higher level. The Idea, what we hoped, planned, dreamed, or thought we were entitled to. The "least we thought we'd get . . ."

Down here is. . .**Reality**

That's what just happened.
The fact. The disappointment, the mis-communication.

See that wavy line going from the Expectations level down to the Reality level? When these two words don't match, it is cause for us to be nervous, agitated, uptight, tense, irritable . . . and angry.

What happens is that one person has a set of Expectations *in his/her mind.* That is the plan. The *result,* now that's something else again. Result is Reality.

Question: Why is it so often that reality falls short of the Expectation?

Answer: Because we had *in our mind* what we wanted to have happen . . . but we did not SAY what we wanted . . . in advance of . . . the actual event.

We "hoped." We "thought." But we didn't *say.* ("I didn't think it would cost *that* much?" "Lady," says the mechanic, "you didn't ask me; you just said 'Fix it.' ")

This is not a lecture. It's an observation. Literally, almost every minute of our working-playing-loving lives, we are *thinking* what "will happen." We live on high Expectations. That's natural. Optimistic. Human. And that's Good!

The people who *Recognize, Choose,* and *Act* are *Realists*. (See "If You Don't Like It Here. . . Get Out!") They are constantly assessing every situation, calculating the odds of getting what they want (without being obnoxious, cruel, or savage). The ones who are NOT disappointed are the ones who Ask, Tell, Say—out front—what they'd like to have happen.

Let's take some regular, ordinary, street level cases of Expectation. Let's play the game of "Whatever Happened To . . ." (A certain customer, for example.)

Once in a while do you wonder why a certain customer just stopped buying from you?

There didn't seem to be any reason you can put you hands on. And the more you think about it the more concerned you become when you think of another lost customer—and another.

What happened?

After all, you *expected* them to keep shopping with you, purchasing policies, appliances, buying cars from you. ("Man, I gave them a great deal.") The reality is they are gone.

What did *they* expect?

Maybe a note. A Thank You. Follow-up. To be included on a special list (see "Direct Mail"). A telephone call to see if they are happy with what they bought. To ask if the service (are you ready?) was "up to their expectations?"

Simple things . . . we didn't do.

Want to know why customers leave? Here is the run-down of a survey made by a national retailing chain who picked at random a list of 100 customers who had not made purchases in a year. They sent out a questionaire*

Here are the replies:

Fourteen had complaints that were not taken care of properly.

Nine were lured away by other stores (better service or lower prices).

Nine moved.

Sixty-eight . . . had no special reason.

(Our interpretation: *No one paid attention to me.*)

In other words: nearly seven out of ten customers you *EXPECT* to come back have left . . . simply because you *let them leave.*

---

*When is the last time you asked your customers what they think of you, your sales people, customer service, or attitude? Maybe you ought to copy down the results of the survey and have it distributed to every person who works for your company. Look to your losses and block those holes. Pay Attention.

That is a difference between Expectations and Reality.

If we *understand* the difference between our *plan* and the *result,* we can then change it to better fit what-we-want.

"But," you might protest, "that's not true of me. My customers are steady."

Really? What's "steady"? Professor George Brown of the University of Chicago analysed the results of the Chicago *Tribune* data on customer loyalty in buying food. Here are the results:

Seventeen percent of the families were loyal to one brand of soup.

Thirteen percent of the families were loyal to one brand of cereal.

Twenty-seven percent of the families were loyal to one brand of concentrated orange juice.

Forty-seven percent of the families were loyal to one brand of coffee.

The rest of the families had little, *if any*, loyalty to one brand.

THEY HAVE TO BE CONSTANTLY SOLD.
OR, YOU HAVE TO BE CONSTANTLY SELLING

Your plan/goal/thinking putting-together your Expectations begins with good selling. And repeat business depends heavily on good selling.

If your customer is sold once, but does not like your merchandise (or you) and does not return . . . this is expensive selling. How do you make the customer return and live up to *Your* expectations?

The best way: think of how you can best *help* your customer. Harry Bullis of General Mills told a convention of Northwestern Life Insurance representatives: "When I go out in the morning, I don't ask, 'How many sales will I make today?' I ask, 'How many people can I *help* today?' "

Hal Stebbins, who has personally written more than a hundred million dollars worth of advertising, offers a "B-complex" for writing: Be human. Be simple. Be sincere. Be specific. Be informative. Be authoritative. Be enthusiastic. Be sure you're understood. And above all, Be believable.*

The good salesman knows his customers better than they know themselves. He can truthfully quote the German proverb, *"Ich Kenne Mein Volk,"* which means, "I know my people."

Only because he has developed this "feel" for his customers—and his employees—can he balance the Expectation and Reality lines to equal positions. And so you must *know* your customer. You must know your merchandise. And, for heaven's sake, your own people. Keeping a handle on these three crucial elements is an on-going, happening-every-minute activity. The top pros know this. They never claim to know all the

---

*Don't fall into the deep trap of thinking that a slogan is anything but—a slogan. "WE CARE" doesn't make people care. It just impresses the president and the advertising department.

answers. But their averages are right up there with Ted Williams's and Babe Ruth's.

Ed Carlson, one of the nation's top executives, did an excellent job running Great Western Hotels. He was hired away to United Airlines. Did he know anything about airplanes? Well, not really, but he was an excellent manager. And quick learner. When he first took the position, his employees would see him walking around the office with a big pin. On it were the letters NETMA.

"NETMA? What's that mean?" a few asked. He smiled and said, "You'll find out."

One day he went to Los Angeles International Airport and saw the lines at the United counter stretching to the entrance of the terminal. He went to the front and saw only one girl. He quickly identified himself as "an employee" of United, and asked if he could help.

"Boy, and how," the overworked clerk said. "Get around here and help." She showed him how to pull tickets and stamp boarding passes. (Presidents don't know about those things.)

Finally, the line trickled down to a manageable few. Carlson turned to the girl and said, "Where *is* everybody?"

She answered, "It's lunch time. Everyone took off to eat. I'm the only one here."

"But," said Carlson, "it's a company policy that everyone cannot leave the counters at lunch time. The hours have to be staggered. Didn't you know that?"

And she shook her head and said, "Nobody Ever Tells Me Anything."

"Right," said Carlson and pointed to his NETMA sign.

We tend to take for granted that if WE know something is happening, the rest of the world knows too. We tend to believe that if we expect something to happen because we have all the plans lined up in our heads, no one will disturb the order.

Wrong.

Most people in our group/organization/customer list do NOT know what is happening all the time. And it is all too true that the people selling for you don't know what is happening—in current advertising, on the radio, TV, or even what direction your marketing plan is taking.

The mangement does. They spend their corporate committee lives hammering out wonderful campaigns, new themes, and new directions . . . and forget two things.

One, that the employees, sales people, and workers are not one-tenth as interested in "what's going on upstairs" as the people upstairs.

Second, the employees don't necessarily listen to the stations and media carefully chosen for the "demographics" of the customers. Maybe the employees have different demographics. How to tell "our" people what "we" are doing?

For several clients we have recommended tapes. Plain everyday audio cassette tapes. Sound only. But what sounds!

Once a month, the tapes are available—for the salesman in their cars so they can listen while they drive, for the cafeterias so everyone hears what is happening on the air, and for sales meetings or just monthly "catch up" sessions. What better way than to turn your management's voice—amateur and folksy—into a "company broadcast" for your best and most important audience: your employees.

That would help accentuate the positive and eliminate the negative NETMA.

For the sophisticated organizations, there is video tape. Expensive, but the way of the future—at least in auto sales. Listen to this . . .

General Motors has just ordered, we have been told, video disc units for all their show rooms. In the most elaborate headquarters production, not only every GM car . . . but each of the *competitive* cars, will appear on these TV-like screens.

Should the prospect for a car inquire about a Spectrum, for example, the salesman pushes a button and accesses a video disc the top pro presentation—in full color, like a TV commercial—the Spectrum story.

Every one of the key sales points is covered by the announcer. And as an expectation that the prospect is "shopping dealers," the competitions's comparative model will be "taken on" by the announcer. Proving, of course, the GM car is superior—in any of several categories.

Doesn't leave much of a separation between Expectation and Reality the company wants presented to the customer, does it?

The point is not to be a GM. Us littler businesses can't do that—yet. But we do have to be "out among 'em," knowing our own people, what they're selling, how they are selling, and who's telling what story.

Training, personal recognition, tapes, seminars, posting current ads, testing, and rewarding our people are all part of getting the Reality line closer up to the Expectations line.

And don't overlook outside Motivators. The good ones (local or national) can pick up the tempo of an audience and deliver the message you want delivered—better than you can.*

Too often your people have heard you too often.

In setting up our Expectations, we must be realistic. This does NOT mean we should not set high goals. We should. But the setting of goals (see chapter on "Goal Setting") is a striving for a *final* result. Steps and check points are necessary to get what we *expect* to happen on the way *to* the goal.

Example: If our goal is to eventually own the most successful men's

*For a twelve point reprint on how *not* to handle professional speakers, write The Great Brain Robbery, 1360 East Rubio Street, Altadena, CA 91001.

clothing shop in town, the step is to have a successful season our *first* year.

If our goal is to be president of the college, our step will be to first earn our masters degree. Then doctorate. Then a full professorship . . . all steps leading toward the final goal.

The problem: too many of us try to short circuit the final goal with unattainable Expectations. Without realistic steps along the way.

We become restless in our situation. We feel if we could only move somewhere else, to another city or country or area or region, our lives would change.

They may. For the worse.

The success in our lives is often right around us, right in the area where we live. Where is it written that all success stories take place in the major cities? Ben Feldman, working out of small Liverpool, Ohio, writes more insurance by himself than *hundreds* of insurance companies! Rembrandt never left Holland his entire life. And Socrates never left Athens.

They had no trouble making their mark on the history books.

One man, Dr. Russell Conwell repeated this theme in his classic "Acres of Diamonds" speech which he delivered as a public lecture more than 6,000 times from 1877 until his death in 1925. He earned an estimated *seven million dollars* in lecturing all on this *one speech*.

The theme was suggested to Conwell in Turkey when he worked as a foreign correspondent for the New York *Tribune*. A Turkish guide on the Tigris River told him the story of Ali Hafet, A Persian farmer who died a pauper. Yet he had spent his entire life searching for sudden wealth.

Shortly after Hafet died, they discovered diamonds on his property.

Conwell interpreted this story into his theme: "Your diamonds are not in far-distant mountains or in yonder seas; they are in your own backyard, if you but dig for them."

His message, repeated over and over, was: Opportunity exists in every backyard, city, and farm, *if* you study the opportunity and create it for yourself.

Turn your Expectations on the world around you. The attainable realities will amaze you!

A psychologist tested more than 10,000 young men and women over a twenty-year period. One basic truth evolved: almost every one tended to think they could *not* do much better.

Think of it: three out of four decided to face life with the "Reality" blocks they set up for themselves. The didn't know the word "Expectations."

Not Booker T. Washington. He said, "I have begun everything with the idea that I could succeed."

Great Expectations!

How does this work in selling?

Like this: Most studies on how sales are made show the great majority of sales are made after the *fifth call to the same customer.*

Should our "expectations" be to make the sale on every *first* call? The "realities" tell us we won't make it. But about half the salesmen quit after the *first* call!

Another twenty-five percent quit after the second call.

Another twelve percent quit after the third call.

One out of ten salesmen keep on calling. And they wind up with eighty percent of the sales.

Who are these people?

Professor McClellan of Harvard University says people are divided into three different kinds: Achievers, Affiliators, and Power People.

What does all this have to do with Expectations vs. Reality? This: If McClellan is right, if there ARE three basic groups of people, we should know *who* they are, *how* they think and act so we can *understand* their Expectations as well as our own.

The three groups: Achievers, Affiliators, and Power People.

ACHIEVERS are simple to identify. They are self-starters. Goal-setters. They *Know* what they want to do. They have been making decisions and working the options all their lives. You do *not* tell an Achiever, "There is only one way to do this." "Really?" he'll answer. "How about . . ." and he'll give you two other options. And he gives them to you "snap!"—just like that.

And Achievers are not afraid or bashful about letting you know where you stand. If you're bad, they'll blast you right out. Then forget it. Move on! They are continually measuring, taking stock . . . of themselves and everyone around them. They have to know how they are doing and where they are going. And for that reason, they hate surprises.

An Achiever is not afraid to cut off people or get rid of them because he knows that where he is going is a tough road and he *has to* get there. Don't play games with an Achiever. He doesn't need the social ramble, how's the family jazz. He knows and feels the value of time. For an Achiever it's a working lunch, a working breakfast, and lets get at it. *Now!*

AFFILIATORS can best be explained by a friend of ours who has a plaque on the wall of his office. This is what it says: "Do not ask me to lead, I may choose not to. Do not ask me to follow, I may make another decision. Walk beside me, and be my friend."

He is a corporate-company man generally. He doesn't like to make waves. He doesn't like to get rid of people. They are important to him. In his office the Affiliator has pictures of family. Talks of family a lot. Is genial. If he has business to give out, he likes to "spread it around," give everyone deserving a share. He is good with staff. He cares. And gets them to work. Very good with compliments and caresses, the business kind.

And he is an important cog in your machinery. Mr. Entrepreneur. He has the patience you don't have. Emergencies are just "today's fires." He smoothes things over . . . maybe after you have created havoc with one of your bull-in-the-china-shop entries and exits.

Don't expect Affiliators to make decisions like Achievers. Give an Affiliator too many options and he's confused. "What do you think?" he asks gently. He likes to get a consensus, to find out where the "other people" stand. You can "help" an Affiliator with his decisions, where you can not with an Achiever. Marvelous in committee meetings. Able to relieve the tension. He mediates, encourages others. Patient. He is a builder. He likes to "belong." It's important for him to be part of the team. And clues? Taking care of this guy or gal can pay you dividends galore— because he or she will be there tending the store and watching the register. Making things run while you are gone.

POWER PEOPLE are people with turf. "This is my desk. I'm the senior vice president. It took me twenty years to get here. Please don't touch anything on my desk. The plaques on the wall? Know how long it took me to earn all those awards?"

He is proud of his possessions. Material things appeal to a Power Person. And he is a *good* manager, competent executive, important leader of the team.

He likes his "perks," as the British say. Give him club privilege, expense account prestige, first class travel and you've got yourself a solid working partner.

Organized. On time. Good at decisions. After all, that's how he got where he is—after twenty years—making the Right Decisions. Politically too. He's one of the boys, but a step away. He has "a good act." He carries title and rank well.

How to handle him? Don't come in unorganized or with a half-vast project. He is analytical. Keen judgment generally. Treats his staff with respect, but a "stick to the rules" guy. Do your job, you can stay with him. But he's the boss.

Can you influence the Power Person? Absolutely. Be prepared. Have your facts ready and clear. Unlike the Affiliator, he is not afraid to make decisions. He wants the back-up, the data, the statistics. Give him the ammunition in a solid form and he'll give you an answer.

There is a speaker's for-fun description of a Power Person: "How about lunch?" he says. "We can drop down to the garage. They give me a spot near the elevator. We'll drive over in my Silver Cloud to a private club where I happen to be a charter member. But . . . we'd better hurry along . . . (looking at his wrist), the old Rollex says . . . it's three diamonds after twelve." Know him?

BRINGING REALITY UP TO YOUR EXPECTATIONS

A friend of ours is in charge of a rather large sales force. All in the home office where he is vice president. "My expectations, "he said," are to come into my office every day and get MY work done. Line up future assignments for my sales force. But the Reality, as you guys say, is completely different . . ." And he told us his problem.

Every few minutes one of his salespeople would come into his office to ask an opinion or decision on some matter, usually very trivial. "That's not the worst part," he told us. "They take half an hour to finally tell me what's on their mind."

We suggested he put his life back in order by using the "Headline Technique."

"What's that?" he asked.

We explained: "It works just like headlines in the newspaper. Nearly seventy-five percent of the people who read the newspaper, read the headlines. But only twenty-five percent keep on reading. The key point: Is the headline important enough to capture their attention?"

"The next time someone from your office comes in to you, ask them for the 'headline' to their question. Tell them to summarize what they want in a few carefully chosen words. Just like the headline in a newspaper."

He agreed to try this technique. He called his staff together the next day and explained from now on when anyone came in his office they were to talk in "headlines."

"If you say 'Next season's shipment may be late,' I'll tell you to come back in a few weeks. If you say, 'The building is on fire and your office is next,' I'll act on it right away."

The next morning, a few minutes after opening, a salesman walked into his office and began a long rambling discourse on a shipping problem. His boss looked at him and said, 'What's the headline?"

"The what?"

"The headline. Tell me the headline . . ."

"Oh, yes, the headline," he said as he left the office. "I'll be back . . ."

A few months later we asked our friend how it was working. "Fine," he said. "Interruptions are at a minimum. They figure by the time it takes them to think of a headline, they can come up with the answer . . ."

Coming up with the answer in *your* life is made easier when you understand the difference between . . . Expectations and Reality.

This *does not* mean to stop dreaming, planning, thinking-about the future. For they *are* your expectations. And you must continue with them throughout your life. For to think only of the Realities of Life is to give up without trying.

Consider the case of the man who failed in business and decided to run for political office as a state legislator. He ran, got beat and figured, well, he really *was* a businessman, so went back into business. And failed the second time around. Back to politics . . . and finally made it to the state legislature. But was defeated when he tried to be Speaker of the House.

He ran for Congress and made it. Only to lose on the rerun. A few years later he tried for the U.S. Senate . . . and lost again. He ran for Vice President of the United States . . . and lost again. Two years later, he again tried for the U.S. Senate and, ah, yes, lost . . . again.

You can see he was building a no-win habit pattern faced with the reoccurring Realities of losing.

But his Expectations continued high. After this last defeat, he ran again, only two years later . . . and became President of the United States.

His name: Abraham Lincoln.

12 *If You Don't Like It Here ... Get Out!*

EIGHT OUT OF TEN are unhappy in their present job.

A survey taken of 600 university students in psychology asked, "What is your most difficult personal problem?" Seventy-five percent said, "Lack of confidence."

A recent study by the magazine *Psychology Today* revealed four out of ten people said they just "happened" into their job.

What does all this mean?

Very simply: very few of us have a real control over our lives.

The reason: Most of the major decisions in our lives are made for us. At least in the beginning.

Take your job. Most of us are where-we-are because of patterns. Graduate from school. Get out of the service. Need a job. Someone says, "I know where there's a job."

Or: "Why don't you call Fred Johnson."

Or: "You saw this ad in the paper . . ."

And so most people work-where-they-work because at first they *needed* a job rather than *choosing* a job.

And some of us are still there.

And after awhile it's too late to start all over.

Is it?

Ab Rosenberg found himself in an unusual position in his mid sixties. He was in charge of Capezio children's shoes. The division went out of business. What could he do? In his mid sixties?

He purchased a declining shoe business in a basement store in New York City's Greenwich Village.

In a few years he transformed a failing business into a success because he enjoyed the buying and selling of fashion footwear.

The upstairs of the building became vacant. The landlord approached Rosenberg, now in his seventies. Would he consider taking the upper two floors, tripling the present size?

"Why not?" shrugged Ab.

Today his three-story Capezio store in the Village does a multimillion-dollar-plus business and continues to grow rapidly as Rosenberg thinks of new and ambitious plans for growth and expansion.

(He does spend some time in his newly-bought Florida vacation home. He purchased it and took out a thirty-year mortgage.)

REMEMBER: IT'S *WHAT* YOU DO, NOT *WHEN* YOU DO IT.

A recent ad from United Technologies in the *Wall Street Journal* put it well:

> Ted Williams at age forty-two slammed a home run in his *last* official time at bat.
> Mickey Mantle, age twenty, hit twenty-three home runs his *first* full year in the major leagues.
> Golda Meir was seventy-one when she became Prime Minister of Israel.
> William Pitt was twenty-four when he became Prime Minister of Great Britain.
> George Bernard Shaw was ninety-four when one of his plays was first produced.
> Mozart was just seven years old when his first composition was published.
> Benjamin Franklin wrote a newspaper column when he was sixteen and was a framer of the United States Constitution when he was eighty-one.

Henry Ford and Abraham Lincoln were both past forty before they started to realize success.

And among those who made it without a college education are Ford, Edison, Eastman, Carnegie, Pulitzer, Lincoln, Franklin . . .

You're never too young or too old.

Age has little to do with ability.

You *do* have a choice in your life. If you exercise that choice, you take control of your life. And if you decide not to make a decision, remember that *IS* making a decision. For no decision is *A* decision. Which is fine. If you are happy and satisfied and that's-what-you-want-to-do and where you want to be . . .

Too many of us stay where we are because we have been brought up to seek approval from others for our actions.

Do you ever say to yourself, "Is what I am doing every day what I want to do? Do I have any other, better options?"

Think about it.

What *do* you like to do?

One sure-fire test is this: in your mind pretend you do not have to report to work tomorrow. You are paid. It isn't a holiday. It's a work day. But not for you. You can do *anything* you want to. What would you do?

Think about that.

Would you write, swim, tend your garden, go to the library, get on a boat and sail? Would you rather tinker with tools and fuss over fix-it projects? Or . . . you decide. What would you really like to do?

Another clue is to listen to Self. What is the repeated wish you express to people? "Someday, I'd like to—" what? Is that the secret but honest goal of your life?

The psychologists have a nasty but effective method of making you admit what you are doing isn't what you want to do. We had dinner with one recently and he asked, as psychologists do, "What is it you want to talk about?" Oh nothing. Just visit. "Well," suggested the psychologist, "whether it's conscious or not, you probably came here for a reason." (Devilish people, these mind-meddlers.)

Protesting, "No" again, we watched him push a paper over, actually the blank side of the place mat in the restaurant. "Write your obituary," he said. What?? "Oh," he said gently, "its just a game. Let's write down, say, the kind of guy you were, what you did, what you wanted to do but didn't get done . . . that sort of thing." The trap and the technique weren't too hard to figure out. But we smiled and started to write.

Try that some night. Do it the honest way. Tell yourself the truth. Then let someone else read it. A close and trusted friend (who else would you share a thing like this with?) Their reading it back—that's the acid test.

Keep it. Tack it on a wall. As you go scrambling through your daily routines, earning money and doing what you've been doing for a long time . . . take a look. Are you doing what you really want to do?

Not too long ago we did a series of once-a-week seminars for managers of a large chain of gift stores. Halfway through each session we would ask the group, "Are you happy in your job? If not, why not quit?" (The first time we shot out that challenge, the president jumped off his chair, but waited, wondering what we were trying to prove.) The managers were startled. They waited "for the other shoe to drop." Was this for real, or some motivation trick?

We explained the question. If you are not happy in your job, and don't enjoy it, you are going to poison the other workers, lose customers, burn out leads and prospects, and in the long run, do nothing but harm to the company that's paying you. So . . . if you don't like it here, both you *and* the company would be better off if you quit.

That made sense to them, and to the president. Because he admitted later, in a company as large as his it's almost impossible, from his level, to find out who is unhappy. (Who is undermining the company in quiet, subtle ways with being discontent.)

At the end of the third week, one of the members of the home office staff who had been attending all the meetings as an observer said, "You know, I've been listening to this same seminar every week. And every time you get to the part, 'Are you happy in your job,' I get a sinking feeling in my stomach. Today I've made up my mind. I'm leaving. And I've never felt better in my life . . ."

A smile from the parents, a nod of acceptance from the teacher, an endorsement from an employer. All that means is "they" approve of what you do. But do *you* approve of what-you-do?

A friend of ours who owns a small advertising agency was flying first class and noticed an older gentleman next to him looking sadly out the window. Tell me about it, said our friend. The older man, startled by this strange neighbor who was apparently reading his mind, told him his thoughts. He was a stockbroker. With a good salary. He lives in Barrington, Vermont, and likes living there. But he works in New York. And does *not* like it there.

The ad-man friend asked him more about his work, and learned that as a stockbroker there was not much person-to-person contact in the job. It was telephone-to-telephone. The young man exchanged business cards with the stockbroker and said he would be in touch.

Three weeks later in New York a telephone communications man entered the stockbroker's office; he returned the calling card the man had given our friend. "You met a man on a plane," said the telephone man. "He is paying for this meeting. I am to find out exactly what equipment you need to move to Vermont so you can work out of your home."

The man was astonished, but agreed to the survey. The brokerage firm was not happy with the move but did not want to lose a valuable moneymaker. Today the stockbroker lives and works out of his home in Barrington, Vermont, still writing transactions. And happy.

The young man thought about what he had done. And wondered if he was like the cobbler who made shoes for everyone else but whose children went barefoot because he did not have the time to make shoes for them?

He thought about that. And then asked his key employees in his California office where they would like to work and live if they could work and live . . . anywhere.

His media buyer said, "On the bay in San Francisco."

His copywriter said, "Baja, Mexico."

His art director said, "San Diego."

His accountant said, "I'll have to stay here because of my other clients."

The young man has a home on the beach with tennis courts and decided he would like to work where he could also play. His secretary said she'd work with him . . . wherever.

Today, each staff member lives—and works—just-where-they-choose.

The young man's garage is filled to the roof with telephonic communication equipment. The cost: almost identical to the rent in the financial tower they used to occupy.

Asked a client of the young man when he heard this story, "That's interesting. But what about motivating your people when they're not here around you. How do you keep them happy?"

And the young man smiled and said, "Think about what you just asked me . . ."

Hank Mitchell was an executive of DuPont. Had a satisfactory position. Played around with amateur theater in Philadelphia. In the manuscript show *The Great God Innis* (starring Arch Johnson, who later became an actor in Hollywood) there was a funeral in the third act, an Irish wake with keening and wailing.

During this entire act, Bob Tornello (now a neurosurgeon in Ohio) was to portray the dead grandfather and lie perfectly still throughout an entire act. Why not cover a dummy body, some nontraditional thinker suggested, and just have the head sticking out at the top. What was needed was a good likeness of Tornello.

Hank Mitchell had dabbled considerably in clay sculpture and fashioned a most remarkable likeness. And by day, Hank went back to his DuPont job. But with this success, he more and more realized he wanted to sculpt. He left his company, studied, and for some mark of his success and talent, have a look the next time you go by a schoolyard or a playground. All those smoothly sculpted animals children ride on, slide on, go under, around and through were Hank's first creations. (And later came grants, studies abroad, and a totally new, *very* successful Second Career.)

The biggest problem with making-a-choice is simply realizing a choice CAN be made. All of us have found ourselves in positions that are uncomfortable and make us unhappy. Instead of trying to come up with a solution to make ourselves happy, we proceed in the old Irish phrase, "to suffer in silence."

Well, some of us do. Others transfer our suffering to others. We complain. We become defensive. We say things we really do not mean. We turn aside helpful suggestions with, "Why don't you leave me alone?" Or, "You really don't understand my problem."

Most of all, we decide the best solution to any problem is to simply . . . complain.

We use one phrase in our seminars that people remind us about when we see them again months or years later that relates to this problem. They say, Remember the phrase about the complaints? Well, I used it on myself (or my wife/husband/friend) and it works. At least it gets you thinking . . .

This is the phrase:

Cut out the complaints and most people have nothing to say.

Read that one again. Say it aloud and remember it.

Cut out the complaints and most people have nothing to say.

Listen to the conversation taking place around you . . .

"Did you see what the president did today! That's a crazy decision!" "What are we going to do about the price of . . . (check one) food, gasoline, heating oil, new cars, houses, clothing . . ." "They sent us the wrong (check one) TV set, dishwasher, drapes, dresses, shoes, china . . ."

Salesmen's worlds are filled with stories about impossible-to-satisfy customers. People talk about ungrateful relatives. When was the last time somebody wrote you a thank-you note? (Or you wrote one?) Or when was the last time you wrote or called to congratulate someone?* Or the bank wrote you a complimentary letter?

One time after dinner Murray's wife Ruth said, "Did you enjoy the steak?"

We said it was OK.

"It was tough, wasn't it?" she said.

"Well, it was . . . a little."

"What do you think of that," she said, "we pay the top dollar for meat and we get tough steak."

"Well, one of those things . . ."

"That's not good business," she continued, "to say he has the best meat and then send over a piece like that. He has his nerve."

Murray suggested she do something about it.

"Do something? What can I do?"

"You see," he said, "cut out the complaints and most people have nothing to say . . ."

"What's that mean?" she asked, annoyed. "Is this one of those things from your seminars?"

"No, really, listen to what you said. You complained about the meat. It was a valid complaint. Now, what are you going to do about it?"

"What can I do about it?"

"Well, let's see . . . how about if we sue the butcher?"

"Sue . . . the . . . butcher?" she asked not-quite believing.

"Sure, we'll tell the court that he advertised tender steaks and they were tough. We may not win, but we'll feel better inside."

"Well, no," she said, "I don't want to *sue* him . . ."

"All right, here's another idea. I'll go to the stationery store and buy some cardboard and magic markers. We'll make some signs—I love to make signs—saying, 'This butcher sells tough meat,' and we'll picket the store starting tomorrow morning . . ."

"Picket the store! Are you sane?"

---

*A fun-loving friend of ours, a very positive guy, picked ten names and sent them all this one word telegram: "CONGRATULATIONS!" Three of them called and carefully inquired, "Ahem . . . ah . . . what *particular* thing did you have in mind?"

"Sure. I just want to do something about it. And not just complain."

"OK, OK," she said, "I'll stop complaining." And then, in her next breath, "But, boy, does he sell tough meat!"

Oh well . . .

The point: stop complaining and do something.

Here's a way to short cut the useless complaints from people around you: as soon as you hear their complaint, look them directly in the eye and ask, "What do you want me to do about it?"

Startled, they will say, "Well . . . nothing, really. I just wanted to mention it."

"Tell you what," you say. "If you have a complaint and want me to do something, say so. Otherwise, don't tell me, OK?"

You'll see dazed looks. Hear mumblings. But—people will stop bringing ritualistic, time-wasting complaints to you . . . and you'll have more time to solve Big Problems.

Othewise you can wind up consuming yourself with worry, which causes heart trouble, high blood pressure, asthma, rheumatism, colds, arthritis, migraine headaches, and a host of stomach disorders in addition to ulcers.

So, in the immortal words of *Mad* magazine's Alfred E. Newman, "What, me worry?" What for?

A recent survey on "Things People Worry About" broke down as follows:

Things that never happen:	forty percent
Things that can't change:	thirty percent
Needless worry about health:	twelve percent
Petty and miscellaneous worry:	ten percent
Real Problems:	eight percent

Conclusion: ninety-two percent of the things people worry about— they cannot do anything about.

Worry is a malfunction of the mind. It is an excuse to do nothing rather than something. And it is contagious. It contaminates positive thinking, and suddenly everyone believes Chicken Little, and they run home to hide before the sky falls.

There was a man who lived by the side of the road and sold hot dogs.

He was hard of hearing so he had no radio.

He had trouble with his eyes so he read no newspapers.

But he sold good hot dogs.

He put up signs on the highway telling how good they were.

He stood on the side of the road and cried, "Buy a hot dog, mister?"

And people bought.

He increased his meat and bun orders.

He bought a bigger stove to take care of his trade.

He finally got his son home from college to help him out.

But then something happened.

His son said, "Father, haven't you been listening to the radio?

Haven't you been reading the newspapers?

There's a big recession.

The European situation is terrible.

The domestic situation is worse."

Whereupon the father thought, Well, my son's been to college. He reads the papers and he ought to know.

So the father cut down on his meat and bun orders, took down his advertising signs, and no longer bothered to stand out on the highway to sell his hot dogs.

And his hot dog sales fell almost overnight.

"You're right, son," the father said to the boy. "We certainly are in the middle of a bad recession."

Worry hampers our ability to think and to reason. It paralyzes the way we act. It increases pain. It is a known fact that seventy-five percent of pain felt while a person is tense disappears when they relax.

Troubles are like a balloon filling up with air. They puff up rigid until someone puts the tiniest hole in the stretched-out skin; then, poof! the tension collapses into nothing . . .

If much of your worry seems to come from your daily work and job and where-you-are-in-life . . . start thinking about change.

How do you do that?

There are many ways that seem to work. Here's one that works for us. We call it the RCA formula. It is not, as you might think, a system conceived and designed by the people who make records and tapes. It stands for three words:

Recognize

Choose

Act

What that means: Whenever you find yourself faced with a problem, you can find the solution if you:

1. **Recognize** the problem. Isolate it. Break it down to its simplest form.

2. **Choose** among the possible solutions. Not just the traditional, "We've always done it this way." Get out of the box. We find that one quick way to establish your own identity in your own business is to transfer concepts and ideas of an entirely unrelated business to yours. Ask yourself, "How can I use that?"

3. **Act.** Ask for the order. The answer. The help. The way to achieve the goal. Thinking . . . Wishing . . . Hoping . . . are things we do in our

mind. The real world is made up of action. Most of us envy the people with the guts to *Act*.

Too many people *recognize* a problem, even *choose* a way to solve it. And stop. That's not enough. There's one more step. You must act: *ask* for the solution by spoken or written word.

What's the worst thing that can happen? You get a "No." And move on to the next problem, the next possibility, or another of your options. "No" is not the end of the world.

Emerson once said, "If a man has good corn or wood or boards or things to sell. Or can make better chairs or knives, crucibles or church organs than anybody else, you will find a broad, hard-beaten road to his house though it be in the woods."

Which should (but will not) put an end to the budding retailers who continue to believe the single-minded and error-filled philosophy of location is everything. They would do well to examine the empty spaces in center cities or shopping centers where well-known major stores no longer exist because their primary goal was location instead of special services or unusual products. Or being where the customers are *today*, not yesterday.

How can this RCA formula help? You come up with answers: not only in your life but in your daily decision-making. Here are a couple of true stories:

We like to stay in the Fairmont hotels. If one of our seminars happens to fall in the cities that have Fairmont hotels, we call in advance to make sure we have a room.

One time we did a show in San Francisco. Our travel agent called with the ticket information but said there were no rooms available at the Fairmont. The reason: IBM convention. "They took every room," said our travel agent.

The problem was easy to *recognize:* how to obtain a room at the filled-up Fairmont Hotel?

What to *Choose* was not as easy. Call the hotel? Try the 800 toll-free reservation number? Play on the sympathy of the assistant manager? All tried in the past and most often found wanting. He could use the RCA formula?

We called the hotel from Atlantic City. This was the conversation:

"Hi. I just left the hotel and was trying to remember the name of the secretary outside the manager's office . . ."

"Sylvia? Is that who you mean?"

"That's the one!" we said. "Thank you." And hung up.

We walked to the Boardwalk. Bought two one-pound boxes of salt water taffy. Made out the address label to "Sylvia, c/o The Fairmont Hotel, San Francisco." And attached a card, "From your secret pal . . ."

A week later we called (*ACT*).

"Hi, this is your secret pal . . ."

"Who ARE you?" she cried out, "Everyone here is wondering about . . ."

Wait. Had she eaten the taffy? Yes. Did she like it? Yes. Great. Now, was she curious?

Yes!

We told the story of no rooms at the Inn. Sylvia laughed and said, "Your reservation is on its way . . ."

And then there was the Sunday in February when the two of us took Murray's wife Ruth to Los Angeles International Airport to catch a flight back to Philadelphia. Since we had half an hour to spare we knew we had plenty of time to pick up tickets and send the baggage through.

When we arrived at the airport the lines were fifty-or-more people long. Ruth looked and said "I'll never get to the front of the line in time. I'll miss my flight."

It seems Chicago's O'Hare Field had been closed for two days. Because of snow storms. It had just opened. And everyone was heading back to the East. All this on a Sunday morning.

Wondering what to do next, Ruth said, "Let's use the RCA formula."

"Terrific," said Murray. "How will we do that?"

And Ray said he would leave the terminal, think of a solution, and return . . . and he was off.

Murray remained with Ruth. The challenge was thrown to him. He could not let his partner beat him. It was an easy problem to *Recognize*. How to get Ruth to the front of the line.

What solution to *Choose?* Go to the head of the line? Not without a physical battle. We need permission to do that, right? Right!

We approached the last person in line and said:

"What time is *your* flight? My wife has to catch a plane to Philadelphia in twenty-five minutes. Can she stand in front of you? She can! Thanks . . ."

Then to the person in front of that person: "Hi, my wife has to catch a flight to Philadelphia in twenty-four minutes. Can she stand in front of you? She can . . . ? Thanks . . ."

And all the way repeated time after time to the front of the line . . .

Once there, we put Ruth in position (with fifteen minutes to spare) and yelled to the rest of the line: "Hey, thanks, folks, you're great!"

As they waved back, in came Considine through the front door of the terminal, standing in the rear of the little electric cars that move through the terminals, and as the driver approached us, Ray cupped his hands and cried out:

"Where's the pregnant lady? The pregnant lady, please . . ."

Ruth, now getting her ticket, nearly fainted as the driver of the car helped her to a seat saying, "Here I am, lady. Everything will be all right now." And we all sat down as the little car went to a special elevator that took us to the loading platform.

One problem solved. With at *least* two solutions . . .

What were the alternatives? Do nothing? Let the plane leave without her?

What are the alternatives in your life? Do nothing? Let life pass you by till you wake up one morning and you're fifty and say, "Where did all the time go . . ."

That's what this chapter is all about.

The point to remember is to take care of yourself. Pay attention to yourself. If you feel yourself getting tense, nervous, angry, irritable, fumbling, starting to worry about . . . everything, pay attention to yourself. Those get-mad reactions are signals that tell you: Something is wrong! It's most noticeable when you're short-tempered with the phone operator, the driver, the barking dog . . . everyone!

Get the habit of being in control of yourself. First it's a conscious move. Then it becomes automatic. A professional athlete's conditioning is a conscious effort—throwing a ball, making a tackle, what-to-do-when. After a while it's automatic. The feeling of being-in-control.

And do not wait until you get started. Do it now! (Winners do.)

Is there a chance you will *not* succeed at whatever move you make? Yes. Who was a champion the *first* time out? Most people do *not* succeed all the time. Even the *great* Idea people. Or the great athletes. Even Ted Williams, baseball's greatest hitter of all time, was only *forty percent efficient*. And yet his .400 batting record is yet-to-be-equaled.

Executives are instructed time and again not to go for perfection. Just get fifty-one percent right and you'll survive. Anything better is frosting on the business cake.

And don't despair over making small decisions. When Val Holwerde, a very talented twenty-nine-year-old lady, was advertising director of one of the largest department store chains in California, someone asked how she could run an ad department, making decisions so fast for newspaper full-pages every day, direct mail choices, plus television and radio "at her age."

Valerie replied (very rapidly), "Too many people make a big deal over which border to put with an ad. My girls bring me in the layouts, I take a look at the options and point to one and say 'Run that.' The store's doing very well. But I suppose I'm wrong some of the time."

> Babe Ruth struck out 1,330 times.

At the risk of some repetition . . . decisions are a matter of practice. And there are notable executives who practice what we are preaching.

Whenever they are asked a question, they give an answer. Not just some dumb, snap-it-off-the-top response. The decisions are usually good decisions. Because . . . they are used to making decisions all the time. With every question asked.

You may find that once you get control of your life and do what you want to do in your life you will experience a few minor failures. So what? How important is the failure compared to staying where you are—doing what you do—unhappily?

Think of that phrase: *Compared to What?* when you feel unhappy about a sale that did not go through, a promotion that did not arrive, a carefully-planned presentation that fell apart in the middle. Can you handle these momentary set-backs?   Our friend Arthur Greene from Atlas Advertising was with a client who was driving his Lincoln Continental in a mad dash to the airport. They were twenty minutes late and, while going down the highway, another driver tried to cut in front. The client blasted his horn and yelled at the driver, got red in the face, and pounded his steering wheel in aggravation. Arthur watched the entire scene and calmly asked, "Gee . . . how do you handle *big* problems?"

Was it worth the aggravation, the worry, the straining of the heart muscles because a car tried to move ahead of him? *Compared to what?*

Art Holst is a referee in the National Football League. At the playoff between the Green Bay Packers and the Vikings he had one job to do: fire the gun to signal the end of the game.

At exactly the right moment, Art pointed the gun to the sky, pulled the trigger . . . and nothing happened!

He blew his whistle and yelled and soon everyone realized what was happening and a few members of the Vikings came over and made references to his family genealogy . . .

Holst was mortified. He was embarrassed as a professional in the field he loved. He felt he had failed.

Norm Schacter, the head referee, consoled Art, put his arm around his shoulder as they clomped down to the locker room, and said, "Arthur, look at it this way . . . there are 800 million Chinese who don't even know this darn game was played . . ."

Compared to . . . what?

Too many people look in envy at other people who are *doing* things, getting ahead, making money . . . becoming successful.

What keeps most people back is not making the simple decision to *try*. And if you try, you are bound to fail the first few times. The best authorities tell us if you do something the first time you are going to make a mistake. So what?

There are 800 million Chinese, a few million each German, Italian, French, and they don't even know you're alive.

If you have any problems, worries, unhappiness, Do Something about it!

If you don't like it here . . . get out! Really.

Do yourself and your company a favor. You are wasting your time (most important to you). You are burning up the company prospects and leads and probably spreading poor public relations with your private dealings with customers when your Attitude isn't right.

Consider yourself and the time you have left. Tom Wilson, president of his own advertising agency in San Diego, California, shocks some people with this example: "If you're fifty, you have 1000 Saturdays left." Figure it out . . . whatever age you are. How many good enjoyable Saturdays do you have?

Makes you want to begin to enjoy your time off, doesn't it? And you should be doing exactly what you want to do. So don't stay where it ain't FUN.

> Whatever you want . . . make it
> happen in *this* lifetime.

13 *Techniques and Tools of Change*

THE MEDICAL DOCTOR READS the latest journals to see what's happening with new techniques, new operations, new medicine so he can Change with the times. The architect faced with rising labor costs and innovative new materials sets aside time to investigate new construction concepts on the market so he can Change with the times. There are certain professional fields which demand their members return for schooling every few years to make sure the staff people maintain their level of knowledge and compete in the ever-changing world.

You are aware of Change, of course. One question is, Can you adapt to Change? And, more important, how can you make Change work for you?

For those who succeed in life, in business, and in the professions, nothing remains the same. Operating costs, housing, real estate escalate Up. Productivity, personal contribution, and profits go Down. Nothing remains at the same level for long, financially, emotionally, or even spiritually.

Those who succeed in sales, promotion, or profit-making do so because they have their antennae out, feeling and receiving the vibrations of everything that's happening in their own world, and in the neighboring worlds of commerce, culture, and humanity. They listen for the changing rhythms, understanding that what was "in tune" yesterday won't "make it" today. What sold yesteryear is dead inventory now.

The successful people are the ones with Adaptability. They are aware of and accepting of Change. They watch and ask, "How are those other people doing that?" They learn. Grow. They jump aboard the bandwagon before it leaves town and before the tune is a distant and fading memory.

The reason most of us are reluctant to Change is because we are comfortable with how-we-are and what-we-do. (Recall the folding of the arms exercise in the Introduction.) Change "feels funny." The psychologists tell us most human beings operate from a Plateau of Complacency. It's only when we are pushed to the brink that we finally change. And that's only because we have to. There is no turning back. Crisis forces Change.

To change you have to stop doing what you know how to do,—and start doing something you don't know how to do.

It's scary. Uncomfortable. Change is Pain. You have to break long-standing habits. And we are fearful of taking chances, because we might fail. Fear-of-failure is the excuse. Inwardly, of course. Outwardly, we have all sorts of persuasive reasons for staying as we were—as long as possible. Which is why so many of us are willing to remain in one job, with one company, a "career"and then X years later (beginning around age forty, the psychology folks tell us), we panic and wonder if Life hasn't passed us by. The mid-life crisis with its heart-freezing "loss of identity." Who am I, really? What am I doing here . . . all this time. Is *this* all there is?

Winners achieve success because they chance it—go for it. That isn't easy for us normal down-here, trying-hard why-take-a-chance types. But look at the few times you've tried (or had to try) something NEW. You probably started full-of-fear-of-failure, or at least "scared to death" in the first-day-of-school shivers. Or new-on-the-job jitters. Now all that is behind you. You are a Pro at what you do. Remember the beginnings? You should. That will be better reinforcement for your future Changes than any rah-rah encouragement you get. It's YOU knowing you can reach farther than you thought was possible. Looking back will give you the confidence for moving ahead. A few mistakes along the way? Inevitable. Slipping back is really part of going ahead. Ask any mountain climber. It's a step at a time. Upward. Outward.

Fight the fear-of-failure syndrome. Champions do. They reach out. In 1966 Bart Starr won every award offered a pro football player. He also failed ninety-eight times—if you count the number of interceptions that year. But Starr didn't think about interceptions. Only completions.

In 1962 Harman Killebrew of the Twins led the American League in home runs. He also set a new record for failure—he struck out more times than any other major league player in one season. But if he hadn't reached far enough . . . there would be no records broken.

William Steinkraus, veteran Olympic equestrian medal winner, was for years ahead of where "he should have been" (like George Blanda in football). When asked how he knew how far to reach, he replied, "Simple enough. I just go too far—and then pull back a little."

Aristotle once said life only has meaning if you are striving for a goal. Robert Browning wrote: "Ah, but a man's reach should exceed his grasp, or what's a heaven for?" The thrill of success knows no description.

Wade Cannon, Santa Barbara expert on Behaviorism says, "Achievers have very vocal and visible goals. They talk about their goals constantly. It's their way of reinforcing their purpose. They hang plaques, keep lists of what they want to do in front of them, ceaselessly check to see where they are and how they are doing.''

Most people tend to settle their lives for what *is* rather than what *can-be*.

Change is Pain.

The reasons for our reluctance to Change fall into three categories: Indexing, Dating, and Etc.

INDEXING: *Relating the problems of the present to the solutions of the past.*

To bolster business for the Easter season, we once proposed a giant fashion show in Atlantic City's Convention Hall. We said this would bring us regional and perhaps national TV coverage. The largest fasion show in the world! Admission would be nominal. Participating retailers would pay for the models and persuade nationally known designers to attend for the publicity.

We put the package together and approached the then-head of Atlantic City Public Relations. A quiet, likeable person who had been in the job for thirty years.

We suggested the promotion. He listened politely and said, "It won't work."

"Why not?" we asked.

"Well, we tried something like that in the 1940s and it bombed . . . "

No amount of argument, persuasion, listing of times-they-are-a-changin' could alter his position. His was the classic, "Don't confuse me with the facts, I've already made up my mind" position. He had heard the idea before. And tried it before. And saw it fail before. Ergo: It must fail again.

What had he done? Taken the concept and Indexed it against his file of the past, pulled out a matching mental computer card, observed where it failed, and therefore, it must predictably fail again. A food chain supermarket operator asks why should he sell plants in his food store? He tried that in 1971 and, across the whole country, only five million plants sold. Hardly worth the effort. . .

But. . .if he looked at plant sales in 1978, he would see the total had jumped to nearly *300 million*! All around him, food stores were opening plant departments and he stood there wondering how-could-that-be and they would certainly fail. After all, *his* Index cards showed there couldn't be that many sold.

Change is Pain.

We also tend to Index *people*. We draw huge generalities around groups and make statements like, "Women like these products," or, "Minorities feel this way," or, "Men are looking for . . . " Not true. Some women. Some minorities. Some men. But not all. And since each of these keeps on changing, so should we. The stereotypes of the past do not work in the present.

Jane Trahey, talented head of her own advertising agency, once chastized the business community for ignoring the tremendous amount of female talent available. Her point: despite the publicity of causes like ERA and movements like NOW, the woman is still a second-class citizen in American business. Trahey's statistics and facts bolster the fact that people will refuse to Change their life or attitude because of something we call *Dating.*

DATING *assumes that women all stay home and take care of children.*

Wrong. Nearly half the women in the U.S. work today. Six out of ten are married and mothers. Today's woman, in fact, has more money to spend (there are more U.S. families with *two* wage earners than one) and less time to spend it.

DATING *assumes everyone gets married and lives happily every after.*

Wrong: Three out of five marriages end up in divorce. In Illinois recently there were nearly five times as many divorces as marriages.

DATING *is saying if you want to buy sporting goods, there's only one shop to buy them: Abercrombie and Fitch.*

Wrong: They went out of business.*

DATING *is saying, "If I'm not here, just leave it with the girl."*

Wrong. What girl? Miss Smith? Ms. Smith? Mrs. Smith? Do they mean Jean Smith? The "girl" changed into a woman as soon as she left her teens—or before.

DATING *is saying people like to shop in great big stores with huge selections and wait on themselves.*

Wrong: Today's supermarket, for example, is designed as a series of

---

*Well, the original firm did. A new group of investors bought the name and opened a shop in Beverly Hills featuring Abercrombie-and-Fitch-style goods but with new merchandising techniques to attract the woman customer. The traditionalists might sniff in disdain. But if the firm succeeds, it will be simply because they knew how to Change.

little stores within one big store. In 1980, for the first time, the number of convenience stores (7-11, Stop 'n Go) outnumbered the number of super-markets; small, quick, but personal shopping. Today's customer is searching for rewarding experiences, pleasure. They want to be wel-comed, said hello to. They want their stores smaller, not larger; intimate, not gigantic. A major West Coast shopping developer has begun to take his two to three thousand square foot rental spaces and cut them in half. He discovered the stores are more successful and do MORE business in a smaller space.

The basic rule of selling applies to creating change: Find out what customers want and give it to them . . . with a solid Reason Why.

ETC.

ETC. means "and others of a kind; and the rest, and so on, and so forth. . ."

We lump groups together in our category of "Etc." The older ones want to know "what's happening to the younger generation." A phrase certainly used by members of the Greek Senate as they met in the Par-thenon.

We can no longer lump groups of people together. Younger or older generations. Blacks or White. Men or Women.

At one time all women/children/minorities/everyone . . . had "their place." No more. Today's equality is defined only in can-they-perform. It happened in the all-white game of baseball when Jackie Robinson was first ridiculed, then harrassed, then booed, then gradually accepted, then cheered, and then . . . elected to the Hall of Fame.

There were those who laughed when the five-year-old sat down to compose and play for the harpsichord. But when the composition was brought to the public, they cheered Wolfgang Amadeus Mozart.

And if mandatory retirement had been in effect for senior citizens at the time of George Bernard Shaw, Giuseppe Verdi, Benjamin Franklin, or Thomas Edison, the world would have been the loser.

Achievement becomes the great equalizer.

So, back to the basic question: How do we handle CHANGE? Ver-ree care-fully. And usually not too well.

How come?

Because people tend to bite off too Big a Chunk. They swear they are "going to turn their lives around." Doesn't happen. The problem is First Failure.

The diet, the drinking, the discipline lasts as long as the new endeavor succeeds. Then comes a set-back. Eat the dessert. Have a couple too many martinis. Miss the racquetball, jogging, or weightlifting regime once. *There* is the moment when most of the Change Challenges fall by the wayside.

A rhythm must be learned when you are changing habits. New patterns must replace the old. Once the beat is broken, you tend to fall back into the old rhythm. "What the hell . . . this is an occasion." Or, "Tonight is a special night." And, "After what I've been through on this week's trip, *no*body would expect me to be on the courts today."

To Change, you should bear in mind two things. First, recognize the trap of that initial downfall. And like they say to the thrown horseback rider—get right back up! Otherwise, the old rhythm takes over. Second, don't tackle Big Change. The secret is small change.

Here's how it works. Wayne Dyer describes it nicely in his book *Your Erroneous Zones*. He calls it the "I'm" circle. It's the tendency to keep going around the same "loop." To change, you have to step out of the loop, much like our example of "getting out of the box."

Picture a circle. At the one o'clock position is your "I'm" statement: I'm not good at varsity sports. At the four o'clock position: "I'd really like to play tennis." Then you loop around past the six o'clock mark to where the eight o'clock mark would be, and you say "I'd better not. I'd look terrible in front of these country club pros."

And here you come up to the eleven o'clock mark saying to yourself "Oh well, it doesn't matter . . . I've never been a varsity player." And inevitably, sooner or later, you will go through the same "loop" again. The next time you watch the players out there, you feel a little envy, a lot of wishing you "were out there." And the redetermination that "I'd really like to play tennis."

Unless you break out of that loop, step away, you go 'round and 'round and 'round. We all do it—in some way. "I always wanted to be a doctor." "I'd give my right arm to play the piano." (Heck of a handicap for starters there.) Or, patting the old tummy, "I've gotta lose some weight. I mean it this time."

Try small change.

Take one lesson. Lose two pounds. Practice against the wall or the backboard for a half hour. Walk, don't jog—for one block. A very small bite. Not a challenging chunk. And put down on paper the plan *and* the first failure. Count on it! Because you will fail in all probability. (If not, you don't need this lecture. You're the exception.)

One fellow made a nice parallel with business. He said, "In business, we have profit and loss statements, every month. What we forecast and plan doesn't always happen. So we start again another month and try again. No big deal. Happens all the time."

Why not the same one month program for your planned Change?

The other question at the beginning was how to make Change work *for you*.

That's a matter of small change, too. How does that work in the personal development sense? Getting better at things you are not terrific at? Feeling more confident with things unfamiliar? Overcoming weaknesses?

There are people all over the place who will teach you anything you'd like to learn—from Bantu to Beethoven, from Inner Tennis to Outer Mongolia. But first you have to enroll. Start the small change by stepping out and stepping up and asking, "May I see the instructor in—," or, "the book on—?"

For personal growth there is Transcendental Meditation, body massage, Rolfing, Silva Mind Control, T'ai Chi exercises, encounter groups, Arica, hot baths, astral projection, primal scream, *est,* and Feldenkreis with his 30,000 body exercises.

The stalwart can try Outward Bound, which offers high adventure and self-discovery through survival courses and mountain climbing, canoeing, whitewater rafting, wind-sailing, or backpacking in the desert or wilderness.

Your choice. Or you can decide to lose two pounds. Walk one block. Hit the backboard and "get started" in a small Change way, like most of us do.

All of these programs are fine. If . . . you remember *Changing* your goals, your habits, your attitudes on life is truly a personal down-deep-inside yourself project.

It is best done alone. Quietly.

William James, the great philosopher, wrote, "Man alone, of all the creatures of earth can change his own pattern. Man alone is the architect of his destiny. The greatest discovery of our generation is that human beings, by changing the inner attitudes of their minds, can change the austere aspects of their lives."

The only thing that's permanent . . . is Change.

14 *Direct Mail*

WHAT IS THE MOST effective way to advertise?

TV? Newspaper? Radio? Magazines?

No. The answer is direct mail.

Direct mail? All those envelopes, brochures, and printed paraphernalia in the mailbox—that no one reads?

Wrong. Somebody IS reading all those envelopes and brochures and printed paraphernalia in the mailbox. Because the people who sent that material to you know exactly what they're doing.* It's an industry spending billions of dollars to insure that their information winds up in your mailbox.

BILLIONS of dollars?

Right. Last year there was more money spent on direct mail advertising than ANY OTHER form of advertising . . . except newspapers and TV.

If so much money is spent on direct mail, how come more people/stores/businesses do not use more direct mail? Last year, less than two cents out of every dollar spent on advertising by individuals or business firms in the United States was spent on direct mail.

If direct mail is so effective, how come so low?

For business firms, the answer is relatively simple. The newspaper advertising man comes in every week and says, "Is your newspaper ad ready?" (And you usually answer, "Uh . . . give me another thirty minutes.") The radio advertising man comes in every week and asks, "Got the radio copy for this week ready?" But where is the direct mail representative who comes in and asks, "Is your direct mail copy ready?"

There is no direct mail representative.

No one. Except you.

Get this: Dollar for dollar you will have no stronger return on your advertising money than in direct mail *used properly*.

---

*Resulting in sales of more than $100 billion dollars or about 20 percent of ALL the merchandise sold in the U.S.

Here's why: It is far, far easier to bring more money from the customer you already have than trying to attract new customers. That does NOT mean you should *not* try to attract new customers. You should. And direct mail will work there too. But the customer you have already knows you, trusts you, believes in you . . . and spends with you. That customer is willing to come and spend even MORE money with you if you simply give him/her a reason to buy. An offer. An invitation. An incentive. A sale.

Insurance salesmen do this by making appointments for "annual reviews" with their clients to "make sure your coverage is what you want and need—now." Because you and your life are in a constant state of change. There are babies born, debts assumed, the threat of inflation. The sale has already been made the FIRST time. This second call, "review" time, is merely "adjusting" your insurance program to fit your present needs. Which means . . . an additional sale. How are these appointments triggered? Direct mail first, often followed by phone.

How does direct mail work? It can take two specific forms: A *general* mailing like the "occupant" throwaways from your local food store or the *specific* mailing with your prospect's personal name and address on the front. That last *personal* approach is the direct mail we are talking about in this chapter. And even though we believe direct mail is the most *effective* advertising medium, we admit it is also the most *expensive*. (Which is true in life, folks.)

Yes, you certainly can have your message seen, read, or heard in other advertising media for a much, much lower cost *per thousand* than in direct mail. But how do you measure results per dollar?

The trick then is to *select* your direct mail audience. For that is direct mail's greatest strength: The selection of your audience.

Use this picture: Newspaper/radio/TV advertising use a shotgun to hit the target. The pellets fly every-which-way hoping they will hit someone, somewhere. Per thousand.

Now picture direct mail advertising as a rifle shot, carefully aimed at a specific customer in a specific location for a specific reason. Pinpoint rifle marketing. It naturally follows the results are higher. And the sales. And the profits. Per dollar spent.

What kind of results can you expect from direct mail?

If the mailing is to a specific person at a specific address, it is not unusual to have a three to five percent return. Doesn't sound like much? Try it this way: If your newspaper has 100,000 circulation and your ad pulled this same five percent, that would mean 5,000 customers poured in to buy your advertised item. Spent money, not just read an ad. And when was the last time *that* happened?

Three to five percent is an average. There ARE direct mail campaigns to a specific list which consistently pull ten to fifteen percent. And there was one campaign we know that pulled eighty-seven percent. Yep, nearly nine out of ten people who received that superb mailer responded. Why?

The campaign was prepared by Dorland and Sweeney Advertising in Philadelphia. Account Executive Rita Sweeney decided to test how direct mail would work for their client, Atlantic National Bank in Atlantic City. They sent out 10,000 gift certificates in bank statements offering a FREE order of McDonald's french fries. And redeemed 8,700! (McDonald's and a bank?)

The results were so staggering, the agency decided to promote the bank's new suburban branch opening with the advertising-dollar-emphasis on direct mail . . . and McDonald's. The pre-opening night-before party brought all the area politicians and society folk to a *black tie champagne* party catered by . . . McDonald's. (Invitation: By direct mail.)

The next day's opening attracted thousands, starred Ronald McDonald, and if you lived in the area you knew about it because all the homes near the new bank branch received invitations . . . through the mail. Opening day's business: More than a quarter million dollars in new deposits. (And lots of free french fries.)

Your direct mail customer is someone who knows you and the service you sell. This customer is *very special.* Paul Fulton, the retail advertising manager of the Chicago *Tribune* once said the success of the small business includes such strong points as friendliness, reliability, service, and, most important, the amount of personal attention lavished on the customer. Your direct mailer serves ALL these guidelines. It gives the customer a sense of "being in" on something before the rest of the world knows about it.

And it IS personal.

Imagine going out on a date with a charming partner. If you wrote him/her a note the next day saying what a great time you had and how much you enjoyed the evening, your partner would feel it was a marvelous compliment and would enjoy reading your letter.

But what if you took that letter and ran it as an ad in the newspaper? Would your date be embarrassed, mad, bewildered, confused? Yes. Or what if you had an announcer read it on the radio? Or the TV? Too public. Same reaction from your companion on the date.

But the letter is fine. Appreciated, welcomed, looked-forward-to being read.

The reason: The letter is private. Between two people. With a far greater sense of belief in the reading than in any other "public" advertising.

Your direct mail message is more accurately "you" than any other advertising medium. It arrives in its own package and is not in competition or conflict with another ad or message as it would be in other media.

Above all, your direct mail piece reflects you more accurately because it does not have to be translated through a whole battery of interference ranging from ad salesmen to printers to typesetters to layout men to radio announcers who certainly do not have YOUR voice.

Direct mail reflects You and your style more accurately than other media because you can "talk" your copy the way you would talk in person. Albert Lasker, the advertising genius called mail Salesmanship in Print. You can use dots . . . dashes—, broken paragraphs . . . just the way you would in a personal conversation. Direct mail is Me-to-You. Not a framed ad with a standard layout. Or a radio commercial delivered by some "big voice" who isn't You. It's a conversation.

Here's what we mean: What would happen if your business did not advertise in the newspaper next week? Or on the radio? How many customers would call up and say, "How come you didn't run a newspaper ad this week?" Or, "How come I didn't hear you on the radio this week?"

Answer: Very few, if any.

But send a direct mail piece to customers and tell them about a special date or a special value or a special offer and forget to send it to a few others and your phone will jump off the hook!

Customers become irate if they think you have forgotten them. You can carefully explain you *did* send your mailing piece to them. That the mailman might be slow. Rain. Sleet. Why should you NOT want them to come and buy from you? Often your excuses have been repeated and you have to send another mailer to them immediately. But you never, never have this kind of reaction from neglecting to advertise in any other media.

Direct mail is very, very personal.

You can make offers to your direct mail customers you would be fearful to run in print. One store sent out five dollar gift certificates to their direct mail list in honor of the store's anniversary. They simply said they wanted to thank their regular customers for shopping with them, so they enclosed a five dollar gift certificate to use for . . . anything. No minimum purchase required. They mailed out 3,000 certificates. And had 800 responses!

A twenty-five percent return! And *every single customer* spent *more* than the five dollars.

Would the same store run a gift certificate with no strings attached in the local newspaper? We asked the promotion people, who just shivered and said, "No way!"

Joe Girard devotes a whole chapter of his book *How to Sell Anything to Anybody* to direct mail. He knows the mail is "his" voice talking to "his" customers. He dismisses the canned, pre-printed mailers put out by companies, even his own, for salesmen to use because he feels that makes him one of the crowd. Joe Girard wants to be Joe Girard. Himself. Separate and apart. And direct mail does that for him.

He admits some salesmen send out Christmas cards which is nice—but which is only once a year. He sends a mailing piece to his customers every month! Each one different in color, shape and size. With no identification on the outside. It arouses curiosity and encourages readership. And makes friends and customers for Joe Girard.

His message is very simple. "Happy New Year—I like you" or "Happy Valentine's Day—I like you" or "Happy St. Patrick's Day—I like you." (See "Four-mula for Success.")

Are there rules to follow to insure success in direct mail?

Well, there is a basic formula. And it works with all advertising you will do. Of any kind. But most especially with direct mail. Use this check list the next time you prepare an ad and make sure your ad has all these ingredients. It's an easy formula to remember because it is an AIDA to you in your advertising and promotion. It works like this:

A—Attention: If you send out a mailer and it arrives, fine. Now, what will make your customer open or *read* what you sent? There must be an attention-getter of some kind. It can be the shape of the envelope. A striking color. Or the pure white "business" serious mail. A phrase on the outside of the envelope that promises a benefit—if they look inside.

I—Interest: After your prospect reads the "headline" of your mailer, what will keep them reading? Your message must contain facts that INTEREST your reader. From savings (a sale) to the description of a product that will save your customer money, time, or effort.

Whatever the benefit, it must be up front. If not in the headline, then in the first sentence. So they will keep on reading.

Most of all, your message must be interesting to read.

Most people have one vocabulary for speaking and another for writing. The speaking vocabulary is natural, easy, believable. The writing vocabulary is stifled, full of long paragraphs. Short paragraphs are easier to read (like the ones on the page). Short sentences are even easier to read. Like this. Or this. Short. Crisp. Effective.

Make your writing, like your selling, enthusiastic. Walter Chrysler once said he would pay more for enthusiasm than any other product. Because he knew enthusiasm sells merchandise.

D—Desire: Your mailing piece should create a desire to buy. It must overcome objections. Make your writing honest. It is too easy to exaggerate, but very unnecessary. The basic facts may seem ho-hum to you, but not to your reader. Remember the advice of Vrest Orton of the Vermont Country Store about whatever you write: "Make sure the story isn't better than the store."

If it is a sale, be sure they cannot say, "Well, it costs too much."

If it is a new item, overcome their reluctance, say why it's worthwhile to make the trip. Offer "free delivery." Extras.

If it is a brand-new design and you are the first store to have it, say so.

Or a wanted product and you are the first salesman to carry it say so.

A—Action: Now they have received and read your mailer. They are ready to buy. Give them a reason to act quickly, a deadline, an immediate advantage for responding—or they will miss this opportunity.

One way: A limited time. One day. One week. Short enough to be effective. Realistic enough to be believeable.

Another way: A coupon for a specific item. A savings on a *wanted* item. More than 80 *billion* coupons were redeemed by American housewives last year. (When a survey was taken on what the American housewife wanted more in their shopping, the majority answered, "More coupons.")

Your mailer can be as simple as a card, an envelope with a letter and a reply form, or as complicated as a pop-up mailer with a three-dimensional effect which is very dramatic . . . and expensive. And impressive.*

Sometimes the expensive and impressive work well. Like this story:

The very large Ogilvy-Mather advertising agency had a client, Cessna Aircraft. Cessna had an executive jet selling for one million dollars each. The agency wanted to reach the prime market, the decision makers. They selected 800 from the list of *Fortune* magazine's top companies.

Now, how could they attract the attention of these busy men? Why, direct mail of course. But how to *guarantee* readership.

Their answer: homing pigeons (nice flying image) and they had 800 pigeons delivered in cages to the 800 prospects.

There was a note attached. The receiver of the pigeon had a choice. "If you want more information, let loose this homing bird who will bring your request flying to us and we will have our key man come to see you about the new Cessna executive jet" or "If you want the cage and bird picked up, call us and we will have a messenger come and take the bird away."

Good. Except the agency experts overlooked one major point. Most New York City corporate headquarters are totally air-conditioned and there is no way to open the windows!

What happened?

1. Some sixty-three of the executive pigeon recipients boiled over, shouted and cursed through their assistant and the telephone saying, "Come get this damn pigeon out of here!"
2. One way or another, released from rooftops, stairwells, or streets, 114 pigeons flew swiftly back to the Ogilvy aviary with the message, "Call me." Good.
3. Final response for the $15,000 cost of pigeons, packing, and presenting to prime prospects: four jets sold. At one million dollars each!

*Write for samples of these pop-ups to Chris Crowell, Structural Graphics, PO Box 666, Essex, Connecticut 06426.

(There does remain one question: If only 177 pigeons were released or returned, what happened to the remaining 623?)

Now, let's go back to what makes people *read* what you write.

Bill Jayme, direct mail writer extraordinaire, did a circulation package for "Behavioral Sciences," the newsletter for *Psychology Today* magazine. He chose a plain brown kraft envelope and created a headline for the envelope:

WARNING: The enclosed materials may be construed as being of an arousing nature.

Some eighteen percent of those envelopes returned unopened to the magazine with enraged written comments—take me off your list!—how dare you?—etc. Bill Jayme smiles as he recalls the story and says, "Now tell me about people not reading the copy on the outside of an envelope."

And those readers who dared open the plain brown wrapper?

So! You opened it anyway, you scallywag, you,—despite the warning on the envelope. Three cheers for you!

And the Jayme hook-'em-right-in-by-their-interest copy said:

If you are engaged in studying the behavioral sciences, an unfettered mind like yours is practically mandatory, a mind that is open, not locked, receptive to new ideas, techniques and possibilities.

A mind that enjoys finding out what others in the field are up to and how their experiences back up against yours. How their findings further your own work.

That's why our envelope says "arousing". . .(And the copy went on to sell the newsletter service.) Wow.

On envelope copy, Jayme's experience says it saves a lot of time "to indicate" the universe they are entering—photography, food, fishing. "You are doing the groundwork, the loosening up," he explains, "as they pick up and read the envelope copy. Isn't this the same principle the salesman uses when he begins a sales call in person—laying out the 'universe,' the general parameters of what he/she *will be* talking about? That's the task of the outer envelope copy."

Another of Bill's classic techniques is the use of "pull-along" words front and back on the envelope which draw the reader from here. . .around to there. . .the back. . .and right on inside.

Example. In a circulation package for a gourmet magazine, he instructed the reader to "turn the envelope over for the recipe on the back." Reader turns over, and there, the recipe begins. *Not* the ingredients, but the instructions. . .which tail off, for lack of space, and continue *inside* the envelope.

The fun part is that as the reader opens the letter inside, the first words say, "And the recipe continuing from the cover. . ." The headline is a *continuation* of the envelope copy! "But," cautions the wizard of words, "don't just presume the reader will somehow carry magically in his or her mind what the final copy was on the envelope. No. You have to orient people, and do that at every step."

In one presentation in Dallas, Jayme included percentages of time he spent in creating the elements of a direct mail package. Here they are (as remembered): fifty percent on the letter and letter copy. Thirty percent on the envelope. (Jolting, but why not when your first challenge is to *get your mail opened?*) And, are you ready—20 percent on the order form. "Well, that *is* the close," murmurs Jayme knowingly, "if you were selling in person, you'd certainly pay attention to how you closed. It's the same thing in the mailing package." And he went on to stress the order card's simplicity, clarity, easy-to-understand instructions, is there space enough for the information you are requesting, and, finally, "checking with someone else to see if you have avoided that awful sin of assumption."

"How many good profitable orders are lost in the presumption, 'Oh, well, everyone knows that'? Too many to think about and terrible to contemplate."

Good advice for the the direct mailer.

To whom do you send your direct mail pieces now that you know how to make them work?

It begins with your own list. That is the most effective. They know you. Can you buy other lists? Sure, you can even rent them. And most major cities in the U.S. have listings for list brokers.*

Most will try to match your product against the "right" list or lists. And most should suggest you "test" a small amount, 20 percent of any list, to see if it works for you—instead of going for broke—mailing the entirety the first time out.

The important point: You are always working toward building your *own* list. Starting with the names who have bought from you previously and then adding to that list either by renting lists, testing others, or buying small space ads in magazines and, everyone who responds becomes part of your list.

QUESTION: Why this importance on having your own customer base?

ANSWER: The more times a customer buys from you, the more "locked in" they become for your product or service and the more friends they will tell.

---

*Or contact the parent organization of all direct mail activity: Direct Mail/Marketing Association, 6 East 43rd Street, New York, New York 10017. They will give you names of list brokers and other material on how direct mail works.

While only one out of three customers repeat purchases with you at the end of the second year, the percentage jumps to sixty percent by the end of the third year. And increases to where, if a customer has bought consistently from you for ten years, you have as steady customers, eight out of ten!

When do you send your mailing piece to these customers?

There ARE months that are better than others. The top months in order of best pull for direct mail are: January, February, October, July, August, November, December/September. The worst months are June, March, April, and May. "They say."

IF YOU live in Alaska, Washington, D.C., Hawaii, or California, your response will be the best in the nation. (The worst: Alabama, Massachusetts, Mississippi, and Iowa.)

And whatever you mail, don't forget to GUARANTEE what you sell. Take a look at all those mail order catalogues you receive in the mail. One item is present in every one: THE GUARANTEE.

In direct mail, the right proposition and the right terms of payment are only two thirds of the reason to buy—a clear, strong GUARANTEE completes the equation.

In 1861, the Austrian foreign minister, Johann Bernhard Graf Von Rechberg was asked to comment upon papers recently drawn with guarantees concerning the recognition of Italy. His answer: "Guarantees are not worth the paper they are written on." (Sounds like Sam Goldwyn.)

The opposite should be true about today's guarantees in newspapers, magazines and . . . direct mail. Make them real!

Guarantees have been around for years, but it was *Good Housekeeping* magazine nearly a half a century ago that made the world-famous claim with its "Satisfaction Guaranteed or replacement of merchandise." Through the years, more and more retailers (often reluctantly) feared guarantees with their products. The reasons were usually: 1. The new state and federal consumer protection laws. 2. The "I offer more than he does" ads of the competition (and so if General Motors guarantees THEIR cars for 12,000 miles, American Motors guarantees their cars for 24,000 miles!) Upsmanship.

Or Downsmanship. . .like the ads for a carpet company in giant seventy-two-point type saying, "Now we guarantee our carpet and put it in writing." The writing was in tiny four-point type (smaller than classified printing) with more than 500 words which said the guarantee did not apply to wear caused by "neglect, willful abuse, improper cleaning, sewer damage, chemicals, pets, rodents, insects, fire, grease, soil crushing, sunlight fading pile, snagging, or defective floors."

Well, you could put a stanchion and velvet rope around the edges of the carpet and let people *look* at it!

Keep your guarantees simple.

Says L.L. Bean, "We will replace it—or refund your money—as you wish."

Spencer Gifts says it nice and simple: "Satisfaction guaranteed or your money refunded." Six words. But what else is there left to say?

There are ten basic reasons WHY PEOPLE BUY. We have listed them here and given you ideas of headlines that might tie in with each of them.

1. GRATIFY CURIOSITY: *How I Made a Million Dollars in Real Estate in My Spare Time.* One thin volume for only $9.95. How did he do it? Can *I* do it? You mean if I buy this book I'll really find out? Wow. Gee. Where's my check book?

Kodak's Klassic from 1890, "You push the button, we do the rest."*

2. COMFORT AND HEALTH: "These shoes are as comfortable as your slippers." The vitamin craze. Warm, fur-lined coats in the winter. Warm, fur-lined gloves in the winter. The medicine man hawking the bottle of elixir that "will cure anything." Rinso's "who else wants a whiter wash—with no hard work?"* and Phoenix Mutual's, "To men who want to quit work someday."*

3. BE POPULAR: "Learn these dance steps and be the life of the party." "They laughed when I sat down at the piano. But when I started to play. . ."* Dale Carnegie's, *How To Win Friends and Influence People,"* Sherwin Cody's "Do You Make These Mistakes in English,"* Listerine's, "Often a bridesmaid, never a bride."*

4. ENJOYMENT: "Sit back and watch (name of team) play in your living room this Monday evening." "Here's a game the whole family can enjoy." Canada Dry's, "Down from Canada came tales of a wonderful beverage."* Coca-Cola's, "The Pause That Refreshes."* Marlboro's, "You get a lot to like. . ."*

5. PRAISE: "Every time a teacher asks a question, the hand raised will be yours because you have this book in your home." Alexander Hamilton Institute's, "The glory of the upward path."* *Ladies Home Journal,* "Never underestimate the power of a woman."*

6. IN STYLE: "They showed these dresses at the show in Paris last month. You can have them today for a fraction of the cost." "Are you still wearing broad lapel suits and wide ties?" The *Book of Etiquette's,* "Again she orders—a chicken salad, please."* (Because she didn't know how to order anything else.)

7. ATTRACT THE OPPOSITE SEX: The Hai Karate cologne commercials showing a man fighting off women because of the scent of his cologne. The ultra-modern fiberglass automobile. The new hairdo. The smaller than possible bikini. Woodbury soaps, "The skin you love to touch."*

---

*The headlines with the asterisk were REALLY used. And are from a collection called the *100 Greatest Advertisements* by Julian Lewis Watkins.

8. HAVE BEAUTIFUL POSSESSIONS: The gold earrings, bracelets, lockets, rings. The antique furniture. The leather-bound books. Steinway's, "Instrument of immortals."*

9. TO BE AN INDIVIDUAL: "There are only twelve of these made this year . . ." "Did you see Tom lately? He looks great!" Cadillac's, "Penalty of Leadership."* (See Chapter 16.)

10. IMITATE OTHERS: All teenagers insist they are nonconformists . . . as they all walk around in their straight Levi's, Lacoste shirts, and Hush Puppies?

If these were the leaders by proven success in the general world of advertising, what about the narrower world of direct mail and direct marketing? How do we find what works in this personal, one-to-one medium?

The Seven Rules of Success in Direct Mail.

Every industry has a leader. One to whom others point as an example of that which is best.

In direct mail, the late Ed Mayer was the unquestioned dean. His Seven Rules for Success in Direct Mail are listed in every course on the subject and form the basis for most success stories in this advertising field. Here they are:

1. What is the objective? What are you trying to sell? The more specific you are, the more effective your return.

2. Address correctly—to the right list. Sending mailers to anyone at random is self-defeating. The more specific the list, the greater the result. If you want to promote your nursery school, you don't send the literature to senior citizens. Conversely, if your book is *How to Enjoy Retirement,* you don't send it to newlyweds.

If your mailing is on a regular basis, have your list "cleaned" with correct addresses every few months. A simple "address correction requested" on the bottom of your mailer will bring it back to you if the address has changed.

3. Tell readers the benefits. Use the word "you" in your copy. Tell the reader in the headline and/or first paragraph the most important benefit they will receive. Back this up with proofs, endorsement, and what happens if they don't act . . . now!

4. Make the layout and copy fit. Selling high-priced merchandise should have a different "look" than selling low-priced items. The Cadillac brochure looks entirely different than the insert from the nearby drug chain in your daily paper. Your mailer should "look" like the item it is selling.

5. Make it easy for the customer to act. Each mailer should call for an action of some kind: inquiry, purchase, visit to your store. Or your visit to them. One way: Set a deadline.

6. Repeat your story. Yes, you told your story in the headline. Yes, you repeated it in the first paragraph. Now, once again, at the end, with feeling . . .

7. Research your direct mail. What were the results of your last mailer? The last three? What pulls best?* Keep accurate records. Test one technique, then another. Your percentage of return will increase as you find out what works best . . . for you.

Earlier you read about Reese Palley's inexpensive nickel direct mailer that brought aboard 700 people to fill two 747s for a four-day Paris trip. Fine. The cost of that jazzy journey per person was $695.

A just-as-dramatic trip was put together, also by direct mail. The cost for this trip: $10,000.

It all began as a simple fund-raiser for the Admiral Byrd Polar Center in Boston. The obvious solution: Fly a planeload of people around the world on a modern-day Byrd expedition. They worked out a fascinating agenda that included flying over the North and South Poles, a stopover on every continent, fishing, hunting, welcoming parties, and receptions with heads of state. The whole trip would take about a month. And the cost would be $10,000. Would anyone buy it?

The budget for the direct mail campaign was (ready?) . . . $5,000.

Hank Burnett, Jr., an independent and direct mail writer, (formerly Dickie-Raymond and then Benson, Stagg and Associates), one of the country's leading creative direct mail experts, asked for the job. It was the challenge that excited him.

He wanted the letter to be signed by Charles Lindbergh or Dwight Eisenhower. Turned down. The editor of the Harvard Business Review and founder of the center to house Admiral Byrd's papers insisted he would be the signee.

Burnett worte a *seven-page letter* explaining the trip in intimate detail plus the privileges and benefits that would be received by each expedition member.

The list was Fortune 500, Young Presidents Organization, jet aircraft owners, and owners of boats over forty feet. Total mailing: 13,600. Total cost: $5,291.18.

Their goal: sixty people at the $10,000 figure.

The response: Nearly seven hundred people responded and seventy sent deposits of $2,500 each. Out of the seventy were selected the final sixty.

From a seven-page letter produced on plain paper with no brochure, no circular, no illustrations, no order form, no reply envelope.

---

*One of the great things about direct mail is . . . if you have TWO good headlines, or TWO offers, you can try both. Mark one A and one B on the response device and keep score by order. Let the response be the judge.

Burnett knew that as he described what would happen to the journeyer in each country, their minds would conjure up pictures to match his words unattainable in any four-color chrome-coated pamphlet. Much like the magic mystery of radio was so much greater than TV where what-you-see-is-what-you-get.

The mystery of intrigue and desire that evolved from the imagination of the mind was what Burnett sold in this most fascinating and effective medium called Direct Mail.*

FICTION AND FACTS ABOUT DIRECT MAIL ADVERTISING

Fiction: "Nobody reads direct mail. They throw it away unopened."
Fact: Eight out of ten direct mail pieces are opened and at least looked at. Direct mail is the *best read* advertising medium.
Fiction: "Most direct mail is just thrown in the mailbox and addressed to an anonymous "occupant.""
*Fact:*Nine out of ten direct mailers are addressed to a *specific* household member.
Fiction: "Most people don't want to receive direct mail ads."
Fact: About seventy-two percent *like* receiving mail.
Fiction: "Most direct mail is coupons that I just throw away."
Fact: If you add up the coupons AND post cards AND small packages, the total of ALL these is about . . . three percent.
Fiction: "Why do we have to subsidise this advertising for the post office?"
Fact: Third class mail is the ONLY class of mail to pay for itself. One out of four postal workers depends on direct mail for his livelihood.
Fiction: "Our mailbox is clogged every week with direct mail ads."
Fact: The national average is three pieces a week.
Fiction: "If most people had the chance, they'd take their names *off* mailing lists."
Fact: The Direct Mail Marketing Association runs periodic ads in national publications offering to take your name off the mailing lists of their 1,700 member companies. Or—if you prefer—to put your name ON lists. So far, those wanting to receive MORE mail outnumber those wanting to receive less.
Fiction: "It's awfully risky to buy from the mail."

*Many people asked what made the Admiral Byrd package work. The best reply was "the thought of immortality." The hidden psychological benefit. The other question was what was the key criterion of the list selection (a big factor in the success of the flight) and the answer was "not only the money . . . but who would have the time to take that much time off." Interesting.

Fact: Mail order volume depends on repeat business. They must have satisfied customers to stay alive. (Notice how direct mailers stress their Guarantee?) And the federal Government has very strict regulations on offers that use the U.S. mails.

DIRECT MAIL GLOSSARY OF TERMS

Direct Mail: Solicitations which go through the U.S. Post Office system, whether in envelopes, as self-mailers, cello-wrap (see-through covers), cartons, or as packages.

Mail Order: Those portions of direct mail which ask for "money back" in cash, check, bank card, or charge, or "bill me later" terms. Mainly the merchandise, catalogue, clothing, or gift categories.

Direct Marketing: *All* forms of solicitation in print, including newspaper, catalogues with order cards, magazines, publications with tear-outs or inserts, "free standing stuffers," and the direct mail medium itself.

Lists: Those compiled by professional list organizations for rental or sale. Lists can be purchased as peel-off labels, computer-generated machine applied labels, or as magnetic tape assembled lists which are printed out by professional mailing houses.

A second type of list source is Response Lists. These are subscribers, donors, buyers, people who have in fact *responded to* offers, solicitations. These are called "known buyers."

Merge/Purge: The process of eliminating duplications between lists. The lists are "run against each other" (usually on high speed magnetic tapes) and a *net name* list is the result of the merging and purging. Cost is an important factor in the *economy* of merge/purge. The question is the cost of "dupe elimination" processing versus estimated savings of postage for mailing to duplicates and the cost of printing production for the packages or mailers necessary to cover the unduplicated (larger) list. The decision to merge/purge a list is logistics (can the lists be assembled in time to purge and still meet a mailing date?) . . . and economy (does the processing cost of merging/purging save enough money in duplicated postage and production costs—paper, envelopes, addressing—to warrant purging?)

Note: Most companies currently do eliminate their own buyers' or customers' names from "outside" (rented) lists when mailing.

Bulk Rate: At present bulk rate is $84 per 1000 pieces regardless of quantity—unless you select presorting to carrier routes at $69 per 1000, but there are complex restrictions on presorting. In order to qualify for bulk rate, you must mail a minimum of 200 pieces; each piece must be identical; they must be zip coded. You must use a bulk permit number (thirty dollar one-time charge) and pay a forty dollar annual fee (January to January, no pro-rates) in order to get the lower bulk rate.

Demographics: Those characteristics of lists—income, sex, telephone ownership, auto ownership, home value, length of residence—the make up of the list.

DMMA: The national headquarters for direct marketing industry. It provides to members and inquirers information, sources, generalized recommendations for all facets of mail, postal regulations, case histories, and performs as a lobby for the mailing industry. The address is: 6 East 43 Street, New York, NY 10017; telephone: (212) 689-4977.

Preference Service: The recent service offered by the DMMA to either have your names removed from or added to mailing lists. The surprising result of nationwide newspaper offers to this effect was more people wanted to be *added to* than removed from mailing lists! Maybe this challenges the myth that nobody reads mail.

Testing: The secret of success in mail. You can test price, copy, offer, charge/no charge, premium/no premium, two for one, and a number of variables. The trick is not to test too many elements of your package at once. (Price versus copy versus offer versus lists all in same test may give you not answers, but total confusion.) Structure your tests simply to discover what you want to know specifically. Some of the terms:

Nth Name: Taking a list and testing a part of it by choosing every 2nd name, every 5th name, every 505th name. "Nth Name" is the term for that technique of choosing a number that fits your budget and purposes.

Cross Section: Simply choosing a segment of the list you or your list broker or mailer feel represents an ideal part of the total list which mailed will give you an accurate reaction to what the rest of the list will give.

Splits: Supposing two good approaches for your mailing package . . . use an "A" or a "B" printed on every other reply device to determine which approach "pulls" the best. Mail every other name. One "A"; one "B"; "A"/"B" right down the list. Literally splitting the list. Record the results to judge the winner of the two approaches. Another split is Urban versus Rural—mainly for product testing.

Pilot: (or initial drop), the term used to indicate the first portion of the testing.

Roll Out: The term for the larger, later mailing after the test has proved that it is viable and probably profitable to proceed. Note: Most test mailings are NOT expected to make money, or in many cases even return the investment. The purpose of the initial test is to determine response, and the degree of response.

Roll outs need not be full mailing to the remainder of the list beyond the initial test segment. Lists can be rolled out in parts, as a method of testing further the validity of the list, offer, mailing. It's like stepping one foot at a time across thin ice. Very carefully is the byword.

Segmenting a List: Selecting out "slices" of the list—by sex, by income, by telephone ownership, donors who gave more than five dollars, customers who bought more than twenty-five dollars worth, people who bought within one year, etc.

Nixies: Mail that could not be delivered. In dealing with list brokers it is wise to get a written statement or policy of the "nixie factor" and have an understanding that you will be rebated (for postage at least) on any mail in excess of their stated Nixie Rate.

Update: The time when the list was last brought up-to-date by contacting the list through one of several methods—address correction, elimination of past customers, recompilation of the list (the new telephone directories put on mag tape and run against the former directory list). Update *facts* are very important to the success of your mailings.

Negative Option: The agreement that "unless notified by you, we will ship." Usually books and publicaitons. Under servere scrutiny of consumer fraud agencies. Check your FTC rules if you plan to use negative options.

Premium Offer: The temptation game of offering "something for nothing." If you do (or try) *this,* we will give you *that* (free or for ten days inspection). Testing of premium versus non-premium must include careful surveying of the "stick rate": How many of the premium sales actually became customers? What was the cost of sale with and without premium? Were non-premium customers gotten at a lower rate than premium customers?

Business vs. Consumer Mail: Obvious difference is that business or industrial mail is directed only to business firms and with products and services most pertinent to that market. The techniques are quite different from consumer mail, and certain list brokers specialize in industrial lists, among them National Business Lists, 162 North Franklin Street, Chicago, Illinois 60606; Dun and Bradstreet (major cities).

Sic: A term for Standard Industrial Classification, a governmental assignment of special codes for every type of industry from Salmon Fishing to Solar Energy companies. With the SIC coding the industrial list companies can provide all or part of any industry by classification and description for the business mailer.

Actives/Expires: The difference between current buyers and those who were buyers or customers. Expires of one company (magazine, for example, or newspaper like *Wall Street Journal*) may work very well for another publication, thus giving Value to expires for testing and mailing.

"Actives" also include "Hot Line" buyers, who are those who have bought in the very recent past and are a premium list for remailing or for testing by other companies. Many of these lists are for sale or rent. Other companies will exchange lists but not sell their lists. Some few refuse to expose their lists to anyone, but the income from list rental is such a large part of the profit for a direct marketing firm (like Carte Blanche, for example), that almost any list is available.

Multiple buyers are also a premium type of responsive prospect for mailing.

Cleaning the List: A term for getting rid of the deadwood, updating the list, addresses, eliminating those who are long past customers, firms or people who no longer exist. There is much money wasted on poor buying of lists (not checking carefully on the updating of that list) and in "not wanting to spend the money to clean the list. Mistake. Look at the absolutely outdated mailings you receive. Total waste of money, postage, paper, and effort. Lists should be cleaned regularly. It pays.

Keys and Match Codes: Terms used to tell you which lists worked, which offers pulled, which segments reacted to your mailings. Almost in every case the keys and codes are printed on the response devices, the order cards, the inquiry piece, etc.

Co-ops: Joint mailings with one company or firm putting together the mailing and then enlisting other mailers (or other departments within a large company or other members of a shopping mall) to "go in with" the mailing and share the costs. Coupons are the most popular enclosures for co-ops with special offers featured on the redemption coupons—which is how the mailers each gauge the response of their offers.

Decoys: Also called "spikes" or "salts." These are names which are invented by the mailer or the mailing list broker which are not able to be perceived by another user of the list. The decoys prevent illegal or multiple use of a reputable list since the mailer or broker receives many copies of everything mailed to that list—at many different addresses. The DMMA and other major mailers serve each other as "drops" or decoys to protect the industry from mis-use of lists.

SIXTY TIPS ON USING DIRECT MAIL

1. *Confidential:* Mark your mailer "confidential" . . . Give it a document "look." Close it with a Dennison seal . . . Don't put a return address.
2. *The "Knight" Sale:* Open your store when everyone else is closed . . . Call it a "Knight" sale . . . Cover has a picture of a knight. Open his "visor" and it says, "We're having a Knight Sale."
3. *Magazine Take-Offs:* Harvard's *Lampoon* received national coverage with their humorous copies of national magazines . . . Copy *Time* or *Newsweek*. Or a trade journal that is well-known in your business . . . Make it different enough so they don't feel you're infringing on their copyrighted "look" but recognizable enough to pique your reader's interest.
4. *Free Money:* Ask your bank where you can buy those little envelopes they give away at Christmas time that you open and it shows the face on the money . . . Make your mailer to fit this envelope and have the face resemble a president on a familiar bill. Well, not too familiar or the Secret Service will be your first customer . . . Great attention-grabber. Especially if you add the magic words "Free Money" on the front of the envelope.
5. *Checks:* Have the front of your mailer look exactly like a check from a local bank . . . Same type faces, only your store's name (The First Gordon's Savings Bank) . . . The check is made out on its face to your customer's name and address . . . And is redeemable as soon as she comes to the store.
6. *Dividends:* Similar to the above but takes the form of "coupons" like the interest from stock certificates.
7. *Confederate Money:* Still a great draw . . . Send for complete catalogue to Historical Documents, 8 North Preston Street, Philadelphia, Pennsylvania 19104 . . .
8. *Savings Book:* Resembles the old-fashioned savings book you used to bring to your local savings and loan. Inside the book is a list of what's-on-sale. Plus a special "dividend" check to start you off.
9. *Credits On Charge Accounts:* Always works . . . Take the inactive charges for the past year and send them a credit on their inactive account towards their next purchase . . . Which must be used on-or-before . . .
10. *Flower Seeds:* Part of the current back-to-basics feeling across the country . . . Everyone likes flower seeds, even if all you have is a small flower box outside your window . . . To find out ideas and costs write W. Atlee Burpee Company, Huntington Park Avenue, Philadelphia, Pennsylvania 15202.

11. *Coupons:* What can we say that you haven't seen in your mail? . . . But they still draw (see your local weekly newspaper supplement) . . . They work as a "cents-off" concept . . . They work as "a credit towards" . . . They work as limit: one to a customer . . . But, most important, they work.

12. *Weekly Specials:* Take a section of your mailing list and mail them "weekly specials" . . . Let them phone them in . . . Food stores do this on an advance basis: "Pick up this circular for NEXT week's weekly specials."

13. *Newsletters:* Chatty, informal behind-the-scenes information. (We were in Rome last week looking for something unusual for you and we found this little shop where . . .)

14. *Playbills:* If it looks like a Broadway Playbill and feels like a Broadway Playbill, it must be a Broadway Playbill . . . Not necessarily. Your mailer invites people to an Opening Night (of your store, of a new line).

15. *Theater Tickets:* A spring-off of the above with special "tickets" inviting you to a special sale . . . Customers will call asking for tickets for friends of theirs to be allowed to come to your store to spend their money. (Say, "Yes.")

16. *Tickets to a Sporting Event:* Similar to the above, but different. The mailer takes the shape of a ticket to a baseball, football, basketball, hockey game depending on the season . . . Or giant size pari-mutual tickets . . . Or, again, tickets to the store's Circus Sale . . . Or World Series Sale.

17. *Print on Wood:* Yes, it can be done if your printer is willing to help . . . Thin balsa wood from your local lumber yard. Bring samples to the printer to experiment before you buy the thousands you need . . . "Wooden you know Gordon's has the most unusual sale this summer?"

18. *Newspaper Reprints:* A news story about your store. A news story about a product you are selling . . . Reprinting a news story gives your product an "authentic" look. Makes it more believable. (I never could understand why readers believed a product was superior when the manufacturer would boast, "As advertised in *Life* magazine." Anyone with the money could make that statement. But, the fact is, the printed word by someone else, gives your product more credibility.)

19. *List of Reasons Why:* People love to read lists . . . "Here's 10 Reasons Why. . ." "Here's 21 Clothing Items That . . ." "Here's 50 Specials On Our 50th Birthday. . ."

20. *Lemon Sale:* Stores have fun listing lemons that didn't move and poking fun at themselves . . . (We bought enough gloves to outfit every child in New York City. We forgot we lived in White Plains.

They sold for $3.00. But grab them for 99 cents.)

21. *Posters:* Everyone buys posters. Make your sale look like a poster . . . Peter Max art style . . . Roll it up, mail it in a tube . . . Someone will frame it in their room and you'll be an every day reminder.

22. *Telegrams:* Did you know the word telegram is not copyrighted? Copy the yellow envelope and print the bold "Telegram" across the envelope and be assured of instant readership . . . Make the inside look like a telegram. All the words in capital letters . . . Use the word "Stop" . . . ("DO NOT STOP, HURRY DOWN.")

23. *Burned Documents:* Write for information to Bob Goldstein, 17 Stonehenge Road, Great Neck, New York 11023 . . . Ask for samples of documents with burned edges and prices . . . Great for raising money to burn the mortgage . . . Or this can't happen to your valuable papers if you have a safe deposit box in our bank.

24. *Mail in plastic:* The plastic sheet protectors from your stationery store make a great holder for your mailer. Your message is right there for everyone to read.

25. *Free Gifts:* Self explanatory but everyone seems to forget the obvious . . . "We have a free plant for the first 200 customers who come to our . . ." Contact your local nursery. Miniature plants in small clay pots will cost you about 30 cents each . . . Several restaurants use the, "Present this ad to your waiter and he has a free gift for you . . ."

26. *Collectibles:* Everyone's a collector these days . . . "Fill out this coupon bring it to the store, and you can win a rare coin" . . . "a stamp" . . . "a bottle" . . . Or mail something that looks like a collectible: Confederate money, Roman money replicas.

27. *Badges or Buttons:* Like the political ones. Especially this presidential year . . . Do a whole campaign on vote for (name of your store)—a Sure Winner.

28. *Gold Nuggets:* Put them in a little canvas bag with your sales message "Discover gold at the savings we have for you during . . ." Or: if gold is a color you're promoting for fashion, for new cars or this year's refrigerator. Available from the same Bob Goldstein mentioned above.

29. *McDonald's:* All are owned by individual franchises . . . They have to check with the home office on what they can and can't do for promotion . . . But if they tie in with you, success is assured.

30. *Photographs:* Old ones of your community 50 or 100 years ago . . . or photographs of famous movie stars from years ago . . . or baseball players from years ago . . . Something that rings a familiar and/or nostalgic bell will trigger interest.

31. *Old Maps:* See your local library. Mark where your store would have been if you were around them. Good take-off for "All Roads

Lead To. . .(you)." Or Have old maps of your town reprinted on parchment paper as a free giveaway "to the first 300 who visit our end-of-season. . ."

32. *Blue Ribbons:* Like those awarded at art shows or country fairs. Print them up, tuck them in your next mailer as the "ticket" of admission for your customers who are the Blue Ribbon choice.

33. *Cartoons:* Walt Disney knew the appeal of cartoons across age brackets. Use them in your next mailer. Originals or well-known. If one of your products is a licensee of a well-known strip (example: Peanuts) have Snoopy or Charlie Brown invite your customers to your next sale, opening or celebration.

34. *Limited Editions:* The Franklin Mint sold nearly $90 million of limited edition books. Everyone's a collector today. What can you offer your customer limited to only-a-few?

35. *Sweepstakes:* Ireland keeps on paying for its hospitals this way. And *Reader's Digest* keeps on boosting circulation this way. New laws make sure you give away that-which-you-advertise. Fine. Say so. Makes the contest more exciting. One effective way: *Everyone wins.* Certain numbers win certain prizes. But everyone else has the same number which is worth something.

36. *Keys:* Send blank keys to your customers which are the "key" to admission to a special store opening—a night, a holiday. Restaurants do this well by making good customers members of a Key Club. Bring it to the back entrance. No waiting for a seat.

37. *Pop-Ups:* Still one of the great visuals of all.

38. *Testimonials:* Put a well-known personality in front of your store and watch sales zoom. Too expensive for a national celebrity? But how about a local TV or sports figure? Or: a simple, "I like to shop here. . ." quote from customers. Ask your attorney for proper release forms, tape their voices, and run the ads on radio and in the paper. You'll be surprised how many people want to boost your store, (and if you don't have too many, better start wondering why).

39. *Credit Card Replicas:* Printed on Kromekote with your store's name, they are an effective replica of the easily-recognized credit cards. Each is worth a specific amount of money on a specific day. And, of course, the envelope has a lead-in line saying, "YOUR CREDIT CARD IS ENCLOSED. . ."

40. *Special Delivery:* Still a guaranteed attention-grabber (if not a guaranteed quicker delivery). To a select group of customers. For a select promotion.

41. *Unusual Stamps:* Contact your local stamp dealer. You can buy all kinds of unusual looking stamps for pennies. Put regular US postage and add these. Or make them part of the message. (Idea headline: "What Do They Mean By 'Stamp of Approval'?") Or, print your

own stamps. Yes, you still need the official US kind as well.

42. *Plain Brown Paper Bags:* Mail "shopping list special" from your grocery store. Annie's Attic in Big Sandy, Texas, uses them to mail their sewing designs.

43. *Airline "Tickets":* Excellent to introduce a new made-in-foreign-country merchandise. Contact an overseas airline for ticket covers. How many will they supply? How many free?

44. *Plastic Records:* Easy to mail and unbreakable. Send for samples and prices to Eva-Tone Soundsheets, P.O. Box 23, 2051 Waukegan Road, Deerfield, Illinois 60015.

45. *Invitations:* To a sale. To a private showing of designer merchandise. To see a new piece of equipment. Make it unusually shaped: twice as big as normal. Or half as big. Or a copy of a children's party invitation. Or. . .

46 & 47. *Special Season and/or Occasion Cards:* Browse through your nearest card shop. Look at the unusual cut-outs, folds, shapes. How can the one that captured your attention be transformed into a mailing piece for you?

48. *Passport Replicas:* Your passport to an exciting world of special merchandise. Also to introduce items from a foreign country.

49. *Zodiac Signs:* Astrology is bigger than ever. Your front cover says, "Turn this page to discover what's going to happen to you on (list day and date of your special event). Inside list a brief summary of the twelve Zodiac signs and include in each synopsis a sentence on how they will be visiting your store to see/shop/buy/select, etc.

50. *Computer Cards:* Available in blanks at low cost for your bank (or, if you're a great customer, for free). Overprint them as "checks" or with a special sales message. Use the new computer type faces for authenticity.

51. *Wooden Nickels:* The old "Don't accept. . ." axiom doesn't hold true for you. You'll accept the ones you've mailed to your customers in exchange for X amount of merchandise during your annual Wooden Nickel Sale. Wooden you like to be here?

52. *Coins:* The special new shiny penny is always a good draw. For a limited mailing, a larger amount. One pharmacist mailed silver dollars to doctors beginning the message with, "We know your time is valuable. But we'd like to buy one minute. We've enclosed payment in advance. The following message will take sixty seconds to read. . ."

53. *Plastic Bagging:* Many manufacturers and some mail order houses send their catalogs in heat-sealed plastic bags. Good for strong visual first-impression impact.

54. *Canvas Bagging:* To mail outsize and bulky items: stones, film, your

sales message wrapped around outside of item. Contact Milheiser Bag for price list.

55. *Wallets:* Not real ones. Make-believe made out of "leather" paper. Mailed flat with your sales message imprinted on the back of the "money" inside the wallet.

56. *T-Shirts:* Take advantage of the T-shirt craze still building. Do you know how many designer shirts sell at double-figure prices with the designer's name imprinted for all to see? Or your store's name? A walking billboard.

57. *Foreign Language:* A message in Italian for Columbus's birthday or in French for Bastille Day to start your summer sale. (Don't forget the English translation.)

58. *Wills:* Reprint or legal document facsimile giving the customer the chance to pick up what has been "willed" to them on a specific date.

59. *Cassette Tape:* You can buy individual cassettes with your sales message for under one dollar each. . .from a local enterprising promoter. For a select group of customers. They will simply have to find a player somewhere to hear your message.

60. *Any Combination of the Above:* Sometimes a little bit of one idea coupled with a little bit of another can have double impact.

For on-going facts, features and stories of direct mail and how it works, write for a subscription to Direct Marketing, 224 7th Street, Garden City, New York 11530. Tell publisher Pete Hoke you were sent by Murray and Ray.

Part Three

15 *Added Value*

THE SATURDAY BEFORE Mother's Day every year, an eastern retail store gives a gift to every woman customer who shops in the store . . . a long stem rose.

A midwestern car dealer sends a personalized "thank you" note to every customer the week AFTER the car is purchased. He includes a signed certificate for the first lubrication and oil change . . . at no charge.

Abe Lipshutz, owner of a fruit and vegetable store in Atlantic City, tosses in something extra every time you shop there. A little surprise. As he's packing up the grocery order, he says, "We got some fine grapes in today. Here, take a bunch home. You'll like them." And he smiles.

Added Value. The unexpected, unadvertised, uncharged-for "extra" that gets people to come back to you again and again and again, *ad infinitum profitum*.

Repeat Business: Come Back! We're Different! You get something extra when you do business with us!

Most customers are not used to receiving "something for nothing," especially if it's not advertised. Bill Veeck practices Giving Something Extra constantly—always keeping the Something back until the last moment.

Businesses are built and succeed because of the extra-attention, something-for-nothing surprises they give their customers.

What do *you do* in your business as ADDED VALUE? What *can you* do—what *can you* supply as an extra to your customers? Are you doing everything you can to use your own product as a giveaway?

All customers, consciously or unconsciously, are thinking, "What's in it for me?" Not you. Me. I am the customer. What is the benefit I, the customer, will receive when I buy from you? I know you will make a profit. What's *my* profit?

One of the great sales training phrases we ever heard applies when any customer arrives at any seller's place of business.

Here it is: I'M HERE TO BUY—YOU TELL ME WHY.

Would I be here if I was not interested in your product, service, store, groceries, automobiles, auto supplies? Why would I bother to come or call your place of business if I didn't have some interest in buying?

I'M HERE TO BUY—YOU TELL ME WHY. And, if you don't make any major mistakes or say some self-centered sentence, I am ready, willing and able to part with my money.

ADDED VALUE simply, *keeps* the customer buying.

Here's how:

Zaberer's was a restaurant twelve miles outside Atlantic City. In the woods. You had to drive to get there. Why would you go to that trouble with dozens of fine restaurants and major gambling casinos in Atlantic City?

Owner Charles Zaberer, not only an excellent restaurateur, but also a keen, smart advertising man, knew he had to give people a reason for coming.

He solved that problem with an advertising phrase still used. On bold billboards beginning outside major cities north and south travelers would see the same slogan on billboards: "Zaberer's —Minutes Away!!"

We once chided Charlie that we saw his phrase on a billboard outside New York City. "Well," he said smiling, "that's only 140 minutes away."

At Zaberer's, ADDED VALUE works like this: when you go out to dinner you have a good idea of how much you expect to spend before you open the menu. How much can it be for—roast beef? Or a sirloin steak? The prices in different restaurants can range as much as five dollars or more. What the menu tells you is what you are going to get for the price you pay—right? Not at Zaberer's.

When Charlie calculated his prices he always left room for "extras" like this:

In his restaurant, the well-trained waitress approaches, and you give her your order. A few moments later she returns with a tray of seafood and this phrase, "Mr. Zaberer would like you to try some new seafood delicacies to see what you think of them."

"Un, no thanks," you might protest, "we didn't order these."

"Oh, there's no charge," smiles the waitress, "Mr. Zaberer is thinking of offering seafood platters and wanted your opinion."

Hmmmmmmmm.

During the meal the waitress will come back with steaming hot small dishes saying, "Mr. Zaberer loves Chinese cooking. He has the kitchen experimenting with some new combinations and would like to have your opinion."

By now you don't have to protest that you didn't order these either . . . and the phrase "Mr. Zaberer would like . . ." automatically means there is no charge.

The waitress might even open a little note pad and ask you if there are any comments on the vegetables, more or less salt, and write down your opinions. (Whether the opinions are acted upon doesn't matter. You are involved and important.)

You think that's all, well it isn't. Following the meal, there is a cheery invitation, "Mr. Zaberer would like you to have an after dinner drink . . ." (That can move a lot of lingering customers from their table to the lounge in a totally happy and expectant mood.) And who would complain about the prices when they have received so much extra for the price they originally saw printed on the menu.

On getting customers to come back, there is no problem especially if there are children. There is always a small gift and often a gift certificate. "Because you've been such a good boy (or girl), Mr. Zaberer would like to have you come back and have your next dinner here *free*. Here's your gift certificate."

Now if you can figure out how any parent can resist the vocal pressure of a seven-year-old *who has been recognized*, and wants to make the twelve mile trip, you'll see that Zaberer understands people—large and little.*

Added Value.

Sometimes Added Value is there all the time, standing around doing its job and you mistakenly assume everyone knows it's there because you know it. *Not* so. Consider the case of the Lifetime Guarantee:

Mahler's Ethan Allen furniture store outside Washington, D.C., had a problem. Their identical competition is another Ethan Allen five-store chain. Both sell the same Ethan Allen furniture. Why should a customer chose Mahler's over the five-store competitor?

The advertising man went through the single store with owner Jim Mahler looking for something "different." There was little choice. All the furniture in every Ethan Allen store is the same. Arrangements are similar. Price equal. What would make a customer chose Mahler's?

The advertising man during his tour peered into a back room and saw several carpenters working on furniture. "What are they doing?" he asked owner Jim Mahler.

"Fixing and finishing customer furniture," said Jim, slightly irritated at this "dumb question."

"Wow. That must be expensive. Don't the customers mind paying all the extra money?"

"Oh, no," said Jim, "it's free."

"It's WHAT?" said the ad man.

---

*When Charlie died at a much too young age, his epitaph was, "Just minutes away . . ." And Johnny Carson, interviewed by Mike Wallace on "60 Minutes" was asked what he'd like on his headstone. Carson smiled and said, "I'll be right back."

"It's free," repeated Jim. "All Ethan Allen wood furniture is guaranteed for the lifetime of the person who bought it."

"You're kidding," said the ad man furiously scribbling away.

Jim looked at him in amazement. "Why are you writing that down? Everyone knows about the guarantee."

"Really?" said the ad man, beaming.

Within a few days, the Washington *Post* carried a half-page ad for Mahler's with the headline, "We guarantee every piece of Ethan Allen Furniture to last your lifetime!"

The ad went on to carefully explain the guarantee and how it worked. In addition, Mahler's would prove that assurance in writing attached to each piece of furniture.

Belatedly the competition took ads saying "Hey! Us too! Our Ethan Allen furniture is ALSO guaranteed for a lifetime." And the consumer answered: "Sure, after Mahler's told us first."*

OK—now Mahler's had to do Something Else Extra.

Jim learned fast. He had a good furniture polish in blank bottles, so he added the label: "Mahler's Furniture Polish for Ethan Allen Furniture." With each purchase, a bottle of this now-special polish was presented to the customer with a little homey "pitch" about using the polish and caring for the furniture. When the something-for-nothing customer needed more polish, where did s/he go to buy the polish? And once there, a short trip around the showroom to see what's new . . .

Lest you start thinking at this point the only way Added Value works is simply to give product away—wrong. It works as well (or better) if you give something of yourself away, or just a touch of the service you can provide at very low cost with very high impact.

Satisfy your customer by making them feel good with something super, above and beyond what they expect. They will be at first incredulous, then leery, then wary, then appreciative, and then loyal customers and friends.

Start tomorrow. With a happy greeting to everyone in the morning. With a "thank you for letting *me* take care of *you*" to your customers.

Give not only extra services and merchandise but also yourself.

That is the best, the truest and the most effective ADDED VALUE of all.

---

*Which has a famous parallel in the beer business: One company was anxious to find a new angle for its advertising campaign. The account executive from the agency was touring the brewery premises and asked, "What are those guys with the rubber suits doing with those hoses with the steam coming out?" "Oh," said the brewery tour guide, "they're just cleaning out the bottles with live steam to make them hygienically pure." "Wow," said the ad man furiously scribbling away (must be the cousin of the Washington ad man). "But," smiled the tour guide, "that's nothing new. All breweries do that." "Yes," gleamed the account exec, "but how many beer drinkers know that?" The headline WE CLEAN OUR BOTTLES WITH LIVE STEAM rolled out across the country convincing beer drinkers that the competition was a bunch of dirty careless brewers, while the other brewers steamed over being caught in the ancient curse of assumption.

16 *Added Value (Reprise . . .)*

THIS IS NOT THE APPENDIX.

Lots of books have appendixes.

Since that sounded like a medical specialty, we investigated and discovered the appendix is *not* a necessary part of the anatomy.

We really didn't like the idea of any part of this book being "unnecessary" and so we have titled this add-on section as "Added Value (Reprise . . .)."

What is it?

When you attend one of our seminars, you arrive early in the morning, sit down at a table and find a portfolio in front of you. Inside are the items we will talk about during the day. (We have mentioned a lot of them in this book.)

But here they are, as a special "Added Value," all put together in the back of the book so you can remember where we traveled and what we experienced . . . together.

The ad at the very end is included because it is one of the best examples of selling-writing ever printed. It has appeared in every anthology of great American advertising. In a recent survey of fifty leading advertising men to choose the ads they liked best through the years, *every one of the fifty judges included this ad*.

The amazing fact: this advertisement appeared only *once:* January 2, 1915, in the *Saturday Evening Post*.

Today more than sixty years later, hardly a week goes by that Cadillac does not receive requests for one or more copies of this ad which was written by Theodore F. MacManus.

The moral of this story is two-fold.

1. No one ever knows when they are creating a legend. We are sure when MacManus sat down to write his copy in 1915, he did not think his work would one day be glowingly judged as one of the masterpieces of advertising/selling/motivation. Professionals constantly do what they do well and try as hard as possible, in the time available, to do the job as well as they can.

From that concentrated intense effort comes good things, fine productions and, rarely, a legend.

The PENALTY OF LEADERSHIP

IN every field of human endeavor, he that is first must perpetually live in the white light of publicity. ¶Whether the leadership be vested in a man or in a manufactured product, emulation and envy are ever at work. ¶In art, in literature, in music, in industry, the reward and the punishment are always the same. ¶The reward is widespread recognition; the punishment, fierce denial and detraction. ¶When a man's work becomes a standard for the whole world, it also becomes a target for the shafts of the envious few. ¶If his work be merely mediocre, he will be left severely alone—if he achieve a masterpiece, it will set a million tongues a-wagging. ¶Jealousy does not protrude its forked tongue at the artist who produces a commonplace painting. ¶Whatsoever you write, or paint, or play, or sing, or build, no one will strive to surpass, or to slander you, unless your work be stamped with the seal of genius. ¶Long, long after a great work or a good work has been done, those who are disappointed or envious continue to cry out that it can not be done. ¶Spiteful little voices in the domain of art were raised against our own Whistler as a mountebank, long after the big world had acclaimed him its greatest artistic genius. ¶Multitudes flocked to Bayreuth to worship at the musical shrine of Wagner, while the little group of those whom he had dethroned and displaced argued angrily that he was no musician at all. ¶The little world continued to protest that Fulton could never build a steamboat, while the big world flocked to the river banks to see his boat steam by. ¶The leader is assailed because he is a leader, and the effort to equal him is merely added proof of that leadership. ¶Failing to equal or to excel, the follower seeks to depreciate and to destroy—but only confirms once more the superiority of that which he strives to supplant. ¶There is nothing new in this. ¶It is as old as the world and as old as the human passions—envy, fear, greed, ambition, and the desire to surpass. ¶And it all avails nothing. ¶If the leader truly leads, he remains—the leader. ¶Master-poet, master-painter, master-workman, each in his turn is assailed, and each holds his laurels through the ages. ¶That which is good or great makes itself known, no matter how loud the clamor of denial. ¶That which deserves to live—lives.

Cadillac Motor Car Co. Detroit, Mich.

Copyright 1914, Cadillac Motor Car Co.

2. Do not let anyone talk you out of what you want to do. Histories of ultimate success come from the determined people who had a dream, a concept, an IDEA whose time had come.

Truth: Most people have only one or two good ideas in a lifetime.
And no one knows how good those Ideas are at the time or when they will catch on. Or to what degree.
Persist.

Don't let anyone talk you out of what you want to do. (See Point 2.) *Do not accept excuses.* Post this list permanently in plain view of your associates.

The Reason it won't work is . . .

1. *We* tried something like that once before.
2. *We'd* have to change our policies.
3. It's never been done in our industry.
4. *We* need a committee to study it.
5. It seems pretty agressive.
6. It's an idea ahead of its time.
7. It might hurt our image.
8. Our President might disapprove.
9. Our competition is sure to copy it.
10. The customers won't buy it.
11. *My* wife thinks it's a crazy idea.
12. The stockholders will be furious.
13. It goes against everything we've ever done.
14. It doesn't go far enough.
15. The idea is too radical.
16. The idea is too conservative.
17. The economy is wrong for it now.
18. *We* might be sued.
19. Who would follow up the leads?
20. *We'd* have to stock huge inventories.
21. What would happen if it worked and we sold out?
22. What would we ever do for an encore?
23. It's over our heads financially.
24. If it works, we'd be swamped by larger competitors.
25. That's pioneers. And you know what pioneers get – arrows in the back!
26. Requires too much consumer education.
27. That's been done before.
28. If it's such a good idea, our competitors would have done it.
29. Why should it work for us when it didn't work for..... ?
30. Do you know how many companies went broke trying to do that?
31. The market is too small.
32. The market is too big.
33. The market is too fragmented.
34. That's not our line.
35. *We'd* be better off sticking to proven techniques.
36. The credit problems would be too severe.
37. Selling to (butchers, bakers, candlestick makers) is impossible.
38. *We'd* be up to our necks in returns.
39. The selling price is too low.
40. The selling price is too high.
41. It can't be good because I didn't think of it.
42. The computer can't handle it.
43. Let's take a survey first.
44. They won't let you.
45. Oh, I thought you were going to say something else....
46. Just leave it with me, I'll work on it.
47. Great idea – but not for us.
48. That only solves half the problem.
49. Don't rock the boat.
50. The last guy who came up with that idea isn't here anymore....

Epilogue:
The Sunshine People

IMAGINE THE WHOLE WORLD bathed in bright, warm, buttery sunshine yellow.

Imagine all the people you meet—smiling.

Imagine what that would do for motivation, for feeling better about yourself, your job, your family and life.

We thought a lot about this, because every once in a while, in our seminar travels, we meet some extraordinary Happy Fella or Gal. Like that wonderful waiter in Brennan's. Or Sylvia at the Fairmont. There are legions of other . . . Happy People.

What if (do you want to play this little game one more time?) people all just smiled, said "Hello" and really meant it when they asked, "How can I help you?"

It's possible.

But it will take a bit of doing.

One man has already proven that. The Sunshine Man.

One day he was driving with a friend in a cab in New York. He smiled, leaned forward and said to the cabdriver, "You are a real good driver." To which the driver snarled, "Yeah? Waddya mean?" (Which, in New York is pretty close to "Thanks . . .")

As they got out, the Sunshine Man reached for money to pay the fare, smiled, and said to the driver, "You really do handle your cab well, the way you manipulated through the traffic, the turns . . ." and handed the driver the fare and a modest tip.

The toughened cabbie looked at the money, raised his head, and said, "Hey, maybe I'll see ya again some time," which was the closest he could get to being friendly. And not a bad try . . .

"What are you trying to do?" asked his companion. And the Sunshine Man smiled and said, "Wait . . . you'll see."

The two walked along the street past a large building under construction. The Sunshine Man looked up and shouted to one of the hard-hat workers atop a steel girder several floors up, "Hey—I'll bet you're proud of that!"

The man looked down puzzled and said, "What did you say?"

And the Sunshine Man smiled and shouted back, "I said I'll bet you're proud of that building. Why, that building will be here for a hundred years after you're gone. And you helped put it there!"

The hard hat smiled and suddenly socked the worker on his right, "Do it right, dummy. Don't you realize this building will be here for a hundred years after we're gone!" and winked at the Sunshine Man and gave him the thumb-and-finger sign for OK.

Stunned, the companion again asked, "What is all this? What's it mean?"

"Wait," said the Sunshine Man again, "you'll see . . ." And then he gave the broadest wink to a not-very-attractive lady who was passing by. She giggled and nearly fell into the street. It had been a long, long time since anyone winked at *her*.

The companion took one look at the Sunshine Man and said, "OK, I give up. What is it with you? What are you trying to do?"

And the Sunshine Man looked at his friend and said quietly, "OK, I'm going to change the world . . ."

And you know what . . . we think he just might!

So, to help him along, we have created the Sunshine People.

What do they do?

Well, imagine a little card coming alive with bright yellow and orange colors. It is a Sunshine People membership card. For handing out to anyone you meet . . . and like.

The words on the front say, "You smiled. You must be one of us." (Who could get mad at that?)

How about you? Would you like to have fun out of life? Feel better? "Get loose" and "connect" with other happy people you meet along the way, on the street, in an elevator, on a plane, at a gathering?

It's easy. Join the Sunshine People. (Write us for your free membership card. Box 3800, Pasadena, California 91104.) And, from that moment on, every time you see someone smile, you make them a member, too.

There are a lot of us now. And there are going to be a lot more.

Have a Happy Day. And a Great Tomorrow. Be a Sunshine Person. Smile at Someone. And if they smile back . . . you'll know they're one of us!

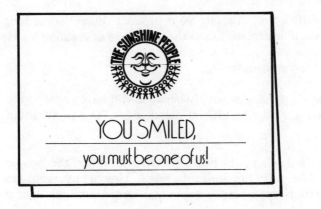

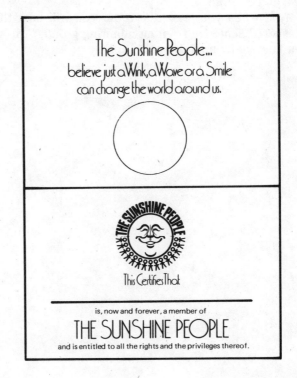

The thrust of this book is to encourage you to think well of yourself. You are unique. The more you are yourself, the less you are like anyone else in the world.

Think untraditionally. Get out of the box. If you don't like what you're doing, get out. You won't starve in this great country. Nor will your family.

Try your idea. Write copy. Promote your product. Invent something new. Collect Ideas. Combine them. Learn the technique of creating Ideas. Work at it. Practice.

Above all: do-what-you-*want*-to-do!

You can make *anything* happen simply because you have come to the end of the book! You are now an official member of "The Great Brain Robbery" club.

Congratulations.

So don't be surprised when, starting tomorrow morning, the people who are part of your every day life notice the slight, almost imperceptible changes in how/what/why you handle every day problems with a new ease and assurance.

And when you leave the room you will hear this now familiar half-whispered sentence from an admiring group, "How did he do that? Do you know how he did that. . . . ?"

Index